PROVOST

PROVOST

Experiences, Reflections, and Advice From a Former "Number Two" on Campus

Larry A. Nielsen

Foreword by D. H. DeHayes

Sty/us

STERLING, VIRGINIA

Published by Stylus Publishing, LLC
22883 Quicksilver Drive
Sterling, Virginia 20166-2102

Library of Congress Cataloging-in-Publication Data
Nielsen, Larry A., 1948- author.
Provost : experiences, reflections, and advice from a former "number
two" on campus / Larry A. Nielsen ; foreword by D.H. DeHayes.
     p.   cm.
Includes bibliographical references and index.
ISBN 978-1-57922-969-6 (cloth : alk. paper)
ISBN 978-1-57922-971-9 (library networkable e-edition)
ISBN 978-1-57922-972-6 (consumer e-edition)
1. College administrators—United States.   I. Title.
LB2341.N49 2013
378.1'11—dc23   2013005908

13-digit ISBN: 978-1-57922-969-6 (cloth)
13-digit ISBN: 978-1-57922-971-9 (library networkable e-edition)
13-digit ISBN: 978-1-57922-972-6 (Consumer e-edition)

Printed in the United States of America

All first editions printed on acid-free paper
that meets the American National Standards Institute
Z39-48 Standard.

Bulk Purchases

Quantity discounts are available for use in workshops and for
staff development.
Call 1-800-232-0223

First Edition, 2013

10   9   8   7   6   5   4   3   2   1

To Sharon

CONTENTS

PART NINE: WHO OWNS THE UNIVERSITY?

PART TEN: BEING THE EX

PART ELEVEN: THE LITERATURE OF THE PROVOST

PART TWELVE: SO YOU WANT TO BE A PROVOST

ACKNOWLEDGMENTS

This book is possible because the United States has an extraordinary system of public higher education. Not only does it provide for the education of regular citizens—like me—who come from anywhere in society, but it provides its faculty members with the opportunity to march to their own intellectual drum. So, that's the big picture.

With more focus, I would like to acknowledge some of the many people who helped me specifically to create this book. First, I have enjoyed working under a great set of bosses, including my department head, Barry Goldfarb and dean (while I was writing), Bob Brown. Second, I benefitted from the confidential and honest review of earlier drafts by three trusted colleagues at NC State, Katie Perry, Dan Robeson, and Dan Solomon. Third, I thank Joe Austin and David Holmes for their advice and assistance in getting matters related to this book in good order.

I am indebted to the fine folks at Stylus Publishing who have literally made this book possible. The publisher, John von Knorring, showed great faith in the idea and execution of the book; McKinley Gillespie kept the process moving efficiently and pleasantly. I hope it works out well for them.

Lastly, I wish to acknowledge the love and support of my family, Sharon, Jennifer, and Amanda. Of course, they supported me during the writing and finalization of the book—including reining me in when I got out of control—but they have lived the life of the university every day right along with me. We are, truly, always together.

FOREWORD

Why would anyone want or be willing to serve as provost? The position and its responsibilities are steeped in ambiguity, contention, swirling institutional challenges, potentially immobilizing debate about critical issues, never-ending shortfall of resources, conflict, and difficult personnel issues. Oh, by the way, just to add a sweetener, it is also a position with an average longevity of about 4.5 years—so job security isn't the reason to do this. Some say it's the toughest job in the academy. In this extraordinary reflection on the role of and experience in serving as provost at a major public research university, Larry Nielsen thoughtfully, and with honesty, wit, and clarity, describes the wonder of the position and helps us all navigate the pitfalls and savor the moments of joy and progress.

Nielsen's years on the faculty and in positions of department head, director, dean, and provost provide him a depth of knowledge and special insights about the inner workings of the academy across several institutions. His uncanny capacity for reflection upon and synthesis of those experiences, including the unfortunate circumstances that led to his resignation, and translation of them into meaningful analysis and prose, lend credence to his advice and make this a book worth reading—not only for aspiring provosts, but also for faculty, deans, and presidents.

The Provost—An Opportunity to Learn

Indeed, the provost gets to live a life of learning to the fullest each and every day. Learning is, after all, the heart and soul of the academy—which at times may be too easy to forget; it's the reason our institutions exist. The learning cuts across academic disciplines, business functions, investment strategies, financial aid challenges and opportunities, people and personalities, and political machinations of assorted types and impacts. Note that I said "the provost *gets* to" rather than "*has* to." The provost gets to enjoy challenges, complexity, and the layered texture of the university and to observe, and perhaps even enhance, the dynamic working surface of the university. As chief academic officer, the provost gets to be embedded from afar in the extraordinary work of the faculty—the learning inherent in our mission of teaching and scholarship and the dynamic debates associated with our commitment to shared governance, academic planning, and strategic institutional evolution. No doubt there are bumps and bruises along the way; you just have to love the work and the academy and learn to endure some frustration in exchange for the opportunity to savor the learning, personal growth, and institutional advancement that is shared by the community. As Larry Nielsen so eloquently describes, the provost position is an exhilarating, yet frequently exasperating job, often bordering on the impossible.

Universities, especially public research universities, are large, complex enterprises with a kaleidoscope of moving parts. For example, The University of Rhode Island, where I currently serve as provost and vice president for academic affairs, is a $750 million-per-year operation for which the provost serves as the chief operating officer. The weight of this responsibility is both mind-boggling and humbling. The university has numerous constituents, including students and increasingly their parents; staff; faculty; deans; vice presidents; the president; system chancellor; board chair and membership; the General Assembly; governor; and, of course, citizens of the state, each having his or her favorite agenda items for which he or she is passionate. It is neither possible nor prudent to attempt to satisfy, or even balance, the competing agendas of so many constituents and still advance the university. University investments need to be strategic and the strategic priorities require collective conception, commitment, and equally important strategic implementation. The provost gets to engage the community and find a way to build commitment. So, the provost gets to lead the charge, uncover the resources, fend off the resistance, and hope the university continues to progress. Nielsen's statement that "people matter most" is an absolute certainty, although that can easily get lost in the dynamic landscape of budgets, credit hours, grant funding, and so on.

Details Matter

No doubt, the president sets the broad agenda, but the provost gets to identify and manage the details necessary to make the agenda real and meaningful. And the details matter immensely. Within the context of that agenda, mostly what the provost can do, actually must do, is stimulate a state of productive "restlessness" in the university community. Universities need to be dynamic places that generate and respond to new ideas, directions, approaches, and possibilities. Restfulness, or complacency, is a killer for academic enterprises that depend on unleashing their intellectual capacity, innovative potential, and entrepreneurial spirit for their success and, frankly, for their resources. The provost, along with deans, the faculty senate leadership, and others, must continually ignite some flames and then encourage and support the faculty to figure out how to move forward in a manner that is viable and effective. Lots of people have great, even bold, ideas, but ideas don't have much meaning if they can't be effectively mobilized and implemented.

As Larry Nielsen so eloquently illustrates in this book, the provost gets to navigate bumpy terrain, even minefields, on a daily basis. To do so successfully, the position demands what I refer to as an "ecosystem thinking" approach to academic planning and policy. *Ecosystem thinking* is a form of strategic thinking that involves understanding and appreciating interconnectedness, complexity, and resiliency (hence the "ecosystem" reference) and the short- and long-term implications of our actions, initiatives, and policies. Most importantly, I think, it involves projecting to the extent possible into the future to understand the unintended consequences of our policies, while at the same time adaptively managing the vagaries and implications of those projections.

Although it sometimes doesn't seem so, most academic policy and protocol is actually well-intentioned and designed to improve some situation in the institution that isn't working well. However, it is not uncommon for many viewing a policy retrospectively to say "What were they thinking?" (or, more likely, "What was the provost thinking?") when examining the implications of the policy years later. This occurs because a new policy or guideline encourages all sorts of behavior changes that may very well extend beyond or around what was intended by the policy initially. The policy may have solved the problem of the day, only to create an array of new challenges. Good ecosystem thinkers can often anticipate potential problems associated with an action before they happen and, as a result, turn challenges into opportunities.

Larry Nielsen demonstrates such good ecosystem thinking. His insights about the life and operations of the academy, illustrated throughout this book, reflect his deep and soulful understanding of the inner workings of the university and his capacity for anticipating potential problems before they happen. However, he missed one potential problem and it turned out to be costly to him and the institution. Always the teacher, he thoughtfully and eloquently shares the lessons from that experience for all of us to ponder.

Grounding in Experience

So, how does one prepare to become the provost or, for that matter, for any major leadership position in a university or other organization? In my view, reading Nielsen's book is a great way to get started. His stories are not only interesting and inspiring, but also reflect the nuance of leadership positions and the broader responsibilities of these complex positions. Furthermore, experience matters and, as Nielsen points out and exhibited through his own career, serving as department head and dean provides relevant and important experience. The lessons he shares at the end of each section are spot-on tips that are worthy of careful consideration. There is also significant emergent collective wisdom that emanates in a more nuanced manner from the integration of his messages, lessons, and ideas.

No doubt there is important job-related experience, but I think there is also a critically important *experience of mind-set and aspiration*—that is, a mindset that includes humility, respect for the position and academy, and a deep understanding of and appreciation for the work of the faculty, shared governance, and opinions differing from one's own. I am not certain that grooming oneself to be provost is meaningful or effective. There is no real grooming—the work in this complex job stems from one's heart and soul—in a sense, it must be a labor of love. Like Larry Nielsen, most of us, whether we applied for the job from an internal or external position or were simply appointed, are and perhaps need to be "accidental provosts." We simply found ourselves ready for something new, complex, and unpredictable for both our careers and our lives. Although we had gained substantial experience through other institutional and national positions, we arrived at the place of the Provost's Office through humility, perhaps even reluctance, but with a sincere belief that we may have something to give rather than something to gain.

Nuance Defines the Job and the Person

Stemming from this perspective, there are attributes or attitudes that may be important for a provost that perhaps can't be learned from grooming or career planning and management. Essentially, effective institutional leaders give up the right to think about

themselves. Or, at the very least, they need to place the institution ahead of their own interests and need for recognition. This
may not be easy for academics who tend to be acculturated to
a reward system that recognizes personal rather than collective
accomplishments. As Nielsen describes throughout this book,
leaders need to understand the working surface of the university,
appreciate the important work of the faculty and staff, and know
that the institution, including its successes and failures, is not all
about them. Borrowing from the central theme of the writings of
Václav Havel, I believe that effective leaders need to spend more
time understanding than explaining, and celebrating the innovative contributions and commitment of those in the university that
actually do the important work of learning, discovery, and community engagement. Moreover, in telling this story, his personal
story, Nielsen has demonstrated these leadership qualities and his
credibility as a thoughtful servant-leader, which is what the work
demands of each of us.

Further, the leadership of academic institutions needs to put
the work of the university into a larger national and global societal context. As such, provosts must comprehend the institution's
responsibilities, challenges, and opportunities through the lens of
the ever-changing economic and political landscape of the time,
and recognize that the whole of society is greater than the sum of
the disciplinary parts in the academy. To lead, the provost must
then find a way to nudge, cajole, create incentives, and remove
disincentives for the community to pursue the large and compelling questions and issues of our time. For sure, this is delicate
work that must be approached with care and respect. It is important, however, to ensure that the work we do as academics has
meaning in the world.

Most academic leaders, especially provosts, establish their
faculty careers in specific academic disciplines or, even more frequently, sub-disciplines within a professional field or academic
department. So, the transition to chief academic officer, with
oversight of all academic disciplines and departments, represents

an intriguing challenge of both understanding and credibility within the academic community. In this context, the provost needs to have the interest and capacity to learn about, appreciate, and communicate with the full array of academic disciplines in the institution. While this may be a challenge, it also represents an extraordinary opportunity. That is, the provost has the opportunity (yes—"gets to") to encourage the exploration of the ever-expanding chasms of important intellectual learning that exists between and among the traditional disciplines and departments. Frankly, we have no choice—society demands that we aggressively pursue such explorations and it is exciting to do so. Whether related to climate change, health and wellness, energy futures, informatics, aesthetics, poverty, or any of the numerous other emerging inter- or, increasingly, trans-disciplinary areas of learning and discovery of contemporary societal relevance, the opportunity to draw upon and integrate knowledge that extends across the university is rich and palpable. So, the provost needs to be curious, imaginative, and provocative, and comfortable in academic worlds outside his or her own areas of expertise. Indeed, in the interest of "restlessness," provosts get to find ways to engage, and maybe even stretch, departments to extend beyond the comfort of disciplinary patterns and assignments. It is clear that Nielsen not only "gets it" in regard to interdisciplinary pursuits, but also managed to successfully navigate this novel terrain.

With his extensive experience in the academy, Nielsen has stated, and I concur, that the university is all about people—their morale, sense of accomplishment, and pride. As such, the provost needs to understand people—who they are and what they do and care about. This, of course, includes sufficient self-knowledge to trust one's own judgment and motivation and to have the confidence to delegate and share responsibility. The entrepreneurial and innovative spirit of the faculty and staff needs to bubble upward. If this spirit is suppressed or frustrated or somehow not encouraged to emerge, the institution and its impacts will be diminished. Simply put, community matters, especially during difficult times—and there will always be difficult times. In fact, we are living in those difficult times in the academy right now. The provost most likely won't be successful by imposing down, but rather by inspiring forward. My sense is that this kind of understanding of the academic soul of a university comes from who we are and our life lessons rather than from grooming or career management.

The Joy of Navigating an Ever-Changing World

Finally, the provost must be prepared for, and perhaps even enjoy, ambiguity because the role is both paradoxical and volatile. Moments of joy can be followed by moments of despair. The Brazilian author Paulo Coelho could have been writing about the mercurial nature of the provost position when he wrote, "Life moves very fast. It rushes from heaven to hell in a matter of seconds." So, one must be prepared for the emotional roller coaster of the job as well. This is another of the many intangibles inherent in such positions. Larry Nielsen reminds us that our universities are large, diverse, and complex organizations and "things will go wrong." As Nielsen points out, the provost "sits in a chair over a trap door. It can open any time." This isn't a bad thing or a good thing—it is simply a real thing. It's part of the job. You need to know it's there, but you can't let it rule you. Just keep moving forward.

In the end, serving in a leadership position at a public research university is an extraordinary privilege. Nielsen captures the special essence of the position, his joy in doing the work, and the honor associated with the opportunity. As he writes in Chapter 51,

> Being provost is a wonderful job, the best job that I've ever had. The joy and honor of making good things happen at a university, not just in your own area of disciplinary expertise, but for the institution as a whole; the reflected pride that comes from successful students, faculty members, and staff; the excitement

of having opportunities, events, and programs flow in so fast
that it takes your breath away; the magic of being at the center
of all that is happening. . . .

Indeed, what could be better than having the opportunity to serve
as "guardian of the soul of the university?"

Read this book and learn about the inner workings of our
universities; the roles and responsibilities of the provost position;
the subtle dimensions of effective leadership; and, equally as interesting, the experiences and reflections of an individual who loves
the academy.

D. H. DeHayes
Provost and Vice President for Academic Affairs
The University of Rhode Island
Kingston, RI

PREFACE: LB2341

Let's begin with a little low-tech geocaching. Visit the stacks in the university library. Take the elevator to the floor that houses works with Library of Congress classifications starting with L, for education. Walk along the stacks until you get to LB, where works about educational theory and application are stored. Now walk down the rows until you get to the shelves containing works between LB2300 and LB2430; these are about educational theory and application in higher education. Bend down and find the works that are labeled LB2341. These, the Library of Congress says, are what you've been looking for—works about the supervision and administration of higher education.

Browse through the holdings. You'll see many books about being a university president, dean, or department head; a row of books about the role of trustees and boards; more books about the financing of higher education than any library needs; and a smattering of books about various subtopics, such as admissions and enrollment, facilities, and curricular reform. But you won't find much about being a provost. If the library is well stocked, it might have a couple of volumes relating to the job of the provost, or chief academic officer. Look carefully, though, because you might miss them. Most people seem to have done so—the biggest, thickest, densest book about the chief academic officer in our library was published in 2004, and I couldn't tell that anyone had ever cracked the binding.

In their initial informal reviews of this book, some of my trusted colleagues suggested that it would benefit from, ah, some scholarship. "Your stories are great, Larry," they said, "but we need some more meat with the dessert you're serving." And when I wrote a publisher and promoted my book on the basis that there just wasn't much out there about being a provost, he was skeptical. Then he looked. And he found—almost nothing.

So, in order to class up this offering, I have reviewed the literature I could find. I don't claim that this review is exhaustive, but I do claim that it was exhaust*ing*. I'm not a scholar of higher education supervision and administration or any of the other subjects that find their way onto the shelves around LB2341. I read most of the books and chapters I could find, and they were full of grand phrases and lofty sentiments and long sentences, maybe even references to various theories of leadership or management; consequently, I didn't get a lot out of them. Nonetheless, being still a moderately capable academic, I've made a pretty substantial little literature review from them. Don't blame me, blame my reviewers.

The literature review is near the end of the book, labeled "The Literature of the Provost." You can go there right now if you wish to learn what others have written. But you'll miss all the good parts.

The few existing works about the provost's job pretty much all begin by regretting the lack of available literature on provosting, scholarly or not. Peggy Shaw Teague (2000, p. 13), writing in her dissertation on chief academic officers of community colleges, said, "The position of chief academic officer in a community college has received much less attention in the literature than that of president or faculty, yet this position has very direct influence on the curriculum offered and the instruction delivered within the two-year college." Karen Doyle Walton and Sharon McDade (2001, p. 85), describing the characteristics of women provosts, wrote that "Despite the irrefutable importance of the CAO, scholars of higher education administration have written little about that position in general, and even less about women who serve as CAO." Walton and McDade make the further point that, while there have been at least five major studies of the university presidency in the 25 years leading up to the turn of the century, only one, which was a broader study of presidents, provosts, and deans, had any comprehensive national data relating to provosts.

The absence of survey data about provosts was rectified in 2008, when the American Council on Education completed a survey of more than 1,000 provosts for their inaugural CAO Census (Eckel et al., 2009). The census is a fine addition to the knowledge base about provosts, and I cite many of its findings in the literature-review section and at various points throughout the rest of the book.

Why such little attention to the provost? I don't believe any silver bullet answers the question completely. Several factors contribute, and let me summarize them here, so you can identify them in the book as they come at you, mostly at oblique angles.

First, the job is internal; so, it deals with the routines of higher education administration. Presidents and chancellors hobnob with the rich and famous; provosts eat Hobnobs at their desks, while considering proposed revisions to the appeal process of the promotion and tenure regulations. Most provosts, I suspect, can't imagine that someone would want to read about what they did.

Second, most provosts, when they finish being provosts, want to do other things besides write books about the experience. As the demographics show, most former provosts go on to one of three roles. They become presidents (about which they can write much more glamorous books), go back to the faculty (usually at their own request, because they are wiped out from the job and couldn't muster the energy or enthusiasm to write about it), or retire (and do something they really want to do, which isn't writing about their insightful revision of the promotion and tenure regulations). In other words, they're either seeking new plums to pick or they're plum tuckered.

Third, provosts come to understand that their experience is idiosyncratic. As David Brown (1984, p. 1) wrote in an early treatise about being a provost, "The position of CAO is defined by its occupant." Overwhelmed by the tasks of the job on a day-to-day and year-to-year basis, provosts don't have the time or energy needed to conceptualize their work abstractly, test their concepts with data from their colleague provosts, and then pen a theory (or theology, more likely) of provosting. Provosts, I suspect, also find it hard to expand their view to see the commonalities of all such jobs rather than the peculiarities of their specific job. When provosts meet, they are constantly asking questions like, "How do you do student orientation? Our approach isn't working," or sharing viewpoints like, "Have you heard how Someplace State counts credit hours? It's bizarre." No theory here, just anecdotal experience that accumulates over time.

Fourth, most provosts come to the position accidentally. I had played with calling this book "the accidental provost," but that seemed to cheapen the job too much. Written accounts mostly describe the path to provost as one that wasn't intentional, but that arose as a faculty member learned that she or he was tolerably good at the administrative game and actually got a buzz from it. So, I think, many provosts haven't dreamed about securing the job since they were nerdy school kids and, therefore, haven't set for themselves an early task of "I'll write a book about this when I get done."

Fifth, provosts don't last all that long. As the demographics show, the average tenure for a provost is under five years. So, individually, a provost may feel that she or he hasn't accumulated enough position-wisdom to justify writing a book as some kind of expert or guru. The position of provost is just part of the academic life journey for most of us, not a destination. Many websites for provosts have a brief section about "what the provost does," but the descriptions are typically operational ("I work with the Faculty Senate Curriculum Committee on changes in degree requirements") rather than theoretical or even strategic. The few postcards we might pen along the provost's journey could deserve to be on the scholarly refrigerator door for a while, but certainly not archived in LB2341.

And, so, the literature of the provost isn't going anywhere fast. The endings of the few existing studies of the provost position pretty much say the same thing, too: We need to study the position more. More statistics, assessment, continuing education, development-for-promising-presidents. It's frightening, isn't it, to think that sometime in the future someone might actually cite Nielsen (2013) as part of the scholarly literature on provosts? [Some real scholars better get busy.]

PART ONE

THE ACCIDENTAL PROVOST

I

I LOVED MY JOB

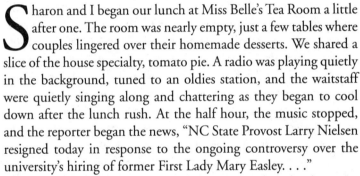

Sharon and I began our lunch at Miss Belle's Tea Room a little after one. The room was nearly empty, just a few tables where couples lingered over their homemade desserts. We shared a slice of the house specialty, tomato pie. A radio was playing quietly in the background, tuned to an oldies station, and the waitstaff were quietly singing along and chattering as they began to cool down after the lunch rush. At the half hour, the music stopped, and the reporter began the news, "NC State Provost Larry Nielsen resigned today in response to the ongoing controversy over the university's hiring of former First Lady Mary Easley. . . ."

We would come to use the term *surreal* to describe the entire set of events that led to my resignation, but hearing about me as headline news will always remain a most surreal moment.

I had never gotten used to the idea that I might be news in any way at all. I was just a goofy, respectful kid, who was good at school and grew up to be a goofy, respectful adult, who got up every morning and went to work. I had a six-month study leave after my resignation, and I still got up early and went to the office most days. I had dutifully followed the typical baby boomer path of moving up the ladder—and I'd climbed pretty high in the academic world. After all, provost is number two at the university. Even so, I never mastered the concept that what I said or did could be newsworthy, or even gossip-worthy. Consequently, I usually said what I thought and did what I thought best.

"How's that working so far?" you might ask. It worked pretty well for the most part, and I've enjoyed a marvelous life and career in the university. But there often comes a time in the lives of many universities when something goes wrong (in reality or appearance), and the world demands that some heads roll. Part of the provost's unwritten job description is to be near the front of the line at the guillotine. I knew that previously in theory, of course, but now, I know it from personal experience.

I loved being provost. I trust that by the end of this book, you will understand that being provost was an enormous privilege for me. Not only did I have universal parking privileges and license to cut into any buffet line with impunity, but I touched the life and purpose of the university with my hands every day. I presented teaching awards, recognized valedictorians at graduation, approved new degree programs, oversaw the design of new buildings, created scholarship programs, expanded international programs, tenured and promoted deserving faculty and staff, cheered and groaned at sporting events, opened art exhibits, brought world leaders to campus, and even took home the trophy for the toy tractor race during Agriculture Awareness Week.

It isn't remarkable that I loved being provost, because I've loved every job I've had at a university. Good thing, since I've spent my entire adult life studying or working at one. My parents dropped me off at Scott Residence Hall at the University of Illinois in 1966, amply provisioned with a new set of dark green towels, a two-volume Webster's dictionary, and an AM-FM radio that brought in stations, if you draped the wire antenna across the bookshelf and out the window. I have spent almost all of the intervening 47 years—except for a tour with the U.S. Army in Vietnam and a sabbatical leave with the Wisconsin Department of Natural Resources—lodged in the world of the public research university: Illinois, Missouri, and Cornell as a student; Virginia Tech, Penn State, and North Carolina State as a faculty member and administrator. A fellow couldn't ask for a much better ride, and I have appreciated every mile of the journey.

The journey has been fun, but the destination was certainly accidental. I never intended to be a provost. Most provosts would probably admit they had never intended to be a provost either. I didn't even know that such a thing existed until after I had my first faculty job at Virginia Tech. I knew there were presidents of universities, for sure, and in my dreamier moments, I probably thought about being one someday (I've always been into positive imaging).

I remember my first real contact with the Provost's Office at Virginia Tech. I had been leading the humanities core curriculum committee for the university (another totally accidental appointment). The committee members met with the associate provost for academic affairs to discuss our recommendations, and as chair, I stayed behind for a few minutes to finish out the meeting. I related to him that I was awed at how he grasped the situation, understanding the ins and outs of putting this new core curriculum thing together. I surely ended with some flattering drivel about how I could only wish to be as articulate about academics as he was. He responded in kind, saying that, to him, I sounded just like a provost. And when the door closed behind me, I'm sure he forgot all about me.

And I did the same, because the career target in my sights was to be dean of a college of natural resources. Eventually, I got there. Sharon and I were in Europe on Penn State business (don't get excited: I paid for my wife's expenses myself), visiting a partner university in Germany and then a donor in France who was considering a major gift to the forestry program. We had reached Paris when the call from Raleigh came. As we returned to the hotel lobby in the evening, the steward at reception excitedly told me that a call had come in for me from the United States, and asked if I would like to return it. I said *yes* and within a few minutes, I had accepted the deanship at NC State. To celebrate, we went down to the lobby again to get some champagne. Except our hotel didn't have a bar, or a restaurant. The only service available was a soft-drink machine, so we toasted the new position by sharing a Coke. That's the kind of hotels we stay in.

It was 2001, and I was 53 years old. I expected to be dean for a decade or so before retreating into the woodwork. No such luck. Three years later, when I heard the reliable rumor that our provost (a former dean colleague) was about to be named chancellor, I called and left a congratulatory message on his cell phone. He called back to say thanks and to ask me if I would help him out.

"Sure," I said, "You know you can ask me to do anything for you and for the school."

"Great," he said. "Would you be interim provost for six months?"

I sat down, stunned. This possibility had never occurred to me. And I didn't want to do it. I'd watched the provost work for the past three years. Actually, for the last three years, I'd watched the last three provosts work—none of them much longer than 16 months. The job appeared to be a man-eater. Being dean was fun, and being provost looked like drudgery—hard and dangerous drudgery.

"But I don't want to be provost," I said.

And that was a big reason he wanted me to be the interim. He didn't want the interim provost to be a candidate for the permanent job. Several deans—the likely ones to be asked to be interim provost—might want to be candidates. A few deans were too new and, I suppose, a couple of others were off the list for reasons I wasn't privileged to know. So, that left me.

"Okay," I said, and another accidental provost was created.

On the other hand, maybe it was destiny.

2

IT WAS DESTINY

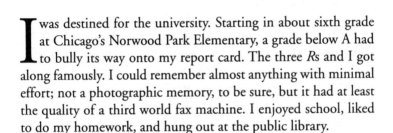

I was destined for the university. Starting in about sixth grade at Chicago's Norwood Park Elementary, a grade below A had to bully its way onto my report card. The three *R*s and I got along famously. I could remember almost anything with minimal effort; not a photographic memory, to be sure, but it had at least the quality of a third world fax machine. I enjoyed school, liked to do my homework, and hung out at the public library.

Perhaps all academics, being born analysts, can pinpoint the significant events in their careers. I certainly can. My next-door neighbor Ronnie and I were playing in his basement when my portable transistor radio blurted out that Russia had launched Sputnik. That was October 4, 1957. Ronnie and I split our attention for the rest of the day between the breaking news (it really was breaking then) and our Monopoly game, and we watched the blinking light in the sky every evening, as Sputnik passed overhead. I was nine years old, and science unseated Ronnie as my best friend.

The resulting space race, not to mention the Cold War in general, led to the need for more scientists, and hence society's continual encouragement for kids like me to focus on science. Unlike today, that encouragement included real opportunities rather than just rhetoric. So, one afternoon, my sophomore physics teacher passed me a brochure about the National Science

Foundation's Summer Science Training Program in field ecology in a distant place called Washoe Valley, Nevada.

A summer course in field ecology would be a dream come true. Every year, my family did what half of the families in Chicago did—take a one-week vacation at a cottage on a lake in Wisconsin. That's where I learned fishing could be boring, but watching the fish that swam around in the shade under our rowboat was fascinating. That's where I discovered pitcher plants, dragonfly nymphs, and red-winged blackbirds. That's when I read Rachel Carson's *The Edge of the Sea* and fell in love with the ocean just as she had—before I'd even seen it.

I usually also tagged along with my buddy's family to do what the other half of Chicago did—take a similar pilgrimage to a lake in Michigan. We reveled in those experiences, collecting every living critter we could find (and sacrificing most of them to science, I confess), conducting what we thought were experiments and generally wreaking havoc on the Midwest's lacustrine ecosystems. One corner of each of our basements became our laboratories. Bug collections, bird's nests, dusty fish mounts, dioramas of natural scenes, and collection equipment made up my world. I was well on my way to becoming a biologist, and the National Science Foundation (NSF) camp coming along at this time was destiny. I took the brochure home to my folks, but my expectations were low.

My parents weren't educated people. Mom dropped out of high school after the ninth grade; Dad finished high school, but claimed he graduated only because they let him sleep quietly in the back row after he had worked all night. Like most in their generation, though, they valued education as the path to a better life for their children. My brother had gone to college, and I was headed there as well. But they had a problem with me—I was their "egghead," better in school than they ever imagined their kids might be. Education was going to take me to places they never expected a young man could go. So, after the normal rhetorical sparring around the kitchen table (ours could have been the inspiration for *All in the Family*), they agreed I could apply for the NSF camp in Nevada. If I could get in and get a scholarship for the train fare from Chicago to Reno, I could go. The fates were kind, and I was accepted, with a free train ticket. That summer in Nevada *was* a dream come true. For six weeks, I studied with scientists from the University of Nevada–Reno, made a collection of mammal skeletons that served me in science fairs and guest lectures for decades, and confirmed my intention to be a biologist. I also wrote my first scientific publication, although I've never had the gall to actually list it on my résumé. Nielsen, Larry. 1964. Feeding adaptations in selected mammal skulls. Pages 84–86, in University of Nevada–Reno, Desert Research Institute, Foresta Publication Number 10 (in the realm of gray literature, this baby is the grayest).

A conscientious faculty advisor at the University of Illinois moved me into the honors biology curriculum after he saw the column of As on my first-semester transcript. That program offered students wide freedom to choose many electives. I took almost all of mine in literature rather than biology, in retrospect a clear sign that I was more of an academic dabbler than a hard-core scientist (and perhaps destined to be a provost).

Let me accelerate the rest of the journey. A mentor at the University of Missouri provided the perfect model of the teaching-research faculty member, and I knew within weeks of starting my MS that I didn't really want to be a fisheries biologist for the Iowa Department of Conservation anymore. I wanted to be a professor. A mentor at Cornell gave me rein to turn my term project into a peer-reviewed publication (a real one this time) that separated me from the other doctoral students coming out in 1977. Imagine that—one publication making the difference between landing a tenure-track faculty job and going hungry.

My department head at Virginia Tech thought he saw potential and gave me many opportunities to explore and understand the university. He said I was "destined" to be a university president (I regret that I've disappointed him in that prediction). A Kellogg National Fellowship fed my cross-disciplinary interests and landed me in the middle of general education reform at Virginia Tech. I'm probably the only fisheries biologist in history who headed the humanities core curriculum committee for a university.

After that, I went over to the dark side: department head, school director, dean, and then provost.

Twenty years later, I'm back as a faculty member.

3

WHO COULD LOVE BEING AN ADMINISTRATOR?

A sk that question—would you love to be an administrator?—to 100 faculty, and you'll probably get 100 consistent replies: NO WAY!

But I could. As much as I loved (and love) being a faculty member, I loved even more being a university administrator. That admission itself is enough to make my judgment questionable, I know, but if you are reading this book, we're probably members of the same questionable-judgment club.

University faculty members come in all shapes and sizes, but in terms of their susceptibility to the temptations of administration, I've observed two main types. First are those faculty members who like to concentrate on one thing and "learn more and more about less and less," as the condescending saying goes. They excel at scholarship, often becoming the disciplinary stars of the university. They can get lost in finding the solution to a geometric quandary, unraveling the mechanism for a biological trait, creating a sculpture, or composing an opera. I recall a statistician who, when asked an interesting question, would turn and stare out the window for as long as it took him to formulate an answer—maybe two minutes, maybe two hours. If you were the person who asked the question, as I was on a particular fall day, this could be an uncomfortable time sitting on the hard chair in his office—but, if you were patient, you would get a complete and insightful answer in the end. Such faculty members make great scientists, engineers, logicians, authors, composers, and artists. The training, apprenticeship, and tenure processes find and nurture these folks as the quintessential inhabitants of the university. They do the real work of the university—they *are* the university. Typically, they keep administration at arm's length and wish they had infinitely long arms.

The second type of faculty members is the group who can't sit still. They like action. They tire of one area of research or creativity after a while and look for new challenges and opportunities across the hall or across the disciplines. They revel in the diversity and variety of the university. They can become great teachers, outreach providers, inventors, and entrepreneurs—even *intrapreneurs*, as the creativity literature likes to call educational innovators these days. As provost, I often had visits from such faculty members, asking for advice about how to get into administration or at least out of their current academic rut.

I am of the second type. I've never liked doing anything twice. Never been to a class reunion, always want to travel to someplace new, can't wait for basketball season after a couple weeks of football season. I've written, cowritten, or coedited four books and always declined the offer to write a second edition. I figure I know the answer, after about 75% of the data are in, and I'm too impatient to wait for the other 25% just to be sure. I like implementing ideas rather than doing research. A few folks will say that my desire for decisions and actions is what led to my unexpected early departure from the provost's chair. They might be right.

I'm not very good at any one thing, but I like almost everything. When in a generous mood, folks call such personalities "eclectic"; when not being generous, they call us dilettantes. The university is an eclectic place, a great place to be a dilettante. Somewhere on campus today, a physicist is bouncing neutrons off a silicon wafer to characterize the nanostructure of its surface; a textile designer is bringing a script to life, by sewing costumes for the characters; a veterinarian is attaching an artificial leg bone to an injured dog; an archeologist is reassembling the shards from an ancient ewer; a science fiction writer is inventing a mind-bending future world; a crop breeder is genetically improving corn plants, so they will thrive during droughts. And all of them are doing their work in collaboration with young students who have the potential to transform our world. As an administrator, and especially as a provost, I got to be part of all that. Who wouldn't love that job?

4

FROM SUBLIME TO
RIDICULOUS

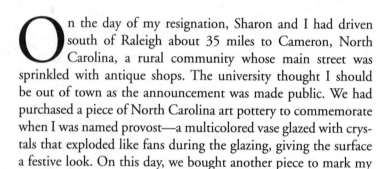

On the day of my resignation, Sharon and I had driven south of Raleigh about 35 miles to Cameron, North Carolina, a rural community whose main street was sprinkled with antique shops. The university thought I should be out of town as the announcement was made public. We had purchased a piece of North Carolina art pottery to commemorate when I was named provost—a multicolored vase glazed with crystals that exploded like fans during the glazing, giving the surface a festive look. On this day, we bought another piece to mark my resignation—this one glazed uniformly in black.

I had told the deans about my resignation at our biweekly meeting that morning. E-mails went to the Board of Trustees simultaneously, then to the executive officers, vice provosts, and the provost's staff. A few minutes later, my notice of resignation was broadcast to faculty and staff, and the university's official notice went on the web.

Bad news has always traveled fast, but in the Internet age, it goes at, well, Internet speed. In what seemed like minutes, my resignation had hit the regular media and the online versions of higher-education publications. I fully understand that the notoriety of the occasion had little to do with me. The notoriety was that the words *governor's wife* were in the same sentence as my resignation.

Colleagues at NC State, members of the Board of Trustees, provosts at other schools, legislators, family members, and friends from across the campus and the country began calling and e-mailing within a few hours. The first call was from a member of the legislature, who told me that he was sorry and to let him know whatever he could do for me. Next was a member of our Board of Trustees, with the same message. Many faculty, staff, and alumni told me one version or another of, "You will always be my provost." For months, no matter where I went—grocery store, swimming pool, church—people would come over to express their regret over my resignation, say how unfortunate and unfair it was, give me a hug, ask me how I was doing. Janitor to corporate CEO, campus cop to restaurant server. I will be forever grateful to the hundreds of people who offered their support and understanding as these events unfolded, especially for their faith in me as an honest and caring administrator.

This event hijacked my career. A hiring decision I had made four years earlier, with the full support of the university administration and accolades from the university and local community in general, had now turned against the university and me. My salary was cut in half, my role shrunk to what it had been twenty years earlier, and, as I've learned, no one has the appetite to give me a second chance at another university.

Sometimes provosts and presidents have to resign because something truly awful has happened at a university. Deaths, embezzlement, academic fraud, racial or sexual discrimination—tragedies like these hit university campuses just as they do all other sectors of our society. After all, a major public university is a small city—ours has a population of about 40,000 when students and staff are included—and cities have problems. Sometimes, though, the reasons for resignations are much less serious. The community gets up in arms about an art exhibit, a faculty member says something inappropriate in class, or someone buys pizza for graduate students off the wrong account.

The ridiculous part of the situation at NC State is that the hiring had been a home run, maybe even a grand slam. I hired the first lady to create a new university seminar series that would bring national and world leaders to NC State. These seminars, as I'll describe in more detail later, were an unquestioned success—and becoming more so with every iteration. But that success was of little consequence in the bigger picture.

The local newspaper had begun to investigate the governor as he went out of office, and my hiring of the first lady was caught up in the process. The paper seemed to be looking for a political connection between my having been hired as provost and my hiring of the first lady as a faculty member. In my resignation letter, I termed any such implications *preposterous* and *groundless*. They were. Eventually, the scrutiny became too uncomfortable for the university, however, and something had to be done. As I will describe in more detail later in the book, I had made the decisions, and I accepted the consequences.

This was a horrible experience. I had never imagined, and I think no one who knows me would ever imagine, that I would be caught up in such a mess. I am a joyful, optimistic man, but this experience knocked much of that out of me for a long time. Perhaps the worst was that it played out in public, and I had no capacity to fight back. Public officials have no privacy, and they are limited in their ability to talk by a range of laws, policies, and gentlemanly expectations. Just when we thought the story had cooled off, the newspaper would run it again. Prompted by the implications of the newspaper coverage, citizens continued to send e-mails and letters to the university and the newspaper, calling me and others out in the most outrageous of terms.

And so ended my four and one-half years as provost and executive vice-chancellor at North Carolina State University. Never had I enjoyed a job as much as I had being provost, but neither had I suffered as much as I did during the last year of my term.

But enough about me. Let's start thinking about the university and its provost.

5

REALIZING POSSIBILITIES

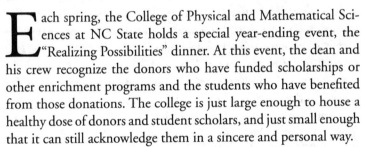

Each spring, the College of Physical and Mathematical Sciences at NC State holds a special year-ending event, the "Realizing Possibilities" dinner. At this event, the dean and his crew recognize the donors who have funded scholarships or other enrichment programs and the students who have benefited from those donations. The college is just large enough to house a healthy dose of donors and student scholars, and just small enough that it can still acknowledge them in a sincere and personal way.

The evening oozes with sincere and personal. The recognitions begin with two students, each talking about a memorable K–12 schoolteacher who helped guide them, inspire them, mentor them to their success in college. On this particular evening, one of the students, majoring in mathematics, talked about her math teacher. To the student, her teacher was like a second mom, someone who paid attention, knew she was there, saw the potential—realized the possibilities, as this night would emphasize. The student cried, the teacher cried, my wife cried.

Then came three students who talked about how the scholarships they received had helped in their lives. One of these students—call him Daniel—was a double major in physics and applied mathematics. Daniel talked about how his father died when he was in middle school and his mother went on disability soon afterward. He and his brother had to earn all the money for their family. When Daniel declared that he wanted to go to college, his brother offered to take care of the family but said Daniel would have to find the money for college himself. Scholarships from NC State donors made it possible for Daniel to attend college, to realize his possibilities. With a 3.8 grade point average, he was realizing them big time. And his dream? When he finished graduate school, he wanted to lead a high school for at-risk children in his hometown, so that his experience could be replicated for many more students in the future. This time, I cried, too.

This book is about loving a job that has the joyous responsibility to help thousands of students realize possibilities like Daniel's. This book is about the experiences I've had and the lessons I've learned as a university administrator, mostly as provost. My hope is that the observations I make will ring true to those who have traveled the same road and will be useful to those who are early in their journey. I also hope that the book might contribute to the general understanding of the American public university.

The American public university may be one of the most important social inventions of humankind. The six universities I've studied or worked at are great examples of the university's success. But an unrelated event made this real for me in the first few months after my resignation.

Sharon and I were visiting our daughter who lives in El Paso. She, her husband, and his family invited us to the opening game of the 2009 University of Texas–El Paso (UTEP) football season. We gladly accepted, as this was the first football season in more than a decade for which we lacked season tickets.

We parked as close to the stadium as we could without paying (we didn't have a VIP parking pass, either), which meant a far distance away. We then joined one tributary of fans walking toward the Sun Bowl. That tributary soon became a river of orange and blue flooding into the stadium. As we walked, we passed a new technology building under construction, designed in the unique and stunning Bhutanese style of the UTEP campus. We passed the library, undergraduate learning center, and buildings housing geological sciences (a big deal at UTEP, home of the "Miners"), computer science, math and other computational programs, and political science.

The school's student body mirrors that of the El Paso community—about 70% Mexican American—and so did the crowd going to the game. The game was for students, to be sure, unmistakable from the revelry occurring across the campus, but it was also for the community. Families filled the bleachers around us, and they were having a fine time, despite the lopsided final score, lopsided in the wrong direction. There we were, invited guests to the love affair between a city and its university. I was never as aware of the importance of a university and the brilliance of the leaders who invented the idea as I was on that Saturday afternoon.

UTEP epitomizes the American public university. Most of us know UTEP only from the sports pages and perhaps as the only Texas university that has won the national basketball championship (1966, a team that is the subject of the motion picture *Glory Road*). But UTEP is much more. It is the largest U.S. university with a majority Mexican American student body. It is classified by the Carnegie Foundation as a research university with high research activity; the National Science Foundation has designated the school a Model Institution for Excellence, one of only six in the nation. Its comprehensive curriculum offers more than 150 degrees. Like most public universities, it focuses on being useful, and it excels at graduating engineers, nurses, and teachers. It supports the El Paso community and economy in scores of ways.

But most importantly, it provides access to higher education and an opportunity for a better life to thousands of Americans every year, rich and poor, well prepared and not so well prepared, traditional and nontraditional, majority and minority. Whether we're experiencing UTEP or NC State or one of the hundreds of other similar public universities in this nation, we're experiencing the best that our nation and our society have to offer. We're helping realize possibilities. How could anyone not love being part of this joy?

PART TWO

MR. PROVOST

6

WHAT IS A PROVOST, ANYHOW?

Move-in day is the Saturday before classes start for fall semester. The chancellor, vice-chancellor for student affairs, and I jump into the golf cart and begin our morning of "helping" our new students move into their dorm rooms.

What a great day—second best of the academic year. Graduation is best, when we happily say good-bye to a cohort of our students. But move-in day is second best, when we say hello to their replacements. Thousands of new students and their parents invade the campus, about to face the unenviable task of wedging into their dorm rooms several multiples more stuff than could possibly fit.

Campus is ready for the challenge though, with hundreds of student volunteers from Greek organizations swarming the residence hall grounds, looking for someone to help—so many student volunteers that they actually compete for something to carry. The officers of the residence hall council are renting lofts so that freshmen can cram even more stuff into their rooms. The chief of campus police is demonstrating acrobatics on his Segway, and the horse-mounted policewomen might ride by at any time, just to make these excited new students understand that there is a higher authority, literally and figuratively. The dining halls are on their best behavior, serving what might just be the tastiest lunch of the semester. Everyone is smiling, sweating, worried, excited, poignant, nostalgic.

Now, up drive three senior administrators in a golf cart borrowed from the women's basketball team. Here's how it goes. The chancellor grabs the most likely grouping, says hello, and starts shaking hands; everyone recognizes him or at least recognizes what he stands for. The vice-chancellor for student affairs peels off to talk to the volunteers from student organizations; they know him. The provost aims for a needy looking family and pounces before they have a chance to get away.

"Hi, I'm your provost. How's it going?" I say.

"Fine," one of them, usually the father, responds, with a question in his voice and eyes. Awkward silence follows, but I'm ready for that.

"Do you know what the provost is?" I ask. Awkward silence follows again, because they don't know whether to fake it and say yes, or admit that they couldn't tell a provost from a fence post. I rescue them.

"See that guy over there? He's the chancellor, right? He's number one, he's the boss, right?"

"Yeah, cool. Look, Dad, there's the chancellor."

"I'm number two, right after him," I say.

"Oh, okay, thanks, nice to meet you. Hey, Dad, let's go say hi to the chancellor."

One person who knows about the provost is Alex Trebek. NC State hosted the College Championship on *Jeopardy!* in 2006. Hosting *Jeopardy!* is about as cool as it gets for a nerd like me. Sharon and I sat on the front row at the taping, and our family and friends across the country saw us, as the cameraman panned the crowd ("Hey, look, Mom, there's Uncle Larry and Aunt Sharon!"). We also got to meet Alex at the reception after the show. When I introduced myself as the provost, Alex said, "Ah, you're the warden!"

Every provost has looked up the definition of their title in the dictionary, just to find out what she or he actually is. Original definition—keeper of a prison—the warden, as Alex said. Some parents appreciate that definition. When asked if they know what the provost is, they are liable to answer that the provost is like the vice principal of high school—the disciplinarian, the person students have to see when they've done something wrong. True in a way, but more for faculty members than for students.

No, I tell the students and their parents, I'm not really like the warden or vice principal at all. Instead, I'm the guy who handles the academics at the university. All the deans, department heads, and faculty members report through me. I approve all of the courses and curricula. I supervise the library, international programs, distance education, admissions, registration and records, diversity, and equal opportunity.

Now they're onto the idea pretty well.

"Ah," the dads say, "You're like the COO, and the chancellor is the CEO. You have to do all the work, while the chancellor gets all the publicity."

"Close enough. But here's a provost pencil, just in case you forget. It has my e-mail address on it. If you have any problems, send me an e-mail."

Over the years, the provost pencils got to be pretty well known. I had them made as a defensive posture and, in true academic form, to be used as a teachable moment. Everyone was giving out trinkets advertising their office or program—maybe mouse pads from distance education, coffee mugs from study abroad, T-shirts from student affairs—except the provost. So I had the provost pencils made. I put my own definition of *provost* on the pencil: "Pro-vost: university official overseeing faculty and curriculum." I gave out hundreds of them.

After a while, I knew we'd made some progress, as evidenced by the following exchange.

"Hi, I'm Larry Nielsen," I'd say to an unsuspecting student. "I'm your provost. Do you know what the provost is?"

"Yeah, he's the guy who gives out those pencils."

7

BEING NUMBER TWO

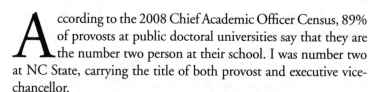

According to the 2008 Chief Academic Officer Census, 89% of provosts at public doctoral universities say that they are the number two person at their school. I was number two at NC State, carrying the title of both provost and executive vice-chancellor.

To be honest, being number two didn't mean all that much; it was mostly ceremonial. Each of the vice-chancellors reported directly to the chancellor, so there was little substantive work beyond that of the provost's specific functions. When someone was needed to represent the university at a general function that the chancellor couldn't make, I was generally the stand-in (for targeted audiences, however, the most appropriate vice-chancellor, dean, or even vice provost was the chosen substitute; a community function, for example, usually was assigned to the chief financial officer or vice-chancellor for economic development). During events when the entire senior administration was represented, the chancellor and provost generally sat together or directly on opposite sides of the podium. The chancellor, provost, and chair of the faculty were the only officials introduced during the graduation procession. The provost attended the closed meetings of the Board of Trustees (but spoke only when invited to).

It did mean that both of us—the chancellor and I—couldn't be out of the country at the same time. When he was out of the country, which was rare, I was officially named acting chancellor.

But in today's world, with cell phones and e-mail, the chancellor was still in continuous contact with his staff. I didn't make any decisions on his behalf; I just signed whatever paperwork needed to be processed.

Once, though, I got to hire the new football coach. I didn't get to choose the coach, of course—no conscientious university would let the provost choose a football coach—but I did get to "hire" him. The chancellor was out of the country when the negotiations ended between the athletic director and the incumbent, and, with sports reporters literally camped out at the football offices, the deal couldn't be kept quiet for the week or so until the chancellor got back. So, I signed the contract with the new coach and kicked off the press conference. Unfortunately, he is no longer the coach—provosts aren't the only ones with short tenures.

My scariest time as number two was when the bonding agencies Moody's and Standard and Poor's came to decide on our ratings for the next few years. This was an early lesson that the university is engaged in more things than a faculty member might imagine, perhaps more than any department head or dean might imagine. We needed to keep our high investment-grade rating, because we had several large building projects on the schedule, and we'd need to borrow a lot of money in the next few years (What, the university borrows money and has big mortgages?). Both the chancellor and provost were new, and the bonding analysts wanted to meet with us, to make sure we were both responsible adults. Our CFO was as nervous as I'd ever seen him. He knew the chancellor was a responsible adult, but the jury was still out on me. Which leads me to the real reason for including this chapter.

Being number two is a pretty good place to be, as long as you remember the one essential rule of being number two: You aren't number one. Collaborative leadership and shared governance are fine concepts, but when the chancellor is in the room, the chancellor is number one, and all the rest of us are distant numbers $1 + x$.

Several years ago, at the beginning of the school year, the student senate had both the chancellor and provost over to address their sessions on two consecutive weeks—chancellor first, of course. The student senate president that year was a creative fellow, and he prepared a brief PowerPoint as the chancellor's introduction. He showed a picture of a 1963 Corvette, as an example of what had been happening way back when the chancellor earned his bachelor's degree. The chancellor remarked that the '63 'Vette was the best machine ever. During the intervening week, I let the senate president know that my vote for best car of that era was the 1964-and-a-half Mustang, and he used that assertion in his introduction of me. Within days, the student newspaper held a referendum—the chancellor's Corvette versus the provost's Mustang. The Corvette won by a landslide. As confirmed by the popular vote, I was not number one.

"I am not number one" can be a difficult mantra for many of us to obey. The shortest route to becoming provost is to have been a dean. The shortest route to becoming a dean is to have been a department head. The shortest route to becoming a department head is to be so type A that, as a faculty member, you take every opportunity to run something for your department. In other words, most provosts have spent a career as the leaders and line officers for their units, serving as number one in their departments and colleges. We get used to having the podium, the seat at the end of the table, the last signature on the form. If we want, we speak first, and, if we want, we speak last, just before we adjourn the gathering.

To be sure, the provost still has a lot of line functions, supervising deans and vice provosts directly and thousands of faculty and staff indirectly. Tenure and promotion decisions, faculty dismissals, honorary doctorate recommendations, and dozens of other decisions at NC State all ended officially on the provost's desk. But the provost got that authority as delegation from the chancellor. All line officers get their authority from the chancellor, of course, but the distance between chancellor and dean or department head was large enough that I had never felt the reality of that delegation directly. The provost's connection is much closer; the provost *literally* acts on behalf of the chancellor.

But the provost is also staff to the chancellor. I wasn't very good at that, having never been staff to anyone before. When the chancellor or his office staff asked for information or analysis or a draft of a letter, I treated his request much as I would any other work that came in—put it on the desk and get to it when I judged it was ripe. Wrong. Work coming in from the chancellor is automatically top priority; all the fruit from the chancellor's tree is picked ripe and has a short expiration date.

Ripe work arrived on my desk in blue folders. "URGENT" read the label on the cover. We couldn't use red folders for urgent work, because everything at NC State is red; whenever we saw red, we'd yell "Go Pack!" and hope for a first down. Inside the blue folder was the nettlesome sticky note with a check mark in the box next to "please prepare a draft for the chancellor," followed by a due date a few days later. I always bristled—didn't they know I had a university to run? And how could something urgent happen every day in his office, maybe several times a day?

Eventually I learned how to handle this situation—give the folder to someone else closer to the issue to take a first crack at the draft (thank heaven for vice provosts). Unfortunately, our efficient vice provosts, much better at being staff than I was, got right on the task and usually had done their "staff work" by the end of the day. Now the blue folder was back, joining its siblings on the pile and screaming "urgent" at me from the corner of the desk. I covered them with something red, so I could ignore them. And, typically, I wouldn't get to the blue folders until someone from the chancellor's office came personally to prod my assistants to prod me. And when *my* assistant said "Jump," I jumped.

The second reason why being number two came hard was that I am a talker. I've never been able to keep my mouth zipped in meetings. I process quickly, and I process orally. During discussions, therefore, my inclination has always been to talk early and often, and I started doing that as provost, even when the chancellor was present. Wrong. When the chancellor and provost are together in a meeting, the person who gets to talk early and often is the chancellor, not the provost. The opportunity to make the first and best response needs to be the chancellor's.

We eventually evolved a system that worked well in those discussions. It had four steps:

- Step 1, I shut up.
- Step 2, the chancellor spoke, usually giving a pretty broad perspective on the topic and allowing me some time to think about the issue a bit more.
- Step 3, he would invite me to elaborate on his comments, which I would do from a more specific, usually academic, perspective.
- Step 4, I shut up again, unless the chancellor invited another comment.

We used that system with Moody's and Standard and Poor's, fortunately, and our bond ratings escaped the review without damage.

Even when the chancellor wasn't present, he got to speak first. Whenever I made a public appearance as provost, on or off campus, I always jotted this acronym at the top of the first page of my text or notes: CFSS. That reminded me to start by saying, "On behalf of our Chancellor and all the Faculty, Staff, and Students at NC State, I am pleased to . . ." The provost always speaks for the chancellor.

Letting the chancellor speak first and getting staff work done quickly are important lessons, but the most important is remembering that you are not the boss. Because the job of provost, as we'll get to next, is to "run the university," one can easily forget that the person really at the throttle is the chancellor. In effective teams, like the one between our chancellor and me, the division of work tends to be clear and unimpaired (I often said we had a great team, because the chancellor didn't want to be provost, and the provost didn't want to be chancellor), but the provost always has to remember that her or his work is conditional on the direction of the chancellor.

The provost's work may be strategic, but the chancellor needs to temper it with an understanding of what is possible. If the chancellor really wanted something in the strategic plan, I put it in the strategic plan—regardless of the fact that it hadn't emerged from the grassroots planning processes we all worship at universities. And when he didn't want something in, I took it out. When I got enthused one day about the possibility of starting a school of osteopathic medicine, the chancellor let me know right away that it was too politically sensitive to even consider. And I never talked about it again.

As I'll cover later, the provost's work is mostly internal, and it is mostly driven by well-practiced processes, with heavy faculty, dean, and department head participation. The chancellor's world, however, is directed much more by the external expectations of the institution. When internal and external matters collide, the chancellor, not the provost, gets to pick the winner. For example, like all major universities, we had a complex, collaborative, analytic system for reviewing and setting our capital construction priorities. It involved volumes of data, dozens of meetings, and transparent decisions, led by a three-person committee, chaired by the provost. Through that process and over a series of years, a new library had reached the number two position on the list. Because the UNC system president allowed only two building requests to go forward to the legislature every year, reaching the number two position meant something important—it meant this was going to be the library's year.

Wrong. Another building had been muscling its way up the list in recent years, scrambling above buildings with less political cachet and now crouching expectantly in third place. That building's supporters found a donor who presented an eight-figure gift to fund half the construction cost, if the legislature funded the other half. Supporters launched a statewide campaign to ensure legislative funding. The chancellor reordered the priorities, moving the library back to third place and out of the money for another year.

(But rest easy—the library rose to first place in the following year and is now completed, thanks to more than $100 million of state funding. It is a signature architectural symbol for our university, our first LEED [Leadership in Energy and Environmental Design] silver certified building, and will be an icon of the modern electronic library for decades to come.)

For these reasons and a list that could go on at some length—academic versus student life, long term versus present, reality versus perception, upside reward versus downside risk—the provost needs to know that she or he acts on behalf of the chancellor, even when the chancellor isn't watching.

Sometimes, not being number one can work to the provost's advantage.

Not long into my provost term, our ROTC staff officers asked me to go along on a helicopter training flight with the cadets (No, the cadets weren't flying the helicopter, just riding in it. "That's okay, then," Sharon said). They knew I had served a tour in Vietnam and hence probably loved helicopters. I was delighted to go along, because the students asked, but my relationship with helicopters was more one of ambivalence than love.

I was given the seat of honor in the ship, just inside the center of the door on the right side, facing backward. The seat is bolted to the floor, and the passenger—me—is lashed into the seat like a baby in a stroller.

It was a lovely morning for a flight. We flew with the door open (have to give the provost the complete experience). With nothing to hold on to and nothing to brace against, the flight was, let's say, dramatic. The pilot was extra courteous and only turned right so that when I looked straight out the door I could see—the ground.

We flew over the football stadium.

"Did you see the stadium?" crackled the pilot's voice through the headphones.

"You bet," I replied. Now can we go land this thing? I thought.

"No, I couldn't see it," said the passenger to my right. Did you have your eyes closed? I wondered. It's that big oval down there with the block *S* in the middle of it.

"Okay, we'll come around again," crackled the pilot.

And we did. In a tighter right turn. Held longer. There was the stadium, right outside the door, 2,000 feet straight down.

I survived, and my stiff upper lip obviously impressed them, because the following summer the ROTC folks called again.

"Provost," they said, "you're a really good sport."

I knew I was in trouble.

"Because you enjoyed the trip on the Blackhawk so much last year, the ROTC cadets have an even better idea for this year."

Uh-oh.

"At this year's Armed Forces Day football game, they want you to jump out of the helicopter and skydive onto the field, waving an American flag and carrying the game ball. Whaddya think?"

Start scrambling, Nielsen, I thought to myself. "I'd love to do it," I said, "but I've never skydived before."

"We figured that," they said. "This would be a buddy jump. You'd be strapped to another jumper who has lots of experience."

Then the lightbulb came on. "It's a great idea, but I'm afraid I would upstage the chancellor, and, as provost, I just don't think that would be the right protocol."

"Bummer. The students were really counting on it. We'll have to think of something else. Thanks anyhow."

Score one for being number two.

8

THE PROVOST IS NOT A DEAN

We've established that the provost isn't number one. The provost is also not a dean. If the provost is number two, what number is a dean? A dean is number 1.5. Or maybe the dean is 1_n. Let's not push the metaphor too far.

Anyway, being dean is a big deal, probably bigger than being provost. The few folks who have written about provosts often note that the provost's and chancellor's jobs are very different from each other; they often suggest that the jobs of dean and chancellor are the ones that are closest in content and style. The dean is the CEO for part of the university—her or his college. Colleges run pretty autonomously, and the dean runs it all—faculty, curriculum, facilities, budget, fund-raising, and public affairs. In the parlance of *Austin Powers*, the dean is mini-chancellor, but without residence halls or a football team. How nice.

I came to NC State as dean of the College of Natural Resources. Colleges of natural resources and the programs within them (forestry, fisheries and wildlife, range management, wood products, paper science and engineering, maybe outdoor recreation, geography, or hospitality management) don't have rating systems like law or medicine or business management. Which college of natural resources is best in the country is hotly debated among the contestants, without much recourse to data or even the pseudo-data that some magazines use to rate schools. But ask anyone with a reason to know, and they'll tell you the NC State College of Natural Resources is about the best in the United States, and perhaps the world. Put it another way—if there were a March Madness for colleges of natural resources, we'd make the final four every year.

So, by extension, being dean of the NC State College of Natural Resources must be the best job of its kind in the country, and perhaps the world. And that would be correct; it is a great job. I only intended to leave the dean's position for six months to be interim provost, and then I was coming right back to what I thought was my dream job. Seems I was dreaming.

Why is being dean a great job? Lots of reasons, but they all boil down to the dean's position in the administrative hierarchy. The dean is midway in the hierarchy of higher administration, getting neither clobbered on the top nor trampled at the bottom.

The hardest job at the university is one step below the dean—the department head. Department heads have all the responsibility for producing the work of the university; they are the plant managers in the educational manufacturing company. They manage directly almost all the people and resources that produce teaching, learning, research, and public service. They have no buffer as they perform that function—every day the messiest operational problems of the university fall into their laps. If all the class sections are full, the department head has to find another faculty member to teach more. If there isn't enough space for research, the head needs to convince two faculty members to share their space. If one of the toilets has been broken for six months, the head hears about it (one head to another). If the marching band has moved its practice field next to the building and now pierces the afternoon quiet with imperfect repetitions of the fight song, the faculty marches into the head's office to complain. Faculty members grouse to the head about parking, student quality, copy machines, academic schedules, heat in the building—no matter what the nature or source of the problem is, it is the department head's problem, not the dean's.

Buffering the dean from above is the university-wide administration—the chancellor, vice–chancellors, and provost. They are the ones who guide the institution as a whole, and, as this entire book relates, they have their own set of problems. They also don't have a buffer, in this case, from the outside world. When things get serious, the world goes right to the top—chancellor@ someplacestate.edu or provost@someplacestate.edu. There is no "dean@someplacestate.edu."

So, deans escape a host of problems, but they sure do have most of the gold. Deans control most of the continuing academic resources of the university. Follow the money, they say, and you'll find where the power is. Follow the money in a university, and you'll end up in the dean's office. They also say that possession is 9/10ths of the law. Deans have 9/10ths of the money, so they also are the law officers of the university—what they say is law. If department heads are the plant managers, then deans are the CEOs of the divisions. I have no difficulty with that state of affairs—in order to produce the real work of the university, deans *need* to control the real money.

Colleges house majors, curricula, and courses, and they manage the faculty and staff positions, facilities, and operating funds (if there are any) to fuel the production. They run research and outreach programs and lead most of the university's strategic initiatives. I often described the situation as a card game in which the chancellor is the bank, the provost is the dealer, and the deans are the players. Each dean will get dealt a hand, some better than others, but at least they are in the game and will end up with some of the chips. Department heads, in contrast, watch the game from behind the velvet ropes; they may or may not end up with any chips, depending on the goodwill and good judgment of the dean.

Part of the reason why deans are so prominent is because the college is the point in the university structure where the most important strategic decisions get made. Most departments can't allocate resources strategically. The typical departmental budget provides an office, phone, and computer for each faculty member; if there is a travel budget, it usually gets allocated by dividing the amount by the number of faculty, so everyone gets something like $627.38 for travel this year. At the university level, the provost needs to be sure that all the units of the university have sufficient resources to be able to perform—so college budgets don't vary a great deal from year to year; in the face of a budget reduction, for example, every college is likely to get a remarkably similar proportional budget cut.

The dean, however, sits at an intermediate level, where she or he has enough resources to matter and is close enough to the actual work to know what is going well or poorly, what needs to be retired, what needs to be born. The dean can take some chances, because in a college of five or 10 departments, at least one of them is going to underspend its budget (more about that later). The programs in a college may even be similar enough that they can be compared and assessed in ways that all the departments and faculty might accept.

Moreover, faculty members expect deans to make decisions. I remember the reaction to my decisions when I was a department head at Virginia Tech and a school director at Penn State. "Who died and made you king?" was a typical comment, expletives deleted. Faculty think of department heads as glorified committee chairs who really ought to just count the votes and do what the majority wants, even if it is a one-vote majority. But when I became a dean, the reaction to my decisions was different: "Oh, okay," the faculty would say, "I guess we better get on with it."

Deans are really the "big men on campus" (or the big women, or big people). Ask anyone who does crossword puzzles. What is the answer whenever the clue is something like "university leader" or "campus bigwig" or just BMOC? The answer is never president or chancellor, never provost, never head or chair. Nope, the answer is always dean, D-E-A-N. Number 1.5.

9

THE PROVOST'S PERFECT DAY

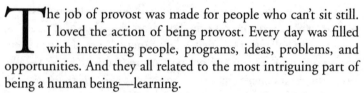

The job of provost was made for people who can't sit still. I loved the action of being provost. Every day was filled with interesting people, programs, ideas, problems, and opportunities. And they all related to the most intriguing part of being a human being—learning.

The provost's job isn't for everyone. If you like having an uninterrupted day, during which you can concentrate on one thing until your spouse calls and makes you come home for dinner, forget being provost. If you like closure—being asked a question and getting it answered definitively in a short time—stay away from the provost's office. If you like working in the abstract, compiling and testing broad generalizations based on the ideal, forget provosting. And if having alligators biting at your ankles prevents you from looking ahead on the path, then best not get on the provost's path.

Here's one iteration of the provost's perfect day:

5–6	Run around the neighborhood
7:30–9	Breakfast with the chancellor and a select group of faculty, just to talk
9–10	Meeting with a dean to plan the hiring of a senior minority faculty member
10–11	Discussion with the architects about the new library design

11–11:30	Call to Board of Trustees member to plan an upcoming Academic Affairs and Personnel Committee meeting
11:30–1	Lunch with visiting delegation from Czech Republic regarding our campus in Prague
1–2:30	Meeting with faculty senate executive committee about—well, to chew on whatever jerky is lying on the table
2:30–3	Coffee with a vice provost, just to catch up
3:30–5	Monthly meeting with student leadership liaison group
5–6	Award ceremony for faculty advisors
6–6:30	Pick up Sharon
6:30–8	Pregame reception in Chancellor's Suite
8–10:30	ACC basketball game (preferably with a win against—well, any ACC win would be fine)
around 11	*New York Times* crossword puzzle before falling asleep

Notice that there wasn't any time for reading or answering e-mail, reading or writing reports—what a perfect day! However, there wasn't any time for getting any real work done, either.

Perfect days didn't come along all that often, but most days when I was provost were about half perfect. Perfection for a provost comes from the combination of moving among many activities, several of which relate directly to the core purposes of the university—education, scholarship, and public service. Perfection also comes from the variety of events. Those activities on the previous list included meetings with one person to 25, and events with 50 people to 19,000 (maybe not quite that many if we were playing Boston College on a cold, February Tuesday at 9 p.m.).

Perfection also relates to being able to feel, really feel, the tangibility of the situation. So much of academic life is about delayed gratification (more accurately, occasionally dribbling in gratification), that actually seeing something happen is an administrative endorphin. Reviewing and helping to revise the plans for the new library building is tangible—you can see and feel that this library will get built, that students and faculty will work, learn, and, in fact, live in the facility, and that your participation helped make it happen. Sharing a meal while talking about the campus in Prague reminds you that there is a building there, with the NC State "red brick" logo hanging from the railing in the courtyard, and that right now our students are there learning—partly because you said yes to the funding needed to make it happen.

I particularly enjoyed the ceremonies we held in the Walnut Room on the fourth floor of our student center. I suspect that every academic administrator comes to like one particular event venue more than others. Just like for Goldilocks, some are too big and barren, some too cramped; some are always hot, some cold; some too formal, lined with portraits of dead White guys in suits; in some the pale green paint is peeling metaphorically off the cinder block walls. I never liked being in the board room at our new alumni center, because it was too regal, not at all in keeping with the practical land-grant personality of the university. A retired CEO of a Fortune 500 company reportedly coveted our board room when he saw it—so you know it's a little over the top.

But I loved the Walnut Room and adopted it as my own. I felt comfortable there, and real. It is far from fancy—low ceiling, fiber-board-backed walnut paneling, stackable plastic chairs, folding tables—so it was the perfect place for events involving units of the Provost's Office. For a lot of our teachers, advisors, office and technical staff, and graduate assistants, this was a big step up from their offices. When it was a big-budget affair, we even had punch and cookies.

And nothing was better for me than an academic award ceremony in the Walnut Room. Academic award ceremonies were always personal, partly because they tended to attract only those being awarded and their families, close friends, and colleagues. Interesting and loving things happened there. An always-inspiring instructor passed out plastic novelties shaped like a pair of hands that, when shaken, made a noise that sounded like clapping, so we could be louder and sound more appreciative; she wrote on mine, "provost's applause assistant." A staff member being honored brought her two-month-old baby, who grandly upstaged the provost during his remarks, to everyone's delight (including the provost's). Sometimes when an awardee couldn't be present, a colleague stood in, standing behind an enlarged photo mounted on a stick so their friend could be recognized anyhow.

The crowd would encourage me to cut up a bit, understanding that this time was just about us—the us who cared about students and teaching. I characteristically abandoned the prepared remarks and spoke off the cuff. I didn't need a carefully vetted speech to express the feelings in that room. We were there as teachers and advisors who loved our work, and there were no reporters present to make us parse our words or disguise our values. I usually had to fight back tears, because handing out awards to these folks went right to the soul of the university. These were the people who nurtured our students in good times and tough times, no matter what their needs and no matter whether their GPA hovered near 4.0 or closer to 2.0.

In the Walnut Room, hugging was allowed—no, it was required. And I loved it. I declared the Walnut Room a "free-hugging zone." Eventually, the regulars got to calling me the hugging provost. Now that's a perfect day.

10

THE UNIVERSITY'S
STAY-AT-HOME PARENT

The provost is the stay-at-home parent for the university (calling it the "stay-at-home dad" is more meaningfully descriptive, but the provost must be the poster child for gender neutrality). The job of the provost is on campus, all day and almost all days. The provost's perfect day that I just described was almost all on campus, surrounded by faculty, staff, students, and others who dropped in for a cup of coffee in the kitchen. I loved it, as I said, but I required some training.

The stay-at-home leash took me by surprise when I became interim provost. As dean, my job was largely external. Get known around the state, country, and world. Meet our alumni and make sure their kids are coming to college here. Visit our donors and keep their donations flowing. Represent the college at professional meetings for all the disciplines in the college, get elected or appointed to regional or national professional positions—and recruit great faculty and graduate students while you are doing it. Serve on committees and commissions for the state and federal governments and figure out who has the money and make friends with them. Participate in academic reviews at other schools and steal their best ideas. Every dean should have a sign on her desk, facing her chair that says, "If you can read this, you aren't doing your job."

Not so for provost. At my first meeting to discuss the interim job with the chancellor, the message was pretty clear regarding the preexisting obligations on my calendar: cancel, resign, delegate. "I need you here."

One of the realities of being provost, therefore, is that you are the operational lead for the academic life of the university. Don't confuse this with grunt work or paper-pushing, although there is plenty of that (not on a perfect day, however). Operations include the highest strategic levels—"what is the proper mix of under-graduate and graduate enrollment?"—as well as the more tacti-cal levels—"we're not going to have the diplomas printed in time for graduation; what should we do?" But both kinds of questions require someone who wakes up every morning focused there, not on his upcoming keynote at the meeting of the Institute for Social Science in Resource Management in Stockholm.

With this realization, the provost needs to change her or his frame of reference for accomplishment and recognition. Most rec-ognition will be internal, and there will be relatively little of that beyond a small circle of colleagues who are actively involved in the same things that the provost does. Associate deans for aca-demic affairs and the vice provost for undergraduate education will appreciate that the provost fostered streamlining of the course and curriculum approval process, but no one else will take much notice—they'll still think it takes too long.

The study abroad office will love the provost for increasing staff, space, and funding to allow them to double the number of students they serve (something he told them to do, as part of the university's strategic goal to be a global university), but no one else will notice. Students will enjoy better service from study abroad, for sure, but they didn't know what services were like before, so they are unlikely to be appreciative now; they'll just have extraordinary experiences that will change their lives forever. Faculty will still find the safety and security requirements for study abroad to be irritatingly strin-gent and the lead time needed for a new program to be excessive. And a number cruncher somewhere—legislature, faculty senate, conservative think tank—will calculate that administrative costs just went up and ask why that money didn't go into faculty positions.

After years of bristling slightly under this system, I've come to accept it as natural. I read the university's website daily, which carries new stories about the university's accomplishments almost every day. Typically, the academic side doesn't show up much. The research program gets lots of recognition, because a faculty member just discovered something important about how Parkinson's disease might be cured or fabricated a car body from old chicken feathers. If we got a massive new grant from the National Science Foundation or the National Institutes of Health that would bring lots of overhead money from Washington, you can bet that'll be on the web. A new patent or spin-off company is economic development, and that flag needs to be waved as often as possible, especially in a public research university. What students are doing shows up all the time—but not usually what they are doing in class. Biking across the country to raise awareness for AIDS research, winning the Jeopardy College Tournament, or pushing a plan to finish the Memorial Bell Tower—those are the kinds of things that make the website.

But provost-office matters are real yawners. Imagine these stories on the website:

"Sexual harassment training for new faculty might keep them out of court."

"Faculty members submit more of their book orders on time this fall than ever before."

"Tenure reviews completed with no grievances this year."

"Reorganization of summer school administration completed."

"Shakespeare classes make people happier all their lives."

You can imagine those headlines, but don't hold your breath about reading the stories. We could probably get some coverage for that last one, if we could actually demonstrate it ("To be or not to be—happy" would get some attention).

The reality is that most of the substantive operational work of the provost travels under the radar. As a colleague recently phrased it, a dean or provost doesn't accomplish things that get listed on a résumé—like a publication, grant, or graduate degree completion. They have to get satisfaction from knowing that they've helped the performance of the enterprise in some way, even if no one notices. Because it's unlikely anyone will.

The flip side is that all of this work is tremendously important and tremendously rewarding. The university wouldn't run for very long if the hypothetical headlines I just wrote and others like them weren't happening every day. The provost just needs to be able to understand the importance and delight in being the catalyst for the changes and improvements that the entire university carries out.

The reward for being provost is to get the system out of the way of students, faculty, and staff, so they can do their jobs as well as they can. Can we squeeze another faculty position out of this budget? Sure! Can we approve new courses with fewer steps? Yes! Can we arrange our financial aid resources to provide for the full needs of our poorest students? Of course! Can we streamline our grievance process just a bit more? You bet! Can we consolidate our campus life sciences laboratories into one big efficient facility? Are you insane? Get lost!

NC State was fertile ground for a new provost when I moved into the office. We had had a rotating door for provost for a long time. The average tenure for an NC State provost had been about a year and a half. Most left for good reasons, but we just couldn't keep one. I was hired as dean by an interim provost, received my first annual review from a provost who started on the same day as I did, my second from an interim provost who followed him after about 16 months, my third from the next provost, and became the interim provost before my fourth. The short tenure of NC State provosts was well known enough to deserve its own political cartoon, a picture of the rear side of the provost's desk, with a trapdoor where the chair should have been. So, my combined service of four years and five months as interim and permanent provost was akin to Cal Ripken's streak of consecutive games played. Not long into my term, every day I came to work, I set a new modern-day longevity record.

The longevity allowed me the time to get at items that a briefly sitting stay-at-home parent could never reach. It takes a few trips through the cycle to get the lay of the land. The first time through, one is just concentrating on the big operational items—conduct the annual reviews, run the promotion and tenure process, allocate the budget (and the budget reductions, as the case usually is), try not to move on the chancellor's lines. The second time through, one might peel another layer off the academic onion—reorganize some unwieldy functions, delegate more to the deans, start a strategic plan, reenergize the honorary doctorate program. After that, the job really gets to be fun—change the academic calendar, decentralize summer school, allocate the budget according to the strategic plan, construct a building, form a center or two, revise the core curriculum (on second thought, never revise the core curriculum).

II

JUST A LITTLE FAMOUS

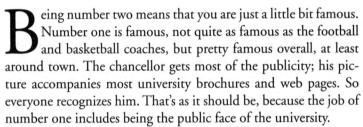

Being number two means that you are just a little bit famous. Number one is famous, not quite as famous as the football and basketball coaches, but pretty famous overall, at least around town. The chancellor gets most of the publicity; his picture accompanies most university brochures and web pages. So everyone recognizes him. That's as it should be, because the job of number one includes being the public face of the university.

But number two is a little famous, too. After all, you're known by a title rather than your name. We only had two people at the university who were known by their titles—the chancellor, of course, and the provost.

Our chief financial officer, who you'll meet often in this book, went one better—he always called me "Mr. Provost."

"Well, good morning, Mr. Provost," he'd say, and then to whoever was with me, he'd say, "Hi, Katie," or Jose, or whomever. He never called anyone Ms. Vice-Chancellor for Research and Graduate Studies or Mr. University Architect. No, there was only one Mr. at the university, and it was me—Mr. Provost. I took it as a sign of affection.

Others left off the Mr., but kept the provost part. I loved hearing the students chanting "Pro-vost, Pro-vost, Pro-vost," as I passed them while running the Krispy Kreme Challenge (two miles from the Memorial Bell Tower to the Krispy Kreme store; eat a dozen donuts; run back). Or the "Hi, Provost," as my path crossed a student's on the Brickyard or the Court of Carolina. Or the rare, but evocative, "Hey, Provost, I want you to meet my folks," at the graduation reception.

Early on, the chancellor and I both showed up at many events because we were new, the organizers asked for both of us separately, and we didn't know the other was attending. We often found that both of us were speaking—not a good idea, unless carefully orchestrated and approved by the chancellor (never give a better speech than the chancellor). So, we evolved into a style where we split the appearances up, with the chancellor naturally taking most of the off-campus and major on-campus slots and me taking most of the lower-profile on-campus slots.

Consequently, as provost, I made hundreds of public appearances, but almost all on campus. Award ceremonies, seminar introductions, international delegations, new program announcements, student banquets and receptions, faculty-sponsored events, poetry readings—sometimes as many as five per day.

The provost also gets the assignments that aren't, let's say, dignified enough for the chancellor to handle. As provost, I

- Was the stooge in the dunking booth during new student week, wearing a cap and gown
- Wrestled a sheep as part of Agriculture Awareness Week
- Rode in the homecoming parade in a tuxedo and gym shoes
- Appeared as *Star Wars'* Emperor Palpatine for the annual student service day
- Got pelted with water balloons for the student chapter of Habitat for Humanity (the CFO spent all his cash attacking me, and even wrote a check so he could keep at it)
- Dressed and gyrated as Elvis for a student affairs staff retreat
- Dressed as the front half of a horse for the business and finance staff retreat (how I got the front half is still a mystery to me)
- Raced toy tractors on the Brickyard (remember, I came home with the trophy)

While any one of these appearances might be seen as a low priority for the provost's calendar, each is a major event for the people involved—planners, attendees, honorees. Because the university runs through the goodwill of these same planners, attendees, and honorees, there is no such thing as a minor event. The job of the provost is to show up, especially on campus, so the people involved know the university cares. To most of them, the provost *is* the university, and showing up is essential. In a very real way, no event is too small for the provost to attend, because every person at the university matters. The university becomes tangible via the presence and participation of the provost. It's harder to blame everything on "them," when one of them is your buddy, the provost.

While I was provost, our Alumni Association started a new tradition for class rings. We hadn't had "official class rings" before, so the Alumni Association, the campus bookstore, and a ring manufacturer got together to create a unique set of designs and styles that only students nearing graduation could buy and then only through the bookstore. We distributed the rings at a ceremony held a few weeks before the end of each semester. The rings actually slept locked in the Memorial Bell Tower, NC State's primary campus landmark, the night before the ceremony.

I spoke at the ceremony each time, with a typical academic message—study hard and make us proud. I also had the delightful task of handing the ring to each student, shaking hands, and posing with the student for a quick photo. We processed a few hundred students through this event in about an hour—only a few seconds apiece walking across the stage and posing for the camera. But when those same students came to the pre-graduation reception, sometimes a year or two later, they and their parents often greeted me by saying, "We remember you; you gave our daughter her class ring; what a lovely ceremony that was." And the daughter would say, "You gave me a pencil once, too."

The reality that the presence of the provost really matters came to me vividly one January day. We were conducting the annual commemoration of the birthday of The Reverend

Dr. Martin Luther King Jr. The event always occurred at noon in our student center auditorium. As always, I was on the stage and gave a welcome on behalf of the university (on behalf of CFSS, that is). Several hundred people had gathered for the event, in a bipolar mood of celebration and anxiety for where we were and where we were headed in our journey to make NC State a welcoming place for all. The speaker was excellent, effectively moving us back and forth across our polarity. That year we were treated to a musical number by an African American preschool (no polarity here, just pure joy). The final speaker was, as always, a student, who, being well schooled by the event's organizer, turned to me and said, "Provost Nielsen, we appreciate you being here today. The presence of the top leadership of the university shows that NC State is serious about diversity." Gulp.

Once, early in my tenure as provost, I failed to appear at an event where I was expected. It was a big agricultural college event. They always had lots of dignitaries at their dinners, and I thought my presence was welcomed, but not required, even though I had said I would attend. My cell phone rang about 7:15 p.m.

"Hello," I said, "This is Larry Nielsen."

"Where are you?" came the reply. "You're supposed to be at our ag dinner."

"Oh," I said, "I can't make it."

"What??? You're supposed to speak! Thanks a lot, Mr. Provost."

I never missed another event that I promised to attend.

Lunch is an important event. I took someone to lunch almost every day, eating at one of the nearby off-campus restaurants. Almost anywhere we went, many tables and booths were occupied by faculty, staff, and their guests (I also used a few places where I knew we *wouldn't* be surrounded by university folks). I'd always work the room, as they say, stopping for a brief "hello" on my way in and out. This often provided a chance for an NC State host to introduce me to a visitor, perhaps an industry partner, donor, international guest, or prospective student—a few seconds invested can transform a "big university" into a small, friendly place. Observing university administrators eating lunch also served to personalize us to our own faculty and staff, giving them an additional connection to the folks "up the food chain." I also reserved lunchtimes regularly for just Sharon and me; consequently, people realized that when I said family was most important, I meant it.

Most of these lunches were times for me to catch up with a vice provost, dean, program director, or other administrator. You hear things at lunch that don't get written down in an e-mail or report. You can convey a perspective or approach that needs to be delivered with a bit of subtlety or finesse. The local merchants appreciate the effort, too. And, for the record, I always paid for myself and my companion and didn't seek reimbursement from the university.

Being a little bit famous is flattering, but it does have its downside. You can't go to Lowe's on Saturday morning before shaving. You can't use the car horn to scold the driver who just cut you off (good morning, distinguished faculty member!). You can't fall asleep in church.

You also get a lot of puzzled stares. At a store or restaurant away from campus, people look at you for a long time, trying to figure out why you look familiar. If they are assertive, they'll eventually come over and ask, "You're from NC State, right? The dean or something, right?"

"Well, yes, I'm the provost."

"Oh, yeah, the provost. What is a provost, anyhow?"

LESSONS ABOUT BEING
MR. PROVOST

1. Nobody knows what a provost is or does. Don't take it personally. If they ask, tell them you're like the COO of a large company.
2. The provost is number two at the university. Don't take it personally. Never upstage the president or chancellor and remember that you always speak for him or her, not for yourself.
3. Being number two has its own rewards. You get to focus on the true work of the university, not athletics or state politics. And you get called Mr.—or Madam—Provost.
4. The provost is staff to the chancellor. So, do the chancellor's staff work—now!
5. The provost is not a dean. Deans are like mini-chancellors, CEOs of their colleges or schools. Provosts just take care of business.
6. Deans have the best jobs on campus; just ask anyone who isn't one.
7. Department heads have the hardest jobs on campus; just ask one.
8. The provost's job is to stay home and run the joint. You must reorient your fundamental interests away from your discipline and toward the university as a whole—and as an organization that needs your continuous attention.
9. But don't expect folks to pay much attention. It's not you, it's the job. Don't take it personally.
10. The provost must love ambiguity and lack of closure, because everything in a university is based on formalized processes, processes with their own sense of time. Hardly anything will get done on schedule.

11. Provosts have little time to do any real work. So, surround yourself with great staff, delegate to them, stay out of their way, and accept their recommendations—most of the time.

12. The provost's job is about action, not extended analysis or reflection. Faculty members get to reflect, and so do former provosts.

13. Showing up matters, so do it all the time. There is no unimportant event for a provost—every one counts.

14. You are just a little bit famous. Don't take it personally.

15. If you want to have a perfect day, hug a teacher.

PART THREE

MONEY IS WAY AHEAD OF WHATEVER IS IN SECOND PLACE

12

A TEXTBOOK EXAMPLE

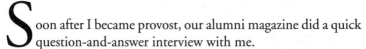

Soon after I became provost, our alumni magazine did a quick question-and-answer interview with me.

"What's the most challenging part of your job?" they asked.

"Money," I answered.

That's a real no-brainer, isn't it? Money is always the biggest challenge, no matter the kind of institution or its status. The top-ranked private universities in the country have billions in their endowments, but they're always looking for more money. So is NC State and every other university. We're either trying to get more money, allocating the existing money, or giving money back to the state for a budget cut. Never doubt that, amid the idealism of our academic environment, amid altruistic careers that are dedicated to learning, discovering, and sharing knowledge, money is crossing the finish line, while everything else is just rounding the final turn.

I can prove that assertion with a textbook example. No, I don't mean a quintessential example. I mean an example about textbooks.

Textbooks are always a battleground on campus. Overall, I think most students hate their textbooks. The most useless question on the student evaluation-of-teaching form is about the textbook. "The textbook was good" might just as well only have choices of "disagree," "really disagree," and "why did you make me buy this doorstop?" Nonetheless, faculty members continue to require textbooks. Faculty members love books in general, and they expect that students love them as well. No matter that the English major will never open his biology textbook again from the moment the final exam starts, or that the biology major won't ever leaf through her copy of *Canterbury Tales* again on a Friday night when she is bored with reruns of *Ice Road Truckers*. Faculty members want students to cherish their textbooks; students want to sell them back to the bookstore on their way home after the final—and for a right nice price, too.

So, we have to keep inventing new remedies to control textbook pain. One remedy is to make sure faculty members choose their textbooks for the next term by the date set by the (evil) bookstore. This isn't too big a stretch in the fall semester, when, let's say, the (evil) bookstore wants next semester's textbook selections by the end of October or so. October isn't too far from January, when the next term starts, and faculty members still have their heads into their teaching.

But it is hard for a faculty member to conceive why textbook orders for fall term need to be in, say, by the middle of April. In April, the farthest thing from a faculty member's mind is what books to require next August—that's five months away, for heaven's sake. Between then and now, we've got summer—write our own book, do our research, teach in Prague, take a vacation, repaint the kitchen, sleep—everything other than choose a textbook. That early spring deadline just seems like some arbitrary date picked by the (evil) bookstore for its convenience. No doubt the list of books just sits around until about August 1, when a bookstore employee stumbles across the list while cleaning her desk and actually orders the books.

As a faculty member, I never understood that early date; I didn't understand it as a department head, school director, or dean. Finally, when I was provost, someone enlightened me. The (evil) bookstore needs to know in April what textbooks will be used in the following fall, so they can buy them back from students at the end of spring finals at a fair price. If the (evil) bookstore knows it can sell the books in the fall, it can pay students top dollar; if the (evil) bookstore doesn't know if the book will be used again, it can't buy them back at all or, at best, they'll buy them at a price that makes students blanch.

Faculty members are notoriously bad at getting their textbook selections to the (evil) bookstore on time, but they have all sorts of good academic reasons for their tardiness. They might argue, with good intentions, that they are going to revise the course over the summer, and they need the time to evaluate several new possible texts. Or they might not know what they will be teaching yet. Many courses don't get instructors assigned until summer, and the department head couldn't be so brash as to assume to know the choices that those instructors will want to make. And the (evil) bookstore is just evil, anyhow. At NC State, this condition manifested itself as about a 45% on-time adoption rate in the spring semester; we did somewhat better in the fall.

Now enters a new university system president, eagerly paying attention to his constituents. Students complained to him about textbooks—they didn't like much about textbooks, including the new book price and the used book buy-back price. The university president told us provosts and our (evil) bookstores to get our textbook acts together.

Tired of the usual solutions, I invented a textbook adoption incentive. Faculty travel is always underfunded in today's university because of the shortage of operating funds, especially in the humanities and social sciences, where most of the university's course sections are offered. So I created a faculty travel fund for each college, with money allocated based on the rate of on-time textbook adoption. Once each college passed the 50% threshold of on-time adoptions, it got $100 for each additional course section with an on-time textbook adoption.

What happened? On-time adoptions in the first spring semester immediately jumped to 75%. That program cost the provost's reserves $140,000, with most of it going to the underfunded humanities and social sciences—and worth every penny, financially and philosophically. The deans and the faculty were thrilled with the travel funds. The bookstore estimated that they were able to buy back about $400,000 of additional books from students, and the (less evil) bookstore was thrilled to pay it.

And the winner is—money.

13

THE PROVOST'S BEST FRIEND

Given that money is the most important vector in the university, here is an essential corollary: The provost's best friend better be the university's chief financial officer.

The provost's office and CFO's office have back doors facing each other across the lobby of NC State's main administration building. Many days, we had more traffic between our back doors than we did through the front doors. Once an interviewer asked me if I interacted much with the CFO, and I answered, yes, we interacted often.

"How much time do you spend together?" she asked.

I answered, "About four hours."

"Per month or per week?" she continued.

"Per day."

In reality, three people oversee the university—the chancellor, the provost, and the chief financial officer, not necessarily in that order. As the three of us at NC State often discussed, ours were the three positions that have as their core responsibility the whole institution. Others, even other executive officers, have institutional roles as well, but they also have loyalties to specific functions on campus (a topic for later chapters). But the CEO, CAO, and CFO spend all their time addressing the entire institution—and they need to be allies.

Let's face it—the CFO can run rings around both the chancellor and the provost, when it comes to money questions. Money comes in from many sources, with many strings attached; it gets parsed out into dozens of buckets (money people seem to like that term, *buckets*, so you might as well learn to like it, too); it gets spent in all sorts of ways; and it is kept track of in all sorts of ledgers. Just when you think you have gotten the hang of it, the money folks introduce some new wrinkle to the formula.

"How much money do we have left?" I ask innocently late in the fiscal year.

"Obligated reserves or unobligated reserves?" the money people reply.

"Unobligated reserves, I guess; what are obligated reserves?" I say.

"Obligations. Now, do you want budgeted reserves, or current balances?" they parry.

"Current balances, I guess; that's what I can spend, right?"

"Depends. Some future expenditures are already encumbered, so there are unobligated expenses that we're already obligated to pay. Current balances also include some accounts receivable that are still within a time frame when they could be realized or not."

"Just tell me how much money we have left," I say.

"Well, we're waiting for this month's allocation from the state budget office, which is due Monday, but we generally don't get it until Wednesday after the university system office looks at it. The system might add or subtract from what we told the state we were supposed to get. Also, although we calculated our budget reduction and are holding it in a separate bucket, the state will make the final calculation at the end of the month, and we don't really know if we have enough or too much in the bucket until then. So, it is hard to say."

I cry uncle. "All I really wanted to know was whether I could say yes to the library's request for a dozen replacement computers," I admit in frustration.

"Why didn't you say so?" they respond. "We have a bucket for library technology that still has money in it. You really need to get better at communicating."

One reality that the provost must accept—and that everyone on the academic side, from faculty onward, must accept—is that the CFO needs a much bigger reserve fund than the provost does. Provosts need a few hundred thousand in reserve in case an opportunity hire comes up or a grant for which he promised matching money actually gets funded. Even in those cases, if there's no money left, the provost just passes on the opportunity.

The CFO, however, needs several *million* in reserve in case a power substation blows up, a classroom building floods, bricks start falling off the library exterior, or a presidential candidate decides to make a campaign stop on campus (all of these were real occurrences within one fiscal year). The CFO can't tell the bricks to get back to their offices and quit their bellyaching, or tell the presidential candidate thanks anyhow, maybe next year.

So, give the CFO a break. It's a tough job. One year, when the budget was particularly dire and we had drained all the available buckets dry, we were still left with a deficit. Rather than glare across the table and tell me that faculty loads just needed to get higher, our CFO said, "Okay, we'll cut the utilities budget by $500,000 more."

"What's our strategy for getting the utility costs down that much more?" I asked.

"Pray for a warm winter and a cool spring." He wouldn't have done that for anyone but his best friend.

14

WE HAVE MORE MONEY THAN
WE THINK WE DO

H ere's the good news: We have more money than we think
we have. Why? Because we spread it all over and give
spending authority to lots of folks who, on average, are
as conservative as a Danish farmer in Iowa.

Here's a painful example. I was presiding, as our policies
require, over the final session of a departmental graduate review. I
was distressed about two things that surfaced in the review. First,
their graduate enrollment was down, in the face of a university
imperative to get graduate enrollment up. Second, the department hadn't used all the money for assistantships that they had
requested and we had allocated to them. It seemed to me that
someone was asleep at two switches.

I asked what the problem was. They said that not every student to whom they had made an offer had accepted, so they had
fewer students than planned and hadn't needed all the money. "Of
course they didn't all accept," I said, "so why didn't you offer more
assistantships to make up for the yield not being 100%?" The
graduate coordinator looked at me as if I were crazy—what if all
the accepted graduate students *had* shown up?

Fearing that this might be a common attitude, I looked further into it.

The university had recently embarked on a mission to increase graduate enrollment (as public research universities often do). Therefore, the vice-chancellor for research and graduate studies and the provost had made a deal—we'd each put $500,000 into a fund to support new graduate students. I transferred my half of the money to him to distribute.

The funds trickled down the administrative chain, from vice-chancellor to dean of the graduate school to deans of academic colleges to associate deans for graduate programs to department heads to graduate program leaders (how can anyone say universities have too many levels of administrators?). At most steps along the way, the responsible party, acting like a good Danish farmer, kept some money in reserve, in case the next level was handled by an irresponsible spendthrift. Add the conservative bent of this particular graduate coordinator, and the consequence was that just about half of the money intended for increasing graduate enrollment actually made it into the hands of new graduate students.

Paul Bryant, author of the 2005 book *Confessions of an Habitual Administrator: An Academic Survival Manual*, relates the following story regarding who keeps money on the side:

> [A] highly respected dean of engineering . . . once told me that faculty members typically believe that their department chair has a secret fund that can finance anything the chair wants to support. The dean said he could assure me that his department chairs had no such fund. The chairs, in turn, he said, believed that the dean had such a secret fund. He assured me that was not the case. However, he said, he thought the provost probably had one. (p. 15)

I don't know anything about the specific individuals or units or university that Bryant refers to, but I'd bet that the dean was winking when he said his chairs and he hadn't kept a little money back just in case. Maybe not enough to "finance anything," but surely enough to do a little here and there, especially for an unusual circumstance.

All the graduate student money that trickled out along the way was used well, I know, so don't start tsk-tsk-ing about fiscal irresponsibility. Some might have gone to other graduate students whose funding ran out unexpectedly, but probably a good deal went to bridge gaps in operating funds. Many university departments start the fiscal year with negative operating budgets—if that is a disturbing thought for you, get out of administration right now—and they couldn't make it through the year without moving funds from some other buckets into the operating-fund bucket.

So, how do faculty members and administrators act when they are entrusted with public funds? The most common approach is to hoard the money. University employees have been hit over the head so often and so hard with the we-don't-have-any-money club, that they've come to adopt a mind-set of scarcity. One department head with whom I worked would complain constantly over the course of the year that her department had no money and couldn't accomplish what it needed. Then, about two months before the end of the fiscal year, she would meet with our business officer and find out that she had a sizable positive balance in her accounts and no good way to use it. "I don't know where that came from," she would say. It came from an unwillingness to spend, based on a fear of running out of money before graduation.

Add the stories that show up regularly in the media about an unfortunate public servant who got crosswise with some accounting rule, and most faculty members and many administrators would rather not have any responsibility for appropriated funds. The most common tendency, then, is to just leave the money in the bank—save it for a rainy day (or a rainy six months). That strategy would be fine if the money carried over from year to year, but in most states, unspent public funds revert to the state treasury at the end of the fiscal year. So, the benefits of being frugal evaporate as the calendar turns over to July 1.

The second approach to public money is to spend it as fast as you get it. This strategy has two phases. First, spend all the appropriated funds really fast, in case the provost, dean, or governor asks for some of them back later in the year. Then you can say, "Sorry, it's all gone. You'll have to get the budget reduction from someone else." Second, overspend—take that negative operating balance at the beginning of the year and just keep riding it down. The overspender is betting that a modestly overspent budget will get covered by the next higher administrative level, probably without anyone ever even asking what the heck is going on. Because most faculty members and administrators are hoarders, they'll have some funding left at the end of the year, which will be used to make the spender's deficit disappear. Spending your budget moderately into the red is a highly efficient strategy in universities. In twenty years as an administrator, I've never seen or initiated a punishment of an academic unit or its leader for overspending the budget.

Of no surprise to those who know me, I am a spender, maybe even a bit of an overspender. I justified my approach with the following analogy to a quartermaster that I learned when I was in the army. I was told that there are two kinds of quartermasters, the folks responsible for outfitting the troops. One kind is proud of a stockroom brimming with supplies, while his troops are marching in worn-out boots and carrying broken equipment. The second has an empty stockroom, but is proud that his troops are well equipped, ready, and able to complete their mission. I determined early that I would emulate the second. After all, we were given the funds to accomplish the mission of the institution—teach students, discover and create knowledge and beauty, inform and advise the community. If every level in the university is underspending their budgets out of well-meaning but dysfunctional trepidation, then we're cheating our aspirations big time. If they weren't going to do their duty, I'd do it for them. So, I stretched our budgets, made lots of obligations, and ran the reserves nearly dry. I allocated new funds early and generously (at least in university terms). I transferred new funds permanently to other budgets, rather than giving out one-time money that would revert to my budget when the next fiscal year began.

Besides, it really wasn't much of a risk. Because the lead time on most university activities is so long, we can afford to skate out on the financial thin ice a bit. We approve new faculty positions almost a year before the actual person arrives, so some chance exists that she or he will never arrive. We commit to cost-sharing on grants at their submission, probably a good six months to a year before they get approved—and most don't get approved. We are only going to get about half of those graduate students to whom we commit assistantships (if we get them all, then we're not selective enough—losing a few to Cornell and Georgia Tech is how we know we're fishing in the right pool). The CFO didn't exactly endorse that idea, and my business officers always watched me like hawks, but it worked fine, because we always have more money than we think we do.

15

WE HAVE ALL THE MONEY
WE NEED

H ere's the second piece of good budget news: We have all
the money we need. That is, we have all the money we
need to do the things that are most important.

I once heard an aphorism that I now use often: Universities
have trouble doing anything for the first time or the last time. I'll
debate the beginning of that statement—universities, I contend,
will do almost any worthy thing for the first time, but not for the
second time. Need seed money? You got it. Need permanent money
to tend the seeds? Forget it. But I'm on board with the second
part—we just can't bring ourselves to do anything for the last time.

If we could do things for the last time, we would have all the
money we need.

Why can't we do anything for the last time? Because we have
a system whose logic dictates the opposite. Here's how it goes.
When a department gets new money, it invariably commits it to
new tenure-track faculty positions, which it fills as soon as possible. This makes perfect sense in terms of self-preservation. If the
department ties up its money in tenured or tenure-track faculty
members, an administrator would need to be a surgeon to extract
it later. Except in the case of financial exigency or the undefined
"major program elimination," both of which universities equate

to suicide notes, a department can count on keeping that money and those positions forever.

When the inevitable next budget cut comes along, the department may be shielded some from the brunt of the budget reductions, because tenure-track faculty can't be readily terminated. But every other department in the college has used the same strategy, so all units are in the same fix. The first thing the dean does is take back all vacant faculty positions, sometimes permanently, sometimes as a hiring freeze (so better fill those tenure-track vacancies as quickly as they occur; early in my administrative career, a particularly kind dean called me one afternoon and said, "Make that tenure-track job offer today, in writing, because we're getting a hiring freeze tomorrow."). After the faculty vacancies disappear and typically with more than 90% of its appropriated budget tied up in salaries, the department has very few choices. Consequently, the department gives up the last of its operating budgets (if it wasn't in the red to start with), lays off additional low-salaried staff members (if any are left), and eliminates as many graduate assistantships as are needed to make up the difference. As a result, the budget becomes even more heavily weighted to the salaries of tenured faculty positions.

When times get a little better and the department gets a modicum of new funds, what does it do? Of course—hire another tenure-track faculty member! We need more faculty members— remember, we lost a vacancy last time—and we have to hire on the tenure-track in order to keep up our research momentum, stay competitive with our peers, and not jeopardize our accreditation. The university is usually complicit in this strategy, because new funds are often allocated as part of some "strategic initiative" or "futures plan." Such plans recognize that the number of tenure-track positions has declined since the last budget cuts (vacant positions went unfilled), so it puts a priority on using the new money to add tenure-track positions.

The existing faculty members need to keep working, of course, and they have become experts in the fields of their academic youth. So, whether or not those fields are still important (yes, I know they are all important—to someone, somewhere), the department needs to continue allocating time, space, and funding to their work. But the new faculty members that the department hires are working in the emerging leading-edge areas of their disciplines. In order to recruit them, the department has committed "start-up funds," a concept foreign to the old-timers in the department but considered essential to the newcomers—renovated labs, six-figure-cost pieces of equipment, staff support, summer salary. To amass the start-up funds, the department has mortgaged itself to the dean, provost, and research vice-chancellor, promising to give up future shares of returned indirect costs and the next several faculty retirements. Along the way, the department has to find ways to cram existing faculty into the now smaller space and carve up whatever budget it still has into even smaller pieces

So, in the end, the department now has maintained or expanded its tenure-track faculty roster, operating on fewer dollars, with less support, in space that is increasingly crowded and with capacities that are distressingly different between the wealthy new and the suffering old.

Why? Because we steadfastly refuse to do anything for the last time.

The poster child for this phenomenon is cooperative extension. Don't get me wrong—I love extension. I've studied and worked in land grant universities my whole life, partly because I love the ideal and reality of extension. Cooperative extension (formerly known as agricultural extension) is one of our nation's most emblematic success stories. The extension idea is to take the knowledge of the university out to the people of the nation, state by state, so that our citizens can work and live better. Initially, extension focused on improving farming operations and quality of living in rural communities; more recently, it has added programs in urban areas, particularly serving lower-income neighborhoods. The concept is uniquely American. Over the century and a half since extension was invented, it has helped all Americans, either directly or indirectly, whether they know it or not.

Over that same time period, extension has built a political constituency for programming that is also uniquely American. It is a grassroots constituency composed of county-based committees and crop-based state organizations (commodity groups, we land-grant folks would say). This is a system perfected to exert maximum influence through the disbursed representation of our state and federal legislatures. As a consequence, should extension say out loud that maybe it would consider eliminating a program that has become low priority because the crop has disappeared or the number of farmers growing it has shrunk dramatically, a political storm would erupt from sea to shining sea. And, consequently, although some programs are ended, most are kept on life support. They just get smaller and less effective—not just the ones that were in the crosshairs, but all the others whose budgets get squeezed to protect the status quo.

External influences might keep the extension service from stopping programs, but internal forces are also at work. In the calculus of pure knowledge, all fields are equal; so, how can anyone make the judgment that medieval history ought to stay and grow, while forensic anthropology must wither and die? If we choose to cut some withering program this year, perhaps mine will be next? Won't reducing a program in our department just make it easier for those other departments to keep theirs? We can eliminate a program in name, but since we can't get rid of the tenured faculty members, we won't save any money, so why do it?

The reason to do it is because there is no other way to run an institution sanely. Unless we are willing to weed out the activities that are lowest priorities, then the highest priorities will never get enough sunlight to grow, and new priorities will never find a place to seed and germinate.

The alternative to stopping whole programs or activities is to keep shaving a bit off the top of all programs—the across-the-board reduction. Everyone (and I mean everyone) says that we should not do across-the-board reductions, but then everyone (and I mean almost everyone) refuses to make decisions that allow anything but.

When I was nearing the end of my term as provost (and, hence, getting a little more frank and impatient in open conversation), I spoke at a budget reduction meeting with a college faculty and staff. I stated that I expected their reduction plan to include eliminating whole programs, vertical cuts as we were calling them, not just the usual trimming around the edges. A well-respected department head took me on.

"It won't do any good to cut out whole programs, because we can't get rid of the tenured faculty members that run them," he said.

"You just have to do it," I said. "And if you come up with a plan that will work but you need some bridging money, let's talk about it." (I had a reserve fund.)

"It would take at least five years before the faculty members that operate a program would be gone, through retirements or taking other jobs," he retorted. "It just isn't feasible."

"All I can say, then, is that five years ago, when times were good, you weren't doing your job. Because back then is when you should have declared that you were ending some program—whatever your lowest priority program was—so today you wouldn't find yourself in an infeasible situation. You should have started eliminating faculty positions in that area as they became vacant, turning the salary dollars into operating dollars, so your department had a way to deal with today's budget reduction effectively. I'm reminded of the saying that the best time to plant a tree was 25 years ago; and the second best time is today. If you aren't willing today to make the commitment to end a low-priority program, when will you ever be ready?"

I'm afraid that the audience's sympathies were with the department head, not with me.

As I write the final draft of this manuscript, our university is engaged in a study of academic programs, looking at various aspects of productivity. The goal, I presume, is to decide if some programs need to be shut down (a study like this would never say such a thing explicitly: Imagine the uproar if the provost said, "We're going to eliminate our least-effective degrees, based on this study."). I have recommended that the undergraduate degree in my own field be closed, for a number of reasons—too small an enrollment, few professional employment opportunities for BS graduates, absence of sufficient course offerings to provide a comprehensive curriculum, and others a little too sensitive to write down. My colleagues can't bring themselves to accept my recommendation, and they have their reasons—it doesn't cost that much to run the program, many university degrees don't have professional outlets, the few students who do want the degree have nowhere else to get it in North Carolina. So, even when the faculty member within the discipline says it is time to put this dying horse out of its misery, the faculty has trouble pulling the trigger.

The reality is that we must always be evaluating what to stop doing if we are to run our universities effectively. We need to say, out loud, that this major or that research area or these extension and outreach programs or these special units or administrative features or these student services have become low priorities and that we are going to stop investing new faculty, staff, space, and money in them. Then we need to actually close the programs down, not because the governor has ordered a budget reduction, but because that's our job, all day, every day.

And guess what? The provost must lead the way.

Then we'll have all the money we need—to do what is most important.

16

THE STRATEGIC DOORSTOP

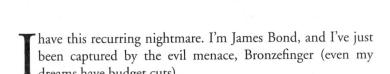

I have this recurring nightmare. I'm James Bond, and I've just been captured by the evil menace, Bronzefinger (even my dreams have budget cuts).

"Killing is too good for you, Bond," he says.

"It's torture then," I say, "what's it going to be? Cutting me in half slowly with a laser beam?"

"No," he says, "that didn't work last time, but I've now perfected the ultimate torture—you're going to chair the strategic planning committee."

Then I wake up screaming.

People everywhere hate strategic planning. I've taught strategic planning for a couple of decades, and I've created or helped create strategic plans for universities, churches, nonprofit organizations, and government agencies. I might hate strategic planning even more than anyone else does. They hate it because it is hard; I hate it because usually nothing comes of it.

Strategic planning involves many capable, well-intentioned folks, spending lots of valuable time crafting an optimistic and exciting vision of the future for their organization. Then they hand it to the boss who says thanks, good job, more later. Later seldom comes.

Later seldom comes because strategic planning is in second place, way behind the thing that is in first place—money. And unless money and strategy are joined at the hip, money wins and strategy loses. This is where the provost and his best friend need to be on the same page. The provost needs to drive the strategic plan, and the CFO needs to get the right amount of money in the right buckets to fund it.

Money gets attached to strategy in one of two ways. Existing money can be reallocated to fund the strategic initiatives, or new money can be allocated up front to do so.

Reallocating old money is risky business. As discussed previously, the tradition and instinct of the university run counter to reallocation. Reallocation implies an adjustment of the relative value of the existing parts of the institution. And because reallocation involves taking away from someone to give to someone else, the threat and insult are double—some programs win, some programs lose.

One of the most reliable complaints about any strategic plan relates precisely to this issue. Many people equate strategic planning with new initiatives, and they ask why we should start new initiatives when we can't even adequately fund the things we're doing now. No, of course we shouldn't stop doing any of the things we're doing now—haven't you been listening?—we should be funding all of them better. So, until we can get all our existing programs up to some definition of full funding, we have no need for strategic planning.

Nonetheless, despite such protests, today's university is going to declare itself in favor of reallocation. The literature on provosts indicates that most provosts are engaged in budget reallocation all the time. Since we're committed to it, we better figure out some way to appear to do it. Because we really don't want to take it on seriously, though, we need to minimize the impact.

An often-used tactic is to create a program whereby each unit only gets, say, 98% of their previous budget, and the provost accumulates the other 2% as a pool to fund the school's highest priorities. If honest, you'll recognize that collecting 2% of the budget is a pretty small increment on which to reorder the institutions priorities. But it gets worse.

The provost then asks all units to write proposals to compete for part of this pool. The eligible topics are usually strategic in name, but written broadly enough so that all the units are relevant to at least some of them. We say that we are strategically focused on such things as economic development, globalization, expanding graduate education, social equity, natural disaster mitigation, or similarly grand and inclusive topics. It is the rare process that gets specific enough to say, for example, all the recovered funds are going to performing arts and renewable energy.

The provost then invents a process that solicits and evaluates proposals for funding under the strategic priorities. The process usually goes overboard in assuring that faculty members have a majority interest in the decisions, via something like the Faculty Assessment Team for Unified Ordination of University Strategy, also known as the Fatuous Committee. Lots of proposals arrive. Fatuous evaluates the proposals and sends its recommendations to the provost; the recommendations are likely to assess about 80% as worthy of funding, 15% as worthy if more funding is available, and a few as somewhat worthy. The provost, sometimes with faculty advice, but more likely with the advice of her or his administrative team, makes the final decisions and distributes the money to the units.

I hate it. My experience is that about 1.9% of the funds end up going right back to the colleges and departments from which they came. An enormous amount of energy and goodwill have been absorbed in a process that has been virtually meaningless to the future of the institution. If the cost of the process itself in faculty, staff, and leadership time were added together, it would probably exceed the total funding that was actually reallocated. I try to remember a principle learned years ago, when Total Quality Management was the strategic rage of the day. The mantra was, "If a step in the process doesn't add value to the product, don't do it." Consequently, I have never used such a cumbersome, inefficient process to reallocate a modicum of existing funds at the institutional level.

Just as strongly as I reject reallocating existing funds to implement strategy, I recommend allocating new funds according to the strategic plan. New funds don't belong to anyone yet, so at least there are no losers to soothe. Tying the budget allocation to the strategic plan will get people's attention, as it did one particular Thursday morning.

The regularly scheduled every-other Thursday meeting of the Council of Deans convened, as always, a few minutes late. After we got the cell phones and PDAs all stowed, the coffee cups filled, and the my-college-is-better-than-your-college banter finished, we began the meeting. Without prior warning, however, I canceled the usual agenda and replaced it with two hours devoted to "compact planning and budget allocation." Compact planning was what we called the execution of our strategic plan.

I had been traveling for about a week, ending with a long plane ride back to Raleigh. Those plane rides always made the deans anxious—something startling might happen if I had too much time to think. In this case, they were correct.

We had just completed the creation of our next three-year compact plan. Each dean had submitted a plan for their college, each vice provost, a plan for their operation. I had coerced our budget folks to estimate how much new money we could expect in each of the next three years from planned enrollment growth and a conservative guess at tuition increases. We had a new university strategic plan with 10 investment priorities and 5 focus areas. And I had a six-hour flight with empty seats next to me. Means, opportunity, and motive!

At the meeting, I passed out copies of the 13-page handwritten document I'd scribbled on the plane. This was my *Jerry Maguire* moment. The plan I unveiled had several features, and each of them tied strategy to money.

First, I introduced a new way to fund faculty positions. We all knew that funding a faculty position with just the salary and benefits was insufficient—it just caused more stress on existing resources. Our new strategic plan also said that we would increase graduate enrollment; because faculty members are the ones who bring in graduate students, accomplishing this would require investing in faculty. So, I suggested that we fund each tenure-track faculty position with enough money to pay salary and benefits (a standard amount, but at three different market-based levels for business, engineering, and everyone else), plus $25,000 for new staff and operating and $25,000 to fund a graduate student. New non–tenure-track positions weren't quite so generously funded, but got the salary and benefits plus an additional $10,000 for staff and operating. This meant that we wouldn't be able to fund as many faculty positions as we might have expected, but we were funding each one honestly.

Second, I committed the faculty positions to meet the core teaching needs in four colleges that produced most of our student credit hours but were chronically underfunded. Thus, the strategic plan solved one of our most nagging problems, because it addressed the investment priority of "improve undergraduate education." Most of these positions were non–tenure–track, because, despite our best intentions to fund as many tenure-track positions as possible, we desperately needed the high teaching productivity that non–tenure-track faculty supplied. We all knew, furthermore, that more non–tenure-track faculty could absorb more teaching, providing new and existing tenure-track faculty more breathing space for scholarship and graduate student mentoring. Also, non–tenure-track positions could be "changed out" as the teaching needs fluctuated.

Third, I committed funds to other investment priorities and focus areas in our strategic plan. Nineteen professional advising positions went out to colleges and various advising programs to "improve student success." International programs got several new positions to meet our strategic goal to "globalize our student experience." Faculty positions went to colleges that advanced programs directly related to our focus areas in environment and energy, human health, economic development, and educational innovation.

Fourth, and perhaps most importantly, these commitments were made in advance for the next three years so that the colleges could begin recruiting early and have the faculty arriving at the same time the money did.

For the first time in anyone's memory, the Council of Deans meeting ended in applause. And the strategic plan ended up in operation. Money still won, but the jockey this time was strategy.

17

THE PROVOST AIN'T GOT
NO ALUMNI

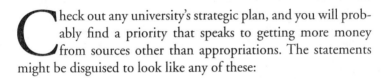

C heck out any university's strategic plan, and you will probably find a priority that speaks to getting more money
from sources other than appropriations. The statements
might be disguised to look like any of these:

- Develop new sources of support for research and innovation.
- Reduce reliance on traditional forms of financial support.
- Expand our engagement with the local and statewide private
  sector.
- Reengage our alumni in the life of the university.
- Diversify and strengthen the institution's resource base.

Let me decode those statements. The first one means faculty
need to get more grants. The second means the state isn't our sugar
daddy anymore; and we can't raise tuition much more either. The
third means do things that business and industry will pay for. The
fourth means get more donations from alumni. The last means we
don't have a clue, but, in the interest of shared governance, we're
going to create a faculty-administrative committee to develop a
strategic approach.

Early in my tenure as dean, the executive officers and deans
had a retreat. At least the chancellor called it a retreat; it was really

a half-day budget meeting. The CFO went through the state budget prospects, which were bad and getting worse. Then the vice-chancellor for university advancement (the chief fund-raiser) profiled our alumni giving. We were doing well in this regard, but most of the money was directed to undergraduate scholarships, athletics, other nonacademic buildings, and a good deal of it was in estate plans we wouldn't see for a long time. The vice-chancellor for research showed us that most federal grants were aimed at medical research, and we didn't have a human medical school (we do have a medical school, but it covers animals other than humans—a veterinary college). The provost showed us where tuition revenues were headed—nowhere fast, and most of the new tuition money had to be used to underwrite the financial support of students who couldn't afford higher tuition. I wrote a note in the margin of the handouts: Nielsen, you are on your own.

At least our college had a constituency. We supplied the employees for one of the largest industries in the state—the wood products industry. Major corporations had paper mills, saw mills, and furniture factories in the state. We represented private forest landowners, and the state is more than half private forest land. We represented the parks, tourism, and sport management folks, and tourism is a big industry in North Carolina. And we had alumni. Lots of alumni, most of whom still lived in North Carolina and loved both the university and college. We also had 80,000 acres of our own forests that we managed for wood production and sales to support our college's students, faculty, and operations.

The college had something else, too. We had a development staff. Three people spent all their time looking for private gifts. They were good at it, and they made the dean spend a lot of his time on fund-raising.

When I got to be provost, I expected that I'd have a development staff. Surely the provost had some help to find private funding for important university initiatives in the academic realm. The university lacked a number of major academic dimensions that our higher-ranked peers had. We needed an honors college, a university fellowship program for doctoral students, a university speakers' series, diversity scholarships, backing for new interdisciplinary degree programs, lots of things. To get them done, we needed private money. To get private money, we needed a development team.

Wrong. The provost didn't have any development staff, and he didn't need any, because he had no development function. I was shocked, but I shouldn't have been. As the literature relates, this condition is almost universal. Most provosts say they have little or no role in their institution's private fund-raising. The reason is that, in private fund-raising, the provost is stuck between a rock and a hard place.

The rock is the chancellor. Remember, she is number one. At the university level, fund-raising is the job of the chancellor and her or his personal development officer, the vice-chancellor for university advancement. High-wealth donors are involved in a lengthy courtship with the university, and they want to be wooed by number one, not number two. Besides provosts turn over much too rapidly to be seen as faithful suitors. More modest donors at the university level are handled by the so-called annual fund, the telephone-based solicitation network run by the vice chancellor and implemented by undergraduate students, who call you at dinnertime. Because the people called are mostly alumni, we enter the realm of the hard place.

The hard place is that the provost has no constituency. Alumni belong to the colleges, maybe even to the departments. Most people remain interested in the university because they went to school there. They come back to reunions of their classes, where they are courted by their old deans and department heads. And they want to give back to the programs from which they graduated and most often for scholarships for starving undergraduate students, just like they were.

And, then, of course, there is athletics. But you know that story.

I thought I could squeeze out of this rock–hard place dilemma. Surely we could find some folks who were interested in the

university, not their home department; some people in the community who weren't alumni but had grown close to the university.
So, I hired a development officer. I was warned that it wouldn't
work; previous provosts had tried this approach and failed; there
was strident competition for any potential donor and the provost
had no tools with which to compete.

The doubters were right. After several years, we had drawn
in a few gifts, but those gifts were typically pleasant surprises or
the result of creative thinking and hard work by one of the vice
provosts. It seemed that whenever we identified someone or some
organization that might be approachable, a check with the university's development database revealed that they had been "claimed
and assigned" to one of our colleges. We have a popular statue on
campus called The Strolling Professor—a facsimile of a chemistry
professor walking briskly while reading an open book. I thought
a Strolling Professor fund would be a great way to raise money for
university-wide academic enhancement projects. Turns out the
Strolling Professor was "owned" by one of our colleges.

In the end, the budget cuts claimed the provost's development officer, and the experiment ended. I don't recommend trying a replication. The law of the universe is this: The provost ain't
got no alumni.

LESSONS ABOUT MONEY

1. And the winner is—money. Don't ever fool yourself that the winner is academics or research or outreach. Those horses run in some other races.
2. As long as money is the winner, use it to modify behavior. It is amazing how little money it takes to get good things to happen in a university.
3. The CFO is the provost's best friend. And it is the provost's job to make sure that it stays that way. Take your CFO to lunch (but don't submit for reimbursement).
4. My brother-in-law says that the race is not always to the swift and the battle to the strong—but that's the way to bet. If the CFO and provost fight, the CFO will win. The provost might win a battle now and again, but never the war.
5. The CFO needs larger cash reserves than the provost. Let the faculty know you agree with that.
6. Almost everyone hoards money.
7. Therefore, you have more to spend than you think. So spend it.
8. The budget always evens out in the end, so don't worry.
9. Go ahead and obligate money for the future, even over-obligate. Many of the obligations won't ever materialize.
10. The provost must be willing to cut programs, because no one else will. Be courageous!
11. You have to cut low-priority programs during good times, or they'll just keep accumulating. Then, when the inevitable bad times come along, everyone will plead that their money is all tied up in tenure-track faculty positions.
12. Strategic planning turns out to be a sham most of the time, because plans seldom get implemented.
13. Reallocating existing funds turns out to be a sham most of the time, too, because a very elaborate and time-consuming process usually puts the money right back where it came from.

14. Strategic allocation of new funds isn't a sham. Because if money gets attached to strategy, the strategy gets implemented.

15. Forget private fund-raising in the provost's office. The provost ain't got no alumni.

PART FOUR
ACADEMICS 'R' US

18

ACADEMICS 'R' US—OR 'R' IT?

This is an academic institution, and, therefore, all of us have academics foremost in our minds at all times, right? Unfortunately not.

But the provost better have. The provost is the chief academic officer, the CAO. The provost carries the academic banner into battle every day, all day. No one else does.

Other administrators care about academics, of course, but they have other jobs to do and, hence, proximate priorities that absorb their time and attention. The chancellor needs to keep the entire universe happy; in a state like North Carolina and a school like North Carolina State University, that pretty much meant he worked on four things—money, athletics, community relations, and economic development—with a real emphasis on the last. We are a land grant university, and therefore, by mission, we need to be relevant to the needs of the state. That is a noble mission, one to which I pledge allegiance every day. After all, I've spent four decades studying or working in land grant schools.

Looked at in one way—the way most faculty members look at it—economic development is part of the academic mission. Our major economic impact comes from the graduates we produce, the folks who have the ideas and skills to transform an economy. Through research, we also produce the knowledge that drives the economy (or might, someday). Through extension and outreach, we share our knowledge so that all people of the state can improve their lives—including their economic lives.

But that isn't what economic development means to many of the people with whom the university's CEO interacts. It means how many jobs did the university help create this year? How many companies were spun off? How much intellectual property was patented and then licensed? How has the university helped bring new companies to the state? How much money did the university contribute back to the state treasury? The chancellor has to have good answers to these questions, with data to back them up.

Athletic directors (AD) care about academics, too. Don't scowl, they really do. They better, because under the late Miles Brand, the NCAA put some real teeth into the jaws of academic requirements for athletes. The AD wants student-athletes to graduate at high rates in quality majors—just as long as they also win a lot more often than they lose.

The same is true for other university leaders. We covered the CFO in the last section; he has a good reason for caring about money (so he can give it to his best friend, the provost). The research office cares about the academic mission, but the real hammer in that office is the volume of external grants, especially grants with full overhead (big NSF grant—fantastic, let's get out a news release; great history book written without grant support—thanks, I'll look at it later). The Student Affairs shop has the specific responsibility to manage the nonacademic part of the student experience. Advancement is about raising friends and raising money, and at the end of the day (or especially at the end of the quarter), it doesn't matter if the money comes in for academic programs or athletics or the alumni building, it all counts. Each of these folks has her or his responsibilities and priorities.

That, according to Cornell, is one of the reasons for calling this person the provost. Back in 1943, the Cornell University governing board entertained an idea to change the position's title from provost to vice president. Cornell's president at the time objected, arguing that the obscurity of the title "provost" served the purpose of separating that position from all the other university officers who carried the vice president-of-something title. The provost was different, more a second president than anything else, but with a focus on the academic soul of the institution (the last are my words, not Cornell's).

So, there it is—the provost is the chief academic officer, warden of all that is academic. This is arguably the most important aspect of the provost's job, to keep the institution's eye on the academic prize. In the 2008 CAO Census, provosts mentioned that, although they spent more of their time on other things, academic matters were their most important function. About half listed ensuring academic quality and advancing the academic visions as two of their three most important duties. They rated nothing higher.

Perhaps my most vivid reminder that the provost may stand alone in support of academics was also the most trivial. We have two graduations each year at NC State, in December and in May. At the December graduation, students didn't get their diplomas handed to them as they cross the stage. Finals always ended just a day before graduation, and our associate deans and registration folks just couldn't run the process from faculty grading through diploma printing and distribution in the 36 hours available. In May, however, a week separated the end of finals from graduation ceremonies. So, through Herculean efforts, we always managed to get personal diplomas to students at their graduation ceremonies.

We also enforced a policy at May graduation that no one could participate in graduation unless they were officially certified as having met all the requirements for graduation. Consequently, a small group of students, sprinkled among the colleges, suffered in a state of purgatory right up to the end—some of them cleared for graduation just before the ceremonies, but others did not. Our associate deans all agreed that the stress of this was unnecessary, occasioned only by the tradition of delivering a diploma at the ceremony. If we didn't give out the diplomas at the ceremony, they reasoned, we could let students participate, even if we weren't sure they actually qualified for graduation. The students could hear their names called, walk across the stage, shake hands with the dean, and make their attending families and friends proud. No harm, no foul.

Therefore, I introduced to the executive officers the idea of eliminating diploma distribution at May graduation. The particular year was ideal. We were changing the printing process for diplomas (from outsourcing to internal printing, in order to meet that year's budget reduction), and the diploma-processing task was going to be Herculean on steroids. The debate over this proposal was rancorous—matched only in my memory by the debate about how many hours we should allow for tailgating before a football game. I heard objections that such a radical change might rankle the alumni, cost us donations, cause politicians to get complaints from their constituents, and look bad in the newspaper. When the votes were tallied, I lost.

The defeat demonstrated that academics aren't us. The 11 executive officers gathered around the table included 5 from academic backgrounds, but 2 of those were present in nonacademic roles. The other 6 executive officers were not academics, and that's how most of them voted. I had naïvely put an academic matter into a forum at which too many other viewpoints held sway. My mistake. Academic matters need to be handled by the provost and his or her advisors, the deans, department heads, and faculty.

This tale does have a happy ending. A few semesters later, an old academic issue once again hit the student leaders' agenda. They wanted "reading days" before finals—more time to study hard and prepare (and they made the argument with straight faces). The head of the calendar committee came to me with a proposal to finally give in to the students and provide two reading days. However, he said, that would mean a tightening of the schedule for spring graduation. Adding two days in the spring would move the last day of finals right up against graduation, just like in the fall.

"Would we still be able to provide diplomas at spring graduation?" I asked.

"Impossible," he said, "just like in the fall."

"Reading days are approved."

19

STRATEGY 'R' US, TOO

Want more good provost news? Not only must the provost's hand be on the tiller of the university, the provost also needs to plot the course. In other words, the provost also has to be the strategist. Want to find a copy of the university's strategic plan? The most likely spot to find it is on the provost's desk, or maybe in the upper right drawer, where he keeps a few important items that he needs to refer to regularly.

With a warped personality like mine, though, a truer sentence would read, "the provost *gets* to be the strategist." When, at an executive officers' meeting early in our terms, the chancellor asked us to start thinking about big ideas for the university, my heart went pitter-patter. I labeled a separate section in my Franklin Covey planner "big ideas" and began jotting notes. Start a medical school, open branch campuses, initiate a music major, double graduate enrollment, abandon the first-year college, establish an international center, build a performing arts center, create a museum about the African American experience in North Carolina, require students to perform a leadership experience. You want ideas? I'll give you ideas.

I know what you are thinking—didn't I say a few pages back that I hated strategic planning? I can explain the contradiction. I hate strategic planning that isn't going to get implemented. Too often, the goal of strategic planning is to produce a strategic plan ("thank goodness that's done; now where were we?"), which doesn't get followed. I recently was asked to help another university as they created a strategic plan. Sure, I said, because I was going to get paid to help, but why are you doing this? They didn't have a plan, hadn't ever had one, but they were coming up for reaccreditation in two years, and the accrediting board now insisted they have a strategic plan. So, could I help them craft one that would fill the accreditation bill and not get in the way of the president's agenda? That's the kind of strategic planning I hate (and they picked another consultant).

But if it's my strategic plan, empowered by allocations from the academic budget, I'm all in.

The provost better be a planning and strategy nerd. Because academics is core at the university, and because the provost is the only person whose job is to protect and enhance the core, the provost needs to grab the strategic planning reins and hold on tight. Many years ago, a strategic marketing consultant told me that when he took on a new university client, he tried to align his reporting with the provost's office, because that is where strategic management is most likely to fall, sometimes explicitly, sometimes de facto.

Without the provost's leadership, strategic direction can emerge from other places, any of which may be suboptimal for the overall progress of the university. The research office will want a piece of strategy and should have one, but too often its thinking mirrors the major grant interests of federal funding agencies. If renewable energy is big now, let's reorganize around a strategic goal for renewable energy research. Or bioengineering, supercomputing, disaster management, or homeland security. Remember the stampede to establish major research centers focused on homeland security right after 9/11? Seen much of that money? Me neither.

The development arm of the university will want a turn at the strategic reins, too, in order to maximize the effectiveness of their fund-raising. The basis of their interest, however, is most likely for ideas they think donors are willing to fund. Also, their strategic priorities will usually be about form rather than function; they talk in terms of undergraduate scholarships, endowed professorships, and building projects, not in terms of specific strategic directions. Student support will probably be on their list, expressed in vague terms; funds for the Gay, Lesbian, Bisexual, and Transgender Center, study-abroad scholarships to Santiago, or additional testing facilities for the disability services office are less likely to be listed.

In a public university, the lobbyist will also want to help set strategy (excuse me, I meant the "state government liaison officer"). The lobbyist is thinking about what the state legislature and governor are most likely to support, however, not what the institution's academic priorities, strengths, or aspirations are; we hope these match up well, but there is never any guarantee. The lobbyist also has a more fundamental strategic interest—the more general a published strategy, the better. Keeping the strategy as vague as possible increases the likelihood that specific programs can slip under some larger strategic umbrella, just in time to match a powerful legislator's interests.

The provost, however, is the senior administrator who has responsibility to make sure the institution is going where society needs it to go. Fortunately, the major trends affecting education in general and any one university in particular are fairly stable and fairly obvious. We need:

- more and better teachers and health care workers;
- a faster form of gaining postgraduate experience than the traditional master's degree;
- students who are globally competent and happy about it;
- more graduates in STEM (science, technology, engineering, and math) disciplines;
- higher graduation rates, in shorter times;
- seamless articulation from community college to university to career;
- online education that is integrated into every student's experience and every faculty member's responsibility;

- to help make the world more sustainable;
- to provide every child the opportunity to escape poverty;
- innovation and entrepreneurship to lead our economy; and
- maybe one or two things particular to your unique mix of programs

There, I've written your strategic plan. You are welcome.

One last thing about strategic thinking. To paraphrase Michael Eisner, the former CEO of Disney and a committed brainstormer: For every ten ideas, one is good; and for every ten good ideas, one is practical. In other words, most of anyone's ideas are useless. Pride of origination has no place in strategy development. The person who can create an idea one minute and discard it the next, if it proves unworthy—that's the person needed at the strategy table.

20

ATHLETES ARE
STUDENTS, TOO

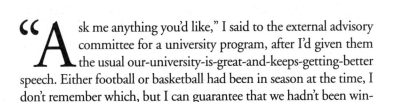

"Ask me anything you'd like," I said to the external advisory committee for a university program, after I'd given them the usual our-university-is-great-and-keeps-getting-better speech. Either football or basketball had been in season at the time, I don't remember which, but I can guarantee that we hadn't been winning enough, so sports were on people's minds. The first question I got, though, was unexpected.

"How can you even pretend that those athletes are students? How can you live with your hypocrisy when you defend them?" I quoted the usual statistics about comparable graduation rates and GPAs, but I wish I had been a little more aggressive in answering, because I have no trouble defending student-athletes. I love student-athletes.

Despite the negative behavior and negative press of a few athletes, college athletes are truly remarkable individuals. You don't get to be a Division-I athlete without being a person who can win in any competition—athletic or otherwise. The time and energy required to practice and perform at this level is astounding. I find it remarkable that our student-athletes can even get up in the morning, let alone get up, work out, go to class, work out, study, compete—and do it all over again tomorrow. If you want to be truly humbled, shadow a student-athlete for a day during their competitive season; my guess is you'll be out sick for the rest of the week.

Soon after I became dean, I met a student studying one of our majors who was a student-athlete, playing on one of our women's teams with a full scholarship. She was also an honors student. She was also a student leader, president or chair of several organizations or functions. In addition to all that, she was a committed community volunteer. After I'd know her a while, I suggested that she ought to take it a little easy on the student organization leadership. I didn't want her to burn out, like I would have if I had been her. She didn't take my suggestion well. She looked at me with an intensity that I wouldn't want to meet on the field of competition. "If you make me stop," she told me, "I'll just go out and find something else to do. I've got to be busy." That's the real story of the student-athlete.

Now, in the spirit of full disclosure, I have to admit that I also love college athletics. Whereas, the pain on the faces of many university leaders is only shallowly disguised while they are entertaining at football and basketball games, I found it one of the best parts of the job. Thousands of us gather in phenomenal facilities (even the older and well-worn stadiums are still wonderful; but, then I grew up watching the Cubs lose at Wrigley Field) to watch world-class athletes compete under the most respectful of rules and traditions. It also helps if you watch from the climate-controlled, snack-enriched, and gaudily furnished chancellor's suite.

We typically entertained two kinds of folks at ball games. One type was pretty oblivious to the contest going on below them; they came to mingle with the right people. The other type came to watch the game—they sat down, anxiously rolled the programs up in their fists, and stayed put (except when the popcorn came out just before halftime). I entertained the latter.

So, maybe the provost's second-best friend should be the athletic director. That certainly was the case for me. NC State was blessed to have a great working relationship between the provost's office and the athletics office, one that I appreciated deeply as provost. Our AD knew that support for athletics among the faculty and academic administrators was just as important as support by the alumni and fans; he also knew that faculty support came from balancing the students' academic ability with their athletic ability. He understood this so well that he attended Faculty Senate meetings whenever he could. He didn't have to attend those meetings; he did it voluntarily, clearly demonstrating that athletic directors have high thresholds for pain and boredom.

Whereas the chancellor has to deal with public response to the win–loss record, especially in football and men's basketball, the provost's realm is the admission and retention of student athletes. By retention, I mean eligibility to compete. Why eligibility? Because NCAA rules for eligibility are generally more stringent than rules for remaining in school (think what you like, but the NCAA polices academics quite well). We managed the academic part of student-athletics via several committees, all coordinated through a device called the Provost's Athletic Roundtable.

We met monthly—provost, athletic director, NCAA faculty representative, director of academic support for student athletes, and several others—to formulate policy, review the academic status of each sport and each at-risk student, and to develop new approaches to improve the success of our student-athletes. This was perhaps the best two hours I spent every month, because we dealt directly with the opportunities and challenges of the "student" part of student-athletes.

One product of our Roundtable was the NC State Athlete Code of Conduct, which I wrote, based on a long, detailed, and technical compliance document that we gave to all student-athletes. Among the thousands of pages that I've written in my career, this is one of those I am most proud of.

Our core commitment to student-athletes was that we would only admit them if we were confident that they could succeed in class and graduate. NC State is a tough school, and it lacks some of the majors that allow a less-rigorous path for continuing

NC State student athlete code of conduct

As an *NC State* student-athlete, I am an ambassador for my university, my hometown, my family, my team, and my fellow students. Because of the respect I have for myself and for them, I will:

1. **Be** responsible for my own actions at all times.
2. **Act** with the highest standards of integrity in all that I do.
3. **Participate** fully in academic and athletic matters.
4. **Earn** my college degree.
5. **Exhibit** good sportsmanship no matter what circumstance I am in.
6. **Contribute** to my community, especially to those less fortunate than myself.
7. **Remain** an amateur, in fact and in spirit, for as long as I am an NC State student.
8. **Treat** my body with respect and care.
9. **Lead**, rather than follow the behavior of others.
10. **Be** a positive role model for my team members, fellow students, alumni, fans and especially the school children that will follow in my footsteps.

eligibility, such as physical education or general studies. We also knew that some athletes required the equivalent of academic coaches to keep an academic focus equal to their athletic focus. Consequently, we, like most universities, had a special program to provide academic support for student-athletes. Unlike many schools, however, we ensured that this program worked well and with integrity, by having it report to the provost, not to the athletic director. The academic buck stopped at the provost's desk, as it should, for athletes as well as for everyone else.

Although holding the academic buck usually meant that I had to say no to someone—prospective or current athlete, coach, or athletic director—sometimes it turned out the opposite. One fall semester, the AD brought a case to me of a student-athlete who had not been doing well in one of our toughest majors—one he wasn't prepared for and shouldn't have been enrolled in (our advising mistake). When he finally accepted his academic limitations, he transferred to another major, but some of the courses from the first major didn't transfer over as required courses (our policy mistake). The consequence was that he hadn't made quite enough progress toward his degree to be eligible to compete during the spring semester (an NCAA rule, but I won't call it a mistake). I was on the student's side and wrote a letter of appeal to Miles Brand, president of the NCAA. No hope he'll waive the rule, they all said.

But he did issue the waiver. The student competed and went on to graduate in the new major (just as he and his Mom had promised me he would). And later the student signed a professional contract.

That's what I call a win-win.

21

YIN, YANG, AND YOU

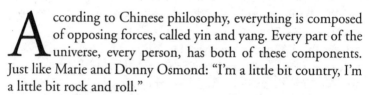

According to Chinese philosophy, everything is composed of opposing forces, called yin and yang. Every part of the universe, every person, has both of these components. Just like Marie and Donny Osmond: "I'm a little bit country, I'm a little bit rock and roll."

The university has its yin and yang as well. Every administrator has some of each. Get the job done today, but do it in the context of the long-term vision. Respect academic freedom, but dismiss the faculty member who won't teach the syllabus. Declare the campus smoke-free, but take scholarship funds from tobacco companies. Only admit student-athletes who can graduate, but make darn sure that they can dribble and shoot.

The university just may be the poster child for yin yang. Our mission and philosophy are rooted in the most noble of virtues, but we've got to keep the place running and on budget. If we fail to balance academic yang with administrative yin, we're out of business.

Please note that I've just defined the academic side of the university as yang and the administrative side as yin. Please note that I include the provost as part of the academic yang. I divide the world this way for good reason.

Yang is associated with the "sunny place," daytime and solidness—of course, that is the academic core, and the academic glow in which the provost basks. Yin is associated with the "shady place," nighttime and unsubstantial—all right-thinking persons would associate that with the administrative context of the university, the realm of other leaders. No value judgment implied here, just the need for some operable definitions (but it is clear to me that yang rocks).

The provost's yang role is to drive the university to do good things on behalf of its mission and vision, to reach for sunny aspirations, to write a strong and transparent strategic plan, designed to advance academics, and then allocate the funds to get it done! The other leaders balance this through their yin roles of keeping the place up and running and in pursuit of mission, aspirations, and strategy, to the extent that all the other pressures will allow. They also need to prevent their yang-y provost from making promises their budget, facilities, computer systems, and support staff can't keep.

I'm sorry, maybe you have to be a little bit yang-y to warm up to this metaphor, but I have to tell you—I love it. It explains so much that I find it irresistible.

For one, it explains the two time frames on which the university operates. The academic time frame, yang-time, let's call it, works pretty much on an annual cycle. We advertise faculty positions in the fall, hire them in the spring, and the new faculty members show up for work in late summer; then we start all over. The tenure and promotion cycle happens once per year. We change tuition only at the start of fall term, based on a series of analyses and consultations that continue all year. It takes us about a year to propose a new course and run it through the review process. Or maybe it takes two years, if we get into a debate about whether a new course on climate change is best offered in meteorology or creative writing.

So, academic yang-time ticks off at a pretty slow pace. I once heard a perfect explanation of the difference between working in a business and working in a university. In a business, when asked how long it takes to do something, the right answer is, "Between now and when the boss wants it." In the university, the academic answer is, "Well, it takes . . . as long as it takes." Figure a year. Like, yang, man.

The administrative time frame, let's call it yin-time, doesn't have that luxury. The yin-time clock ticks along like the "Minute Waltz." Most work has to get done right away. The payroll has to be done now, or we don't get paid; the experimental mice need to be fed and watered now, or they die; the traffic lights need to get fixed now, or we don't get home for supper; student records need to be updated now, or no one graduates on Saturday; the e-mail system needs to get fixed now, or, or, or—else!

As a consequence, the operating styles of the provost and CFO are very different. It seemed like a day never went by without my best friend, the CFO, needing to see me—just stick my head in between meetings or before lunch or for sure before I leave for the day. It used to irritate the yang out of me. But, of course, he was right, and I knew it—he had questions that needed answers in yin-time.

"Faculty salaries need to be entered overnight to make the October paychecks (like you, Mr. Provost, promised); do you want the promotion bonuses to go to all faculty, or just tenure-track?"

"The merchandise licensing revenue is up again; do you want to keep the same proportion going to study abroad or the same dollar value?"

"We just had a small fire in a chemistry lab, no one hurt, but we had to evacuate the building and we're moving classes around for tomorrow morning—just thought you should know."

"The legislative budget office called and wants to know how many 'middle managers' we have, by five o'clock; who on this list of 1,000 is a middle manager?"

(By the way, the responses were: All faculty members; Proportion; Thanks; and Staring blankly at the list.)

My issues could wait, though, since they generally traveled in yang-time. So I seldom dropped into the CFO's office unannounced, with some crisis in tow. I could usually save up a list until our next regular weekly meeting. Then I'd hit him with my list.

"When we start the new masters of analytics program next year, we're going to need a full-time, dedicated 40-student classroom; where will we get it?"

"The library will fill up its storage capacity in two years; then what?"

"I advised the chancellor to sign on to the commitment to move the university to become carbon neutral, and he did—just thought you should know."

(The responses were: What?!; What?!, WHAT?!, all followed by a series of other typographic symbols.)

The yang of academics and the yin of administration impact operations in many other ways, too. I committed most of the academic budget years in advance, according to a strategic plan. The CFO kept a good supply of cash in uncommitted reserves, to handle emergencies that came along regularly.

The provost's schedule filled up with dozens of recurring meetings for committees, task forces, and other groups that I chaired or attended; they were often scheduled months, sometimes years, in advance and probably occupied 75% of the daily calendar. Once something hit my calendar, it was as sticky as a gecko's feet. The CFO had to keep more flexibility in his day to handle those emergencies; if his calendar were solidly booked, odds were that some emergency would come up, and he and his staff would be rearranging those other appointments all day long.

I checked my e-mail when . . . when it was time; the CFO checked his continuously. Sharon was the only person who called me on my cell phone; his rang all the time.

Likewise, the chancellor's office was pretty much embedded in yin. It's a very real-time place. A legislator, trustee, reporter, community leader, or major donor wants their questions and concerns handled now, not "when it's time." The chancellor has several speeches to give on most days, and he needs the facts checked now. His day is embedded in anticipation of some athletics revelation—whether good or bad, it demanded attention. Because the chancellor and CFO operated in similar time frames and usually on nonacademic items, they were in constant communication.

My interactions with the chancellor were much more scheduled—academic matters could wait until the next regular weekly meeting. To be honest, I envied the camaraderie that developed between the chancellor and CFO, because of their similar personalities and work needs. I was always confident that the chancellor respected my leadership of the academic matters of the university—he would have checked on me a lot more if he hadn't. But on a day-to-day basis, he was more occupied with other issues and other people.

Sometimes being yang is a lonely job.

22

SPEAKING OF STUDENTS

A s the champion for academics, the provost also needs to be the champion for students. I've devoted an entire section later in the book on the point that people are the most important part of a university, but let's spend a little time on a particular kind of people right now—students.

In the hallowed halls of administration, it is sometimes easy—and sometimes convenient—to forget about students. In early December, ask a person walking down the hall in the administration building when classes end. Most won't have a clue, because the presence or absence of students doesn't change their jobs very much, at least not in the near term. They are much more likely to know when the agenda is due for the next Board of Trustees meeting. I often showed up out of uniform—in an NC State polo shirt rather than coat and tie—on the first day after graduation or during fall break, just to shock people into remembering the academic rhythm of the university. How yang of me.

Along with a distorted view of the calendar, administrators can also develop a distorted view of students. Our exposure to students was pretty sanitized—we mostly interacted only with the cream of the crop (and, of course, occasionally the sour cream). We met with student leaders regularly. They are generally excellent students, often supported on merit-based scholarships that relieve any need to work part time. They are also highly verbal, self-confident, and motivated; that's how they got into leadership positions. But they sometimes reminded me too much of Michael J. Fox's character on *Family Ties*.

So, while I respected all of the student leaders I worked with, the one I liked the most was the "Pirate Captain." One spring, to the dismay of the politicians-in-training, who tended to rule student government, a fellow came out of nowhere to run for student body president. He campaigned in pirate garb, sported a plastic parrot on his shoulder, and said "aargh" a lot—and in an unexpected manner that should make us all confident about the next generation, he won. He was the most representative student body president I'd ever met. He was initially shy, always soft-spoken, obviously ill at ease in the formal ceremonial settings he had to attend, treated my wife with genuine (not fawning) friendship, and was, most of all, just a regular guy. He didn't accomplish much, but that was okay with me. Other parts of student government were apoplectic and spent the year trying to impeach him. Like, yang, man.

Along with elected student leaders, we were also surrounded by other high achievers. We met with our prospective Rhodes, Goldwater, and Udall Scholars, paraded award winners in front of alumni groups, attended banquets for academic all-stars, put the medals around the necks of Phi Kappa Phi inductees. Even when I taught as provost—special one-credit-hour seminars when I thought the schedule could handle it—I taught small sections of honors students. Most of these exceptional students will not shrink from telling you, definitively, what students think and want.

I often wondered, however, whether they were speaking for the average student, the ones trying to keep their grade point averages in a decent range while they shuttled between school and work. Were our internship programs serving all of our students well, or just the cream of the crop? Were all students finding out about financial aid for study abroad, or just the ones who had special advisors through their honors or scholars courses?

So, the provost needs to keep students at the front of her or his mind—and to remind others to do the same. One of the best ways to do this is a theme I'll return to later—show up a lot. Woody Allen is often quoted as saying, "Showing up is 80% of life." I usually misquote him by raising the figure to 95%, because showing up is one of the things I did best. When students asked for me, I went. When a department or college asked me to attend a student-oriented program, I said yes (for faculty and staff events, also). When asked to hand out awards to students, I was honored to do so.

And that includes graduate students. Ask the imaginary person-on-the-street to picture a university student, and they will almost always imagine an undergraduate student. The same is true for student-affairs professionals. Because we usually have a "graduate school" that watches over graduate student matters, I've perceived that the student affairs shop generally sees its role more focused on undergraduate students.

But graduate students are about one-quarter to one-third of the enrollment at most public research universities, and most schools' strategic plans call for increasing that proportion. Graduate students both need and deserve the provost's attention. A good portion of graduate students will be from other countries. Associating with the provost is especially meaningful for them, because the separation between student and administrator in non-U.S. universities is much wider than in ours.

The most important aspect of interacting with students, however, is to treat them like adults. They can see through bureaucratic doubletalk just as easily as faculty can, and it is just as fatal. I've found, however, that students are sponges for thoughtful perspectives about the university. They know little about the inner workings of the university, so even the most basic messages will be received as powerful learning opportunities. Five minutes discussing how tuition fits in with the total budget of the university can supplant eighteen years of misinformation—and just might get back to parents in a way that could influence their voting on the next higher-education bond referendum. A brief explanation about free speech policies on campus can prevent a lot of bellyaching about the campus preacher. A few words about scholarships being specifically available for study abroad may get some students in the program who never thought they could afford it. If, after speaking at a student gathering, the provost leaves the students with the impression that he is a thoughtful, caring, and open person, he will have supporters for life—folks who chant "pro-vost" as he jogs by.

Treating students as adults is a good idea for another reason. A lot of them *are* adults, a lot more than used to be. Now that I am back in the classroom, I am regularly reminded that the university isn't just for eighteen- to twenty-two-year-olds. On a recent Veterans Day, I asked all the veterans in the class to stand up so we could acknowledge their service; along with me, about 10 others stood, out of the 80 or so in class. The needs of these and other adult students are vastly different from so-called traditional-age students. One student recently sent me an e-mail apologizing for missing class, because her three children had come down with the flu in the most inconvenient way—one right after the other. Some other professor can tell her that she can't have an extension on her assignment, but it won't be me.

23

IN THE SERVICE OF
ACADEMICS

A common debate on campus is the proper balance between direct investments in teachers and indirect investments in academic support services. How much central advising should we have? How many admissions folks do we really need? Do we need a graduate school at all? What do those people in international affairs actually do?

I endorse the adage, "Where you stand depends on where you sit." That is actually almost the title of a book you'll find in LB2341 (Smith, 2006). It applies fundamentally to our opinions about academic support services. As a faculty member, department head, and even dean, I had little use for the academic services of central administration. We did all the work with students out there, I thought, so why did we need all those budget-sucking central offices?

Where I stood as provost gave me a much different perspective. I marveled at all that had to be done and that we had such capable people who knew how to do it—and did it, all day every day, no spring breaks, no sabbaticals, no teaching gigs in Prague.

Consider financial aid. Just the words *financial aid* strike terror in the hearts of knowing administrators. If faculty only knew what these folks actually did, they'd bow when a financial aid advisor walked by (not to worry, they don't walk by—they're chained to their computer monitors, eating a lunch of cheese crackers and a diet drink while they work). About half of all students get financial aid of some kind in a public research university; every need-based program has its own eligibility rules and limits, and the feds alone have more different programs than anyone but a financial aid expert can juggle; merit-based aid requires all sorts of applications and judging programs (some even done by departments and colleges, but most done centrally); aid to athletes is a topic all its own; international students have a passel of other requirements; and so do graduate students.

Through all this, the financial aid people take in the data, judge the validity of the requests, disperse the funds—and wait for the kickback. I've been party to the unfathomable skill, patience, and diplomacy that financial aid professionals display day after day after day. And this isn't just bureaucratic fuss. Without the work of these offices, students wouldn't be in school. These folks are on the frontline of the educational process. They are the cow-catchers on the train of higher education.

Early in my term as provost, the chancellor gave me the task of developing a financial aid program that ensured that our poorest students (in economic terms) would get all the money they needed to attend NC State. I handed the project to our director of financial aid. At first, she came back disappointed, because she couldn't figure out how to do this while leaving all other programs intact. No, I said, that wasn't the task—take care of our most needy students completely, even if it meant moving some funds away from other students.

She smiled, and her faced glowed at the chance to make this happen. Given that mandate, she found the way to reconfigure our need-based aid so that the neediest 20% of our student body got all the money that they needed. She then went farther and designed a special advising program so that these students would also get the academic and socialization assistance they would probably also need. The program, known as Pack Promise, now serves about 1,000 students per year, with a retention and graduation rate comparable to that of our entire student body. This could not happen, would not happen, if left to individual departments or colleges.

Now let me shake my provost's applause assistant for some folks who never get much credit—the college's associate deans for academic affairs. I have the utmost respect for these folks, even though I chose to spar with them regularly. I contend that associate deans for academic affairs are the most knowledgeable people in the university. They sit at the crossroads of almost all academic matters. They move effortlessly between university requirements, rules, and processes on one hand and the reality of student and faculty needs on the other. They hold ex officio seats on almost all functional (and dysfunctional) university committees, so they know what ideas and changes are floating around. As provost, whenever I needed informed opinions on how some yang-y idea might actually affect operations, I met with the associate deans. Now that I'm a practicing faculty member again, whenever I need to know how to do something, like substitute a class on an advisee's degree audit, I call the associate dean's office.

Associate deans will be glad to talk about one vexing problem that affects academic support. In fisheries science (my home field), we have a riddle about algae growing in a pond. If algae growing on the surface of a pond double in area every 24 hours, which is often the case in the middle of a hot, humid summer, how full will the pond be on the last day before it is totally covered? The answer is half full. In other words, algae grow really fast, and once it gets going, there's no stopping it.

Academic support programs can grow like algae, too. Offices get created, and staff members get hired to solve problems, real problems that colleges and departments can't deal with. Retention and graduation rates aren't as high as desired, so let's assign some folks full time to this problem, maybe even hire a presumed expert from another school or educational think tank. Then new programs get started to solve the problems that the last solution created. Maybe we find out that retention rates of freshmen are too low, because today's students are too embarrassed to come to an advisor; so, let's create an online advising service. And so on.

My favorite example of academic algae gone wild is the small-grant program for faculty. Every office wants to support faculty, and they know that faculty members need a little incentive to explore the services or mission of an office. So, they start a small-grant program. At NC State, last time I looked, we had small-grant programs in international affairs (to develop new study abroad courses), distance education (to develop new online courses), research (to run small projects that can develop into overhead-yielding grant proposals), instructional technology (to improve classroom teaching), outreach (to encourage faculty to take their expertise into the community), and service-learning (to get faculty started in that subject); I'm sure there are others. Put all those funds together, and we could fund a bunch of graduate student stipends, something that would really help faculty!

At least faculty grants are supporting faculty. If left unchecked, however, academic support can grow to just support itself. We had a teaching improvement center at NC State that began as a faculty initiative to help faculty members learn to teach better. It functioned successfully for many years, but then the leadership turned over a couple of times, the staffing became more professionalized, and the mission began to drift. When I finally closed it, the teaching resources it offered were being used almost exclusively by graduate students. That's fine, of course, except that we had another program in the graduate school to help graduate students learn how to become effective teachers. And another program in distance education to help faculty members learn to teach over the Internet. And another to help faculty teach writing and speaking better.

I have to admit being partially to blame for some of this as provost. NC State needed to enhance its reputation as an institution beyond the border of North Carolina. Several academic support units at the university happily reported to me that they were highly regarded for their work by their peers across the region and nation. If that were so, I reasoned, then a little bit more investment might establish one or more of them as the go-to places in the country for expertise in their particular missions, thereby making us famous and maybe kicking us up a few notches in the polls. So, I invested additional resources in academic support for student-athletes, the African American cultural center, and the service-learning program.

Unfortunately, when the most severe budget crunch hit, these enhancements were prime targets for cuts. The service-learning program was the most troublesome for me. Service-learning is an important element in a university like NC State—a land grant school in a major urban environment—and we had built a substantial reputation from the ground up. In response to the growing attention that service-learning was garnering among educators everywhere, we created the Center for Excellence in Curricular Engagement. Fancy name, new digs, national advisory board, aggressive leadership, high profile. We forgot one thing, however—making sure that we were impacting the folks at home while we were also establishing our reputation beyond the campus. As a consequence, when I asked deans for ideas of things that should be cut, the overwhelming first choice was service-learning. Although they endorsed the concept and practice of service-learning, they saw little value in the infrastructure we had built. Closing the center and releasing the four professional staff put a sad but necessary exclamation point on the final days of my term as provost.

24

GRADUATION DAY

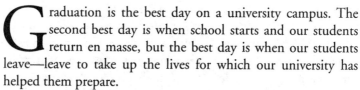

Graduation is the best day on a university campus. The second best day is when school starts and our students return en masse, but the best day is when our students leave—leave to take up the lives for which our university has helped them prepare.

But before they leave, we have a grand party. Ours is hosted at the basketball arena, which holds a pretty big crowd. We graduate more than 3,000 students every fall and spring, all dressed to kill in their ridiculous caps and gowns. The only ones more ridiculous are the faculty members, who are dressed even more bizarrely, with their hoods trailing out behind them in every color of the rainbow. With any luck, the audience will be treated to a few faculty members who graduated from British universities, who parade in dressed like Beefeaters.

Yes, it is all ridiculous, but I have to admit that the pageantry is also engaging. In vivid colors and velour puffy-armed robes, graduation highlights that this academic activity we've been embedded in is quite different from the rest of life. It may be uphill or downhill from here, but this hill has been special.

The provost plays a big part in the ceremony. I processed in just behind the chair of the faculty, who carried the university's mace (no, I don't know why we have a mace, but it is cool). Only three names get mentioned as we walk in—the chair of the faculty, the provost (this time without the Mr.), and the chancellor. I imagine people whispering, "Don't you remember? He gave you a pencil."

In our big ceremonies, only the doctoral students walk across the stage, where the provost hands each one an empty diploma sleeve, as though it were a diploma. Many students decorate their caps, but the doctors of veterinary medicine are the champions. Farm scenes, inflated examination gloves, stuffed animals, and, in one case, a cage with a pair of live mice, totter on the mortar boards as the graduates negotiate the stairs. Occasionally I would know one of the recipients, and she would give me a hug in front of all those people.

I introduced each college's dean, who then asked the candidates for degrees to rise and presented them to the chancellor. The chancellor conferred the degrees, ceremoniously raising his hand and blessing them, "with all the rights, privileges and responsibilities thereto." Whatever those might be. Lots of people gave short unmemorable speeches, and one person gave a long unmemorable speech. The a cappella choir asked us to join them in singing the alma mater ("the words are printed on the front cover of the program"). Then we recessed.

At NC State, though, we have another graduation, not so grand, but just as important. Later in the afternoon, we graduate the students who have completed our two-year associate's degree, housed in our College of Agriculture and Life Sciences. I loved this graduation—partially because I awarded the degrees. Yes, "by the power vested in me by the Board of Trustees," I granted the graduates all their theretos. I never asked when and how the Board of Trustees actually vested their power in me, I just accepted that they had and ran with it.

But the real reason I loved this ceremony was that here was graduation on a human scale. Not much pomp or circumstance—the music came from a CD in a boom box—but genuine appreciation for the life-changing nature of a college education, even a two-year one. The ceremony was brief, another blessing. We didn't have any unmemorable speeches, although I couldn't resist waxing unmemorably for a few minutes when I was handed the podium. Each of the thirty or so graduates received her or his diploma, a real diploma this time. Almost all of the graduates received several diplomas, because most were double or triple or even quadruple majors.

Each student then got a moment at the microphone to thank whomever they wished. Most thanked their parents, God, a teacher or two. Their words were few and a bit redundant—these agricultural folks aren't usually big talkers. One memorable student limped up to the microphone on crutches, one leg immobilized to the hip in a plaster cast, and proceeded to thank "my parents and grandparents and my in-laws." He then labored back to his seat to resounding applause.

The emotions of the graduates and their family members, sitting on the folding chairs behind the graduates, were as real as the skills the graduates learned during their time at the university. Many people wonder if we should be offering a two-year degree at a big important school like NC State, but to me, this is the American public university at its best—serving the people, making the knowledge real, reaching out to the people of the state who need most what we have to offer.

I watched the student in the cast all through the rest of the ceremony. He wore a pained expression on his face, and I worried that he might have reinjured his leg while walking to and from the microphone. No such (bad) luck. After everyone had spoken and the dean was preparing to give his final remarks, the student rose painfully to his feet, pivoted on his cast, and yelled back to the crowd, "I forgot something—I also want to thank my wife."

And now maybe we know why he was on crutches.

LESSONS ABOUT ACADEMICS

1. The provost is the academic leader for the university. Everyone else has another job.
2. The provost is also the strategic leader for the university. If someone else is trying to do it, the provost needs to throw the mutineer over the gunnels.
3. The strategic plan needs to be backed by money. That's the only thing that makes a strategic plan meaningful—and just might keep people from hating it.
4. Most of your ideas are bad or impractical, so be prepared to discard them as fast as needed. Relax about this, because most of other people's ideas are bad, too.
5. Athletes are students, too. Your job is to make sure they remember that—and that their coaches remember it, too.
6. So, make the athletic director your second-best buddy. But don't make the CFO jealous.
7. The university fights with itself all the time—is it about noble, long-term vision (yang) or getting the job done on time and within budget (yin)? Good news—the provost gets to be yang-y most of the time.
8. The provost runs on academic time, so nothing much is ever an emergency. The CFO and chancellor run on right-now time, and almost everything is a crisis. Learn to live with the difference.
9. The provost can commit budget long term and permanently. The CFO can only commit right now and one-time. Learn to live with that, too.
10. Make others in the administration remember the academic rhythm of the university, because they're prone to forget. Besides, it's a great excuse for casual Friday on any day you'd like.
11. Pay attention to students. Whenever you are asked, show up. Students will love you for it.

12. Pay attention to average students, too. You can get starstruck by the smart, talented, glib, and assertive ones. Most students, though, are average—just like you.

13. Pay attention to graduate students, too. They can get lost in the instinctive focus on undergraduates.

14. Pay attention to "adult" students, as well. And cut them some slack; they are trying to make it in an institution not designed for them. This is especially true for returning military personnel.

15. Associate deans for academics rock! They know more about how the university works than anyone. And if they ever manage to agree on something, implement it right now.

16. Central academic support functions also rock. But hardly anyone will appreciate that except the provost. Deans often think these functions are frivolous and redundant.

17. They have a point. So watch central functions, like a lion watches the wildebeest herd, and cull the old and weak.

PART FIVE

FACILITIES AND OTHER EVILS

25

SPACE, THE FINAL FRONTIER

I f possession is 90% of the law, in general, then possession is 99% of the law, as it relates to space in a university.

Nothing matters quite so much in a university as space. Budget is important, but budget is promiscuous; it loves you today and then moves out next year. Besides, everybody has their hands all over the budget before you get to hold it. Graduate students are important, but today faculty members have to generate most of the money to support them. The way one gets money is to get grants; the way one gets grants is to demonstrate promising results; the way one gets promising results is to do advance work in—space. Title is nice, too, but we all know that titles are what universities give out when they want to convince someone to take on extra work without extra pay ("We'd like you to become the director of our new Global Sustainability Initiative, in addition to your other duties, of course.").

Yep, pilgrim, when it comes to space, the university is just like the Ol' West. He who has the biggest gun gets the most space. Once you stake your claim and successfully ward off the squatters with a verbal ambush or two, your deed will never be challenged.

Space is about as close to a sacred cow as the university gets. Just about everything else today is up for grabs. We'll reallocate budgets and vacant faculty positions, sometimes even filled faculty positions. We'll collapse departments or colleges or administrative service units, and we'll redraw the organizational flowchart whenever the leadership turns over. We'll revise the general education program (albeit grudgingly). But touch the space inventory—not a chance. In 20 years as a university administrator, I've done all those things and more, but I never hauled a faculty member into my office and said, "Please vacate your laboratory by next Tuesday. I'm assigning it to someone else."

On the rare occasions when we must reallocate space, we make a big deal out of it. At NC State, we manage space through a three-person committee, composed of the provost as chair, along with the CFO and the vice-chancellor for research and graduate studies. Every decision is treated as momentous. Moving one room in a building from the inventory of, say, the Industrial Engineering Department to the Office of International Affairs requires the university architect to do a comprehensive study of the effect, including perhaps a motion-triggered video camera to verify or refute the department's claim that it uses that room all the time. We probably have to agree to renovate some other space for the vacating unit, as ransom for their acquiescence. We gather all the evidence, call a meeting at which we listen to witnesses from all interested parties, collaborate on the options, and, finally, vote. Three senior officials of the university actually *vote* on who gets this 300-square-foot room. How can anyone say we have too much administration?

An interesting anomaly in the literature on the provost's job is that space allocation is almost never mentioned. Space showed up nowhere in the 2008 CAO Census in regard to major work elements, most important work elements, or even most frustrating work elements. Yet the space resource is one of the most valuable in the university. In the state of North Carolina, more than half of all state capital resources are owned by the University of North Carolina. A huge chunk of that space is academic—classrooms, laboratories, offices for faculty and academic staff. So, who is managing all this space if the provost isn't?

The answer, I'm afraid, is no one. In the decentralized culture of the university, space gets parsed out to hundreds of individual units. Each of those units uses the space for their own needs, and they guard the space ferociously. If the unit has grown or wishes to grow, it barks loudly about its need for more space. If the unit has shrunk, it won't ever say a word about space, pretty confident that letting the sleeping space dog lie is a really good strategy. So, existing space will often sit vacant or underused as the university spends tens of millions of dollars building new space.

The provost isn't likely to see this herself, though. For one reason, the provost isn't very likely to take a walk through a random building, nosing around to see what space is being used well or poorly. When the provost does come around to a college, department, or center for an announced visit, the unit will have cleaned up the poorly used spaces and will have people sitting at every desk and looking through a microscope at every lab bench when the provost's parade passes by.

Here's a tale of the lonely lecture hall. The hall held about 100 occupants, a size of room that the university desperately needed, especially in the part of campus where it was located. But it was in horrible shape—broken seats, 1950s technology, asbestos tiles dangling by one corner from the ceiling. The university classroom program would fix the room up, they said, but then the room would need to go into the university's classroom inventory rather than being "owned" and scheduled by the academic unit that occupied the building. That's a nonstarter for the owners, who weren't about to give up control of the place, even if it was in ruins. The unit did use it for a few hours every week and claimed, of course, that those functions couldn't occur anywhere else—and they were essential. So, the room sat lonely for decades, like Boo Radley's scary house, slowly succumbing to the laws of thermodynamics. All the while, we built new buildings with new 100-seat classrooms all over campus. The story ends happily, however, because we eventually pulled everyone together and convinced them that there was a win-win here. We agreed that the room would get renovated, would get scheduled by the university, but would give priority to the home unit's needs. Now it is a beautiful, functional, well-used room. But notice that I didn't decree anything, rather I negotiated with the "owners."

In the chapters about money, I wrote that we have more money than we think we do. What's more, money is also appropriated anew every year; and if we have any left at the end of the year, the state makes us give it back. So annually, near the end of the fiscal year, we start moving money around to balance the accounts. If one unit doesn't spend all their money, we use it for another unit or another purpose; if one unit overspends, we cover the transgression with unused money from another unit. And we have staffs of accountants and business officers at several administrative levels who watch this process scrupulously and make it all come out right, to the penny.

Not so with space. No one comes around near the end of every year, looks into every space, and asks whether or not it is being used. No one moves people around from crowded offices to sparsely occupied offices, to balance the load; no one moves experiments from one crowded lab to an empty one down the hall.

No one does this, but someone should. At NC State and probably at most schools, we actually do the first step pretty well. Our facilities folks know how much space we have, of what kinds, assigned to what units. We have combined the space inventory into bigger units, usually colleges and vice-chancellor kingdoms. We've created a set of algorithms that calculate space needs according to the number of students of various kinds, faculty and staff, and other functions. We've compared the space needs to the space inventory and calculated the assigned space to needed space ratio. Some colleges have only 70% of the space they need, some have 120%; the same for other functional areas.

But then we stop. We never make the college with 120% of the space it needs give up space to the college with only 70% of its needs met. Why not? For many reasons, some of them actually sensible. For example, every respectable college is projecting that it will grow in some way—more undergraduates, graduate students, research, community service—so its space needs will catch up to its inventory. Also, a college may have just gotten a new building assigned to it, after having been short on space for generations; of course that college instantly has excess space. We'll also argue that the algorithms aren't sensitive enough to catch the subtleties of space needs, or sometimes even the gross differences; a construction engineer working on the structural integrity of steel beams needs more space, perhaps, than an inorganic chemist working on the structural integrity of nano-fibers (or maybe the reverse—some of those nano-analyzers are pretty bulky). Use of space also has a temporal dimension; a specialized laboratory might get used only a week every month, but it certainly can't be used for freshman English the other three weeks.

All of this may be logical, but I think the real reason we shrink from reassigning space is because it's hard and we don't want to do it. Taking space away from one user to give to another user is a win-lose proposition, and we hate those.

26

SPACE ASSIGNMENTS DON'T DIE, THEY JUST FOSSILIZE

The folks who grow space roots in a university are tenured faculty members. Their space gets assigned to them early in their careers, typically, and they don't like to move. For good reason. Faculty members accumulate stuff. They deal in information, and, at least until recently, information was preserved on paper. Consequently, we collect paper in all its forms—books, reports, pamphlets, data sheets, old lecture notes, old exams, old course records, graduate student theses, letters from friends, old slips of paper containing a scribbled idea for a research project.

Every department has one—the faculty member whose desk looks like a paper incarnation of Jabba the Hutt, a mountain of seemingly random papers, letters, newspaper clippings, and the like. My colleague who lived like this was miraculous. Ask him a question about ruffed grouse in Europe, and he would gaze thoughtfully at the pile, say, "I saw a newspaper article about that when I was in Ireland," grab the tiniest protruding corner of a page buried in the stack, and start pulling. After a brief struggle for ownership—Jabba or him—out would come the clipping. The article might be from 2011 or 1974, but he could find it.

We are especially fond of "gray literature," the reports that come out of government agencies, institutional centers and laboratories, nonprofit groups, and professional committees. We are fond of gray literature, because only a few of us have copies, and it is the basis of our specialized knowledge and, hence, power. So we hoard it. We might even read it someday. One of my mentors at the University of Missouri had a huge office in the style of old university buildings, about 20 feet square and 15 feet tall, with floor-to-ceiling built-in oak cabinets and bookshelves. He worked sitting on his chair, hunched over, writing on the seat of another chair in front of him—the only two surfaces in the entire room that weren't occupied by a teetering stack of gray literature. The fact that he perfected one of the most important freshwater fisheries management strategies of the late twentieth century—the slot length-limit—based on that gray literature shouldn't be dismissed. But his office was a death trap.

When I returned to the faculty, I inherited the office of a colleague who had recently moved to an administrative position. He had been in the office for about 20 years. I had visited his office a few times when I was dean and was a little concerned by how small the space seemed in my memory. Sharon and I moved my stuff into the office on a Sunday afternoon, and when I first opened the door, I was shocked at the size—it seemed gigantic (now, don't get excited, it is absolutely standard-sized; I got no special deal on office space). The next week, colleagues kept stopping in, ostensibly to welcome me back, but mostly to see what the office looked like since the previous occupant had moved out. "Don't you have any stuff?" they all asked, either directly or by the questioning look in their eyes.

But offices are mostly the same—150-square-foot cubes, filled with stuff—and everyone needs one. Everyone, that is, except emeritus professors. Did I just hear a collective gasp of disbelief? Am I suggesting that retired members of the faculty should *not* keep their offices? No, no, we couldn't do that; it is an inalienable right of the faculty to keep their office until, well—just until, and maybe even a bit longer than that.

That's because every emeritus professor is going to keep working, and they need their offices. They have a couple of graduate students still several months from graduating, a few grant reports to write, and some committee work they really want to get finished completely. And, of course, they are going to write that book they've been talking about for years (a book about being provost, perhaps?). Besides, they need time to clean out a career's worth of stuff—might be some gray literature in there worth passing on to the next occupant.

For a while new emeritus faculty members are pretty conscientious about coming to the office. For one thing, most haven't planned what they are going to do after they retire, so they just keep coming to the office every day, out of habit and with the encouragement of their spouses to get out of the house. They see their remaining graduate students through to graduation, maybe write the grant reports, might even look through the committee notes (that can wait until next time). And they start cleaning out their filing cabinets. But they have to keep most of those files as the basis for the book they're going to start writing soon. Then we start to see them just once a week, then once a month, then once a semester at the fall picnic or holiday party.

Meanwhile, the office fossilizes, lonely and forlorn, filled with long-fossilized stuff. The phone sits there, too, along with the data connection, at $34 per month, all waiting to become fossils. And the new faculty member that replaced the retiree is stuffed into the old supply cabinet, waiting until a real office opens up.

Now the altruistic department head unknowingly engages the battle. He suggests to the retired faculty member that the department needs the office, and she needs to get her stuff out of it by the end of the month. She explodes with indignity; after all those years of loyal service, this is how you treat me? She also starts coming back in again for a while. Her colleagues don't want to make her mad, and, besides, they're going to need their offices once they retire. If the department treats her so shabbily, it'll probably treat them the same way. So, to paraphrase Machiavelli, space reallocation has enemies of the folks who are going to lose space now and disinterested observers of the folks who are probably going to lose space in the future.

Office space, however, isn't the real problem in space utilization at a university. Offices are small, cheap to build, and pretty well interchangeable. Research space is the problem. Unfortunately, the practice surrounding office space is typically replicated with research space. Give a faculty member a laboratory, and it is theirs for life.

Why does this happen? First, of course, because faculty members are the machines by which the university turns raw materials into products—knowledge, learning, community improvement—and those machines occupy space. Second, because we work in an amazingly benign evaluative environment, years, even decades, go by before we are ready to assert that a faculty member has reached the end of his or her productive life.

Third, and the topic of this chapter, is the way space is managed within a university. Most of the space is assigned to colleges, and the colleges assign space to departments. Within departments, the heads or chairs assign laboratories and other work spaces to individual faculty members. Most current department heads won't recognize this as their prerogative, however, because all the space had been divvied up several academic generations ago, and it hasn't come back on the market. So, we have a system in which faculty members hold de facto deeds to the space that they occupy, deeds they were given when they first joined the university, or deeds they got when the department was fortunate enough to acquire new space in the distant past.

Most administrators and most faculties are unwilling to challenge this approach to space management. As with most aspects of university life, the right of the individual faculty member to decide what and how to teach, what and how to study, and how to allocate their time are all of a piece—a piece called academic freedom. Reassigning space, which means taking it away from one faculty member and giving it to another, is perceived as a violation of the rights of the faculty member to pursue their scholarship at a scale and pace of their own choosing. The space itself is considered a necessary tool of their right to choose what to study; if the space is taken away, the faculty member no longer has the capacity to pursue her or his current or future research. Hence, the institution is attempting to direct their work or, worse yet, to censure their work. Consequently, the space generally stays put.

One of the bitterest disputes I've seen at a university was between a faculty member who was no longer using a laboratory and a department head who reasonably wanted him to vacate the premises. The faculty member said no, he would not move out of "his" laboratory; the department head padlocked the lab to make the point that the lab belonged to the university, not to the faculty member. The faculty member filed a grievance, and the case went to arbitration. Is it any wonder that a savvy department leader, especially if she thinks of herself as a department chair (rather than a head), will shrink from engaging any such Pyrrhic warfare? In her defense, she would say, "That isn't what I get paid to do."

The consequence is that a significant part of the university's physical resources are underused. A laboratory occupied by a research-active faculty member might be filled to overflowing with graduate students, post-docs, and research assistants, falling over each other on inadequate bench space that makes them prone to errors and safety risks. In the adjacent laboratory, a single graduate student, probably paid on a teaching assistantship or not supported at all, might work alone among boxes, shelves, and cabinets stocked with obsolete equipment and expired supplies. Or, worse yet, the adjacent laboratory might be dark, having not been used for its intended purpose for years.

Here's a corollary to this space dilemma: Bad uses of space drive out good uses. Remember all that stuff that faculty members collect? Eventually, the office gets full. So, the overflow goes into laboratories. Boxes of reprints, data sheets, old samples, drafts of manuscripts that eventually became published papers—or rejected papers—sit on laboratory benches or in sample rooms. Departments as a whole suffer from the same malady. If you buy new chairs for the office staff, you've got to do something with the old chairs. They probably go to graduate students, whose chairs are most likely an OSHA violation. Can't just throw those chairs away, though, because they might be on a property inventory somewhere, and someday somebody from facilities might show up and ask you to produce those chairs. So, just stack them up in the laboratory no one is using—or maybe in one of the emeritus offices. Colleges act the same. A few years ago, our space committee walked through facilities that one of our colleges was renting—high-cost laboratory space they claimed was indispensable for their research program. We found it filled with old furniture.

You ask, of course, why would a college whose budget is being reduced at every turn keep paying rent for space that is filled with old furniture? The logic is flawless. If the college gives up that space, someone else will get it. What if the college needs it sometime in the future? No chance of recovering it from the new occupant—because possession in a university is 99% of law.

27

NEW SPACE IS JUST ON ITS
WAY TO BECOMING
OLD SPACE

You'd think that having lived through generations of dysfunctional space allocations, we'd be smarter about new space. We ought to treat new buildings and renovated spaces as university space, without assigning them to individual units or faculty members. In fact, some universities are now building new research facilities just that way. They create facilities for particular but general topics—life sciences, biotechnology, information technology, nanotechnology—which remain assigned to the university; individual faculty members are provided space for particular lengths of time for particular research projects (usually based on receiving big federal grants with full overhead). But, in the main, we still allocate space the same old way.

NC State, like many universities over the last decade or so, has happily experienced a building boom. The state—its government and voting populace—were insightful during the last recession to realize that pumping capital funds into educational projects would do two things at one time, improve educational capacity and rescue the construction industry. It worked spectacularly. Through a very generous state bond issue, the University of North Carolina system received about $3 billion in construction and renovation funds; NC State ended up with about $500 million. We built new facilities for research, teaching, and administration; renovated buildings that were generations out of date; improved and extended our physical infrastructure; and beautified the campus. We chose the work purposefully and strategically, through a comprehensive space plan. As described earlier, the space plan was a brilliant piece of work by our institutional planners and architect's office. We projected enrollment and research growth then converted those projections into their space equivalents. And we did it all out in the open, with plenty of input from the university community. However, we made one understandable and traditional mistake. We projected it all from the most common currency of university management—the college. Colleges, of course, based their needs on the inputs and interests of departments. In the end, most of the space was allocated to individual colleges and then on to individual departments. So, right from the moment of publication of the space plan, individual departments and colleges took ownership of the new space. Having taken ownership, they were invested in ensuring that "their space" didn't shrink or fall in its position on the priority list.

We benignly neglected the "university" in our space planning. We didn't allocate research space, for example, to the strategic research priorities of the university. We were heavy into biotechnology—still are—but no biotechnology research building appeared on the list. We also ignored several other academic functions that needed space, like interdisciplinary programs, the library, study abroad, and admissions. We ignored major facilities gaps that stand in the way of our reputation as a comprehensive university—performing arts center, international center, art museum, faculty club, child care center, ecumenical chapel.

One particularly painful lapse was a new student center. Our student center was built in the 1970s, when our student body was half the size it is now. We have loved our student center to death. Prospective students always want to see the student center, and ours suffers badly in comparison with those of universities that have invested in this essential facility. Several institutions within the UNC System used part of their bond funds to build or remodel their student centers. But not NC State, because our mantra of decentralization led to allocation built from the ground up around colleges.

Even during the planning process, the territoriality and ownership of individual units came forward—and I was in the gang. I was dean of a college that was allocated part of one of the new buildings. Most of the remaining space in the new building was assigned to another college, but a small piece, maybe 10%, was assigned to a university-level research and outreach center. The university also desperately needed classrooms at our end of campus, and we agreed. So, we designed three large classrooms into the building—one for each college and one for the university. As the planning proceeded, we came to the inevitable task of reducing the size of the building because the budget was insufficient. The college co-chairs met, and we developed a joint strategy to thwart the university. When we appeared before the space committee whose mission was to trim the building, we each fought for our own space, supported the other college, and attacked the allocations to university needs. We won. The space committee chucked the space allocated for the university center and for one classroom, the one allocated to the university. High fives all around for the college representatives; institutional interests be damned.

The seriousness of this problem shows in the reality of the cycles of action for different kinds of resources. When a new strategic priority develops at the university, we need to assign resources to that priority. The provost can get faculty in place within about one year. Faculty positions are relatively small chunks of budget that get allocated annually. Enough of them turn over every year so that we always have some vacant positions to reassign if necessary. Need a new faculty member who is an expert in renewable energy sources? Abracadabra, it's done. And she can be hired and working, even with our elaborate processes, in one year or less.

What if we need a new renewable energy research building to go along with that position and a number of others in a new "energy cluster"? Or even just an energy research building to address our overall priority of "energy and the environment"? We have no way to respond quickly. We have a capital plan that has priorities set years ago and campus units that have been waiting for a generation to get their next bit of space. Bump the college-based building that has slowly climbed to the top of the list over two decades in favor of a university-controlled energy research building, and you invite a no-confidence resolution.

The consequence is that space is a constant problem, with the availability of adequate space often lagging years, maybe decades, behind the need. Departments and individual faculty members jury-rig the situation as best they can, often with altruistic faculty sharing or sacrificing for the sake of their new faculty colleague and her research emphasis.

The real nomads in a university are functions like computer support or undergraduate academic programs. These folks don't need specialized space, so they can be booted around at will. They aren't tenured faculty, so they also don't have much status within the power structure of the university. The staff, who don't get paid very much, turn over pretty regularly, so they don't have much seniority and can't put up much of a fight. Tell them they'll get air conditioning that might work or a toilet on the same floor as their office, and they're ready to pack. To be embarrassingly honest, as provost, I actually lost track of a few units in undergraduate affairs for a while. They had been splintered in various locations, but they were slated for some renovated consolidated space. While they were waiting for their new space to be completed, however, their existing spaces were being torn down, used as temporary homes for other displaced programs, or had been reassigned and were needed now. So, they were truly nomadic, moving around every few months, ending up in places with dubious-sounding names like the Old Laundry Building.

28

THE WORST TWO-WORD PHRASE IN THE UNIVERSITY VOCABULARY

N o, it's not what you're thinking. It's not "post-tenure review" or even "strategic planning."

The worst two words in the university vocabulary are *value engineering*. These words strike fear into everyone who has ever planned a public university building project. Value engineering is the step when the project goes from great to good, maybe all the way to mediocre. Architects blanch at the sound, and faculty members question their administrator's mental competence when it happens.

Value engineering is the ultimate space euphemism. What it really means is that there isn't enough money to build the project the way everyone has planned and is anticipating. Therefore, you've got to start chopping. But, we're ahead of ourselves. We have a lot of calculations to do before we get to value engineering.

First, we have to plan the building. Planning begins with what architects call "the program." I had trouble with this from the beginning, because to me a program is molecular biology or graphic design. We house a program in a building. To architects and space planners, however, the program is the set of spaces that you need for your, er, program. But, okay, that's fine, because this is the fun part—the first step is thinking of all the spaces you'd like to have, regardless of the budget.

Next, we have to fit the program into the building. Let's say that we have $30 million for a building and space costs $300 per square foot; so by math so simple even a provost can do it (with a calculator) you get a building with 100,000 square feet. Hold on, are we talking about gross square feet or assignable square feet? Gross square feet means every bit of the building, from the mechanical rooms to toilet stalls to the widths of the walls. Assignable square feet means spaces to house the work that you listed in "the program." At a rate of $300 per square foot, we're talking about gross square feet.

But our real interest is assignable square feet. Not a simple matter to convert one to the other, however, because the ratio of assignable to gross square feet is a design feature. A lower proportion of assignable square feet means a roomier, grander building, with open atriums and spacious gathering spots for students outside classrooms, interior stairways, wider hallways, some interesting organic shapes to the spaces. A higher proportion of assignable square feet means a cereal box. Let's assume a nice building design, with an assignable-to-gross ratio of 0.6. So, the assignable space for the program is about 60,000 square feet.

But, wait, we've forgotten about a whole set of costs that have to be paid before getting to the building itself. The site needs to be prepared, infrastructure needs to be run, parking spaces need to be built (and parking ain't cheap), designers and architects need to be paid, the central staff overhead needs to be covered, furniture needs to be expensed, and a contingency needs to be set aside. Sustainability needs to be built in; today, it's pretty much déclassé to build or renovate anything to less than LEED silver standards. Maybe public art has to be added; some states have a 2% holdback for that. How much are we talking about here, in total? About 30% to 35%; let's call it one-third. So, the funds available to actually *construct* the building are about

$20 million. So, we get just about 40,000 assignable square feet for the program.

Now is when the faculty is starting to question their administrators' competence and ethics. Because they heard $30 million and $300 per square feet about two years ago when all this planning started, and they did the math—a 100,000-square-foot-builidng. What happened to their beautiful spacious new building? It's now less than half as big as "promised" when the naïve provost or dean said, "We have $30 million dollars at $300 per square foot." Are we evil or just stupid?

But the real drama hasn't even begun yet. A prominent architect who worked with us on a major building once tried to get our building committee back into reality. He said there are three elements of a building design project—quality of space, quantity of space, and cost. The client, he said, gets to set two of those, but the architect gets to set the third. If the client has a defined budget and wants a certain quality, then the architect says how much space he can build. If the client has a defined budget and wants a specific amount of space, the architect says what quality the space can have. If the client demands a certain amount of space at a set level of quality, then the architect licks his chops, because his budget is unlimited! At the university, because the budget is capped by the funder (generally the legislature or a private donor) and the quantity of space is enormously contentious, the quality is usually what has to give. Enter value engineering.

Value engineering is the process of trimming all aspects of the building down so that it will meet the budget (remember, money is way ahead of whatever is in second place). The first step is changing the assignable-to-gross ratio. Cut down the public space, narrow the hallways, get rid of the atriums. Instead of 0.6, make it 0.75. That way we can still get 40,000 assignable square feet, but in a building whose gross size is 80% of the original. It will still sound okay to the faculty and staff, because they didn't lose any of their space with the changes. Only they are now going to get a cereal box. Now, get cheaper materials—no wood paneling, no tile floors, no domestic or sustainable sourcing, just whatever is on state contract. Next, cut out the furnishings; we can move in the old stuff, or we'll promise to find donors to buy us furniture. Use standard contractor landscaping rather than native, climate-appropriate plantings. Cut the number of high-definition monitors in the laboratory classroom from two to one. Forget recycled products, because they cost more than standard. Scale back the innovations for energy conservation, because operating costs don't come out of the same budget as capital expenses. Let the LEED standard drop from silver to bronze, and don't pay for the actual certification to be done, just say we would have achieved bronze if we had applied.

Value engineering is one of the most disappointing activities that I've had to manage as a provost or dean. Most administrators get to design and occupy no more than one building in their careers. You get no do-overs. The new building for our college is a fine functional building, but nothing about it is special or distinctive. A natural resource building should scream "Conservation of natural resources!" from the moment someone walks through the door. It should have terrariums and aquariums, planters with unique native species; it should have photo exhibits of natural treasures from around the world. We should have had LEED platinum certification, not hypothetical bronze. But, when faced with value engineering, I chose to preserve space and give up quality. We got a very functional cereal box.

At first, I railed against the incompetence of people who were not able to estimate the cost of a building accurately enough to prevent this folly—after all, they were the professionals, the experts at this sort of thing. Even recognizing that some of the cost elements were outside their predictive ability, it seemed that our university leadership (meaning me) ought to be honest and courageous enough to cut the initial size down to make aspirations meet capacity.

Ah, aspirations! I hadn't considered aspirations, those contagious little beasts. I now realize that we inevitably raise our expectations to beyond our capacity, no matter how hard we try to keep them in line. We're all good enough at math to see what is happening. Begin with a planning process that is keeping the aspirations in check, and people quickly realize that there might be some wiggle room—and they start to wiggle. Everything gets a little bigger, a little grander. And before long, the program, fed by voracious aspirations, has now outgrown its available budget and then some. It isn't the architect's fault, or the project manager's—neither of them has authority to take on the faculty. It is just human nature, starting when Adam and Eve decided to upgrade to the next housing division over from Eden.

You might as well accept it—someday you're going to get value engineered.

29

PRIVATE BUSINESS WOULDN'T
DO IT THIS WAY

How many times have you heard: "If I ran my business the way you guys run the university, I'd be out of business in a week." Of course they would. And if we ran the university the way they run their business, we'd be in jail in a week. Private business is private; what they do is their own business. They follow the laws and rules that we've set out for private enterprise. But university business is public; what we do is everyone's business. And we have to follow the laws and rules we've set out for public institutions.

And now might be a good time to rail a bit about one of the most disingenuous statements one will ever hear about the people who run a university. Rookie trustees and advisory board members, along with many in the community, often deride university administrators—and faculty members, too, if they are feeling especially self-righteous—because we have never had to "make a payroll." The implication is that we are given money that other people make, via taxes and gifts, and then we just spend it like irresponsible teenagers. Having to hear such tripe is galling enough, but we have to endure it silently, because to make our case would be untoward.

No businessperson in her or his right mind would ever agree to operate a business under the conditions we are handed at the university. In business, if a product is selling well, you make more of it, raise the price, open new sales and manufacturing facilities; if profits start to get tight, you pressure the suppliers to lower their price, cut down on the size of the product, employ lower-cost workers; if a product isn't selling well, you stop making it, lay off the staff, and start doing something else. All the while, you are growing equity in the business and the facilities, taking profits, including big ones when things are going well, giving and taking bonuses. And it isn't anyone's business except your own.

The public university can do virtually none of those things. Tuition and fees are set by outsiders; students even have a role in deciding their tuition (imagine asking customers to vote on the price they'd like to pay for their curly fries?). New degree programs have to be approved by layer on layer of overseers—so forget about timely entry into an emerging academic market. Old degree programs have to be continued for years beyond their useful life, so students who started years ago can finish (even though they are unlikely to do so). Opening new facilities is controlled by another set of overseers, and politics dictate that one can't offer competitive degree programs in the turf of a neighboring university (with bold type in North Carolina). Personnel matters are hemmed in by generations of accumulating regulations, mostly set by the state, not the university. Good luck trying to get new facilities for an educational program that has doubled or tripled in recent years; unless the politics are right, it isn't going to happen.

A good example of the consequences of this operating environment is the construction of university buildings. Almost everyone thinks that the way the state (or federal) government builds buildings is stupid. It takes too long, costs too much, ends up with poor quality. My experience is exactly the opposite. Despite my angst over value engineering, I believe that the processes in place at the university—which the state government largely dictates—produce excellent results in a reasonable time at an acceptable cost. Given that we will always have budgetary constraints, then what we get and how we get it make a lot of sense.

Here's my logic. Just like every hiring, firing, admissions, graduation, and curriculum decision I ever made as provost is considered everyone's business, so is all of our construction and renovation work. Just like many members of the public, legislature, and, especially, alumni believe they know better how to run the university in general, they will also believe that they know better how to build, repair, and operate our physical plant. So do most faculty members. Consequently, all decisions will be second-guessed, in public and often in the media, by lots of folks. Because construction and renovation decisions are big-ticket items that affect the powerful construction industry, and because most trustees and donors have overseen similar projects in their own spheres, people really like to watch how we build things.

So, we are pretty conservative and process-driven. Decisions need to be checked and rechecked. We get a price estimate on a building design from a designer, then another from the builder, and then we have an independent estimator do it. Typically, all three are different, and we work with all three to get them reconciled—and only then do we start signing contracts and excavating for foundations. We do every project up to code. This is especially irksome on renovations, which invariably require us to renovate systems well beyond the particular space that we're aiming to improve. The rule is, if you touch one brick, you've touched the whole wall.

As we build, we're rather like the Fram Oil Filter commercial from years ago—we figure that we're either going to pay for it now or pay more for it later. So, we opt for now, when we have the funds allocated. Most people, even within the university, don't understand that capital expenses can be paid only from the specific capital funds bucket for that project, not from operating funds or other capital buckets. Moving money from one bucket to another requires approval by the legislature, or at least an oversight agency outside the university. The whole cost of the building has to be paid now, from its own bucket; we can't leave the parking lot for next year with the hope that "you'll find the money someplace."

Next time someone tells you that we should run the university like a business, tell them to go get value-engineered.

30

SNOW DAYS

"We need to talk about emergency procedures," said the university's safety guy.

"What emergency procedures?" I said, "I'm only the interim provost."

"Well, for example, winter is coming, and you are the person who decides whether or not to cancel classes and close the university in bad weather. You know, snow days."

"I thought that was the chancellor. He's number one." My adrenaline was starting to rise.

"Nope," he said, "that's the provost. You know, the academic guy."

"Right, I'm the academic guy. What do I know about whether or not to close in bad weather?"

"Don't worry," he said, "you really don't have to do anything except approve the recommendation we make. We have a process. Our folks are out at 4 a.m., working on the parking lots and pathways, so they know what conditions are. And we have a network of people who provide us information. We talk it over with the CFO, and then we call you, if we think something needs to be done. Public affairs will have an announcement ready to go. All you have to do is give us the okay."

"Great," I said, "I'm relieved. You bet I'll follow your recommendations."

I was still a bit concerned, though, knowing that the announcement about closing would go out under my name. It actually read something like this: "In consultation with the chancellor and chief financial officer, Provost Nielsen announces that the university will operate under winter weather advisory level 4. . . ." Or level 1, 2, or 3, whatever the case might be.

My concern became reality a few days later. The weather had been playing nice for the first two weeks of my appointment, but January 19, 2005, would be different. The forecast called for some light flurries around midday. I went out for lunch and a haircut about twelve, as a few flakes were falling, the kind of snowflakes they show in Christmas specials on the Hallmark Channel. I was in a great mood—it was Sharon's birthday and I actually had gotten her a present already. The weather was exhilarating, and I felt like a king, at least an interim king.

I came out of the barbershop to a markedly different picture. The sidewalks and parking lot were pretty well coated in a light, icy snow, and I slid to the car. As usual, I used back roads to make the half-mile trip back to the office, so I didn't realize what was happening on the main streets until I had to cross one. Traffic had ground to a halt, backed up now as far as I could see in all directions. I slithered into my parking spot and then into the building.

The back door to the CFO's office was cracked open an inch—always the signal that he needed to see me as soon as I returned. I knocked, walked in, and said, "The weather is getting pretty treacherous out there."

"Yes," he said. "The chancellor was just in. After his luncheon downtown, he sat in traffic for half an hour, then parked his car in a bank lot and walked the rest of the way back. Traffic is backed up all the way to the Capitol. And look at the weather map—the forecast has changed, and there is a line of freezing rain and sleet on top of us."

"Well," I said. "We better invoke the process that determines whether we should issue an adverse weather advisory."

"What process?" he asked, looking at me like I was from some other university, or universe.

"You know, the process that health and safety has for making weather decisions."

"Here's the process: Whaddya wanna do?"

We wouldn't get anything right that afternoon, but no one else did either. We decided to keep the university open for another couple of hours, hoping that the storm would pass (that's what the weather radar looked like), and the road crews would improve conditions by late afternoon when folks would be heading home. No such luck. The freezing rain eventually stopped, but the coating of ice wasn't going anywhere. The roads stayed impassible until the next day. A usual 20-minute trip for commuters took hours and, in many cases, the whole night. People stayed the night in convenience stores—so they could use the "conveniences."

Making the call on weather may be the most thankless job in the university. Literally. No one ever thanked me for closing or staying open. What they did was call or write to complain. If we closed, faculty members were upset because the teaching schedules went haywire, especially if a test had been scheduled. If we stayed open, commuters were angry—we would typically get a call that our decision had resulted in someone having a traffic accident. Commuting students—and we have many who drive a long distance—had the same reaction. If the K–12 schools were closed and we were open, we created a child care nightmare for hundreds of employees.

Bah, humbug.

31

HOW THE PROVOST FROZE CHRISTMAS

The budget needed to be cut. The budget always needs to be cut. We wouldn't be good public servants if we weren't looking for ways to reduce expenses, especially if what we cut out can be classified as "waste."

Our facilities folks had a brilliant idea about how to cut some waste. The university virtually closes down over the Christmas holidays, basically from graduation through the start of the next term in early January. Teaching faculty members on nine-month appointments don't have to be around—so they aren't. Faculty members and staff on twelve-month appointments mostly take leave during a portion of that time, usually the whole of the non-holiday days between December 25 and New Year's Day. We realized that if we turned down the heat in most of our buildings during some portion of that time, we'd save a truckload of money. We'd actually save many truckloads of coal—which cost a truckload of money—and reduce our greenhouse gas emissions. We calculated we could save around $350,000 with two weekends and a week of lower temperatures.

So, here was the plan. We told all the units of the university that they could close their offices during that time and that everyone could take leave if they wished. The university employees—at least most of them—were ecstatic about that, because the few people who normally had to work in order to keep this or that office open were being given permission to take off. We still had to keep some folks around, essential services like police and a skeleton facilities crew—and the basketball coaches. We also had to keep some of the buildings warm, if they housed experimental animals or plants or ongoing experiments that were temperature-sensitive.

The CFO and I sent out the notice under both our signatures, as we did with all nonacademic matters (so that everyone understood we were best friends). The feedback was great. So, my best friend and I settled down to a long winter's nap. He left town for his holidays, which he extended for several days into the new year.

Little did we know that this would be news. State workers in North Carolina are not unionized, but an effort to form unions is always in the background. Union organizers used this circumstance to protest against harsh treatment of workers, because some workers—those who chose not to take leave—had to work in subhuman conditions. The news media interviewed a few. They complained that their fingers were so cold they couldn't punch the computer keys; they had to wear so many layers of coats that they couldn't move their arms.

So, here we were again—front-page news. All of the complaining personnel were nonacademic, but their supervisor—my best friend the CFO—was nowhere to be found. It was warm where he was. It became hot where I was. As spokesman for the university, I tried to explain that we had this all worked out and we were sorry for the conditions that we had created for a few people. It basically sounded like I said, "Bah humbug."

A few weeks later, I received a photograph in the mail. It resembled the Grinch, but with my green face photo-shopped where the Grinch's should have been. The banner emblazoned across the top read, "How the Provost Froze Christmas."

A postscript. The plan that year was an interim step on the longer-term strategy to completely close down the university during the holidays. We now add a former "floating holiday" to the week between Christmas and New Year's, arrange the other holidays appropriately, and require all employees to take one or at most two days of their normal annual leave during this time. So now, no one works except essential personnel. And we save hundreds of thousands of dollars per year, depending on the weather. Not only do we freeze Christmas, but we freeze the utility bill!

LESSONS ABOUT FACILITIES AND OTHER EVILS

1. Space, not money, is the university's biggest problem. We manage money well, but we're not so good with space.
2. We assign space down to the smallest organizational unit, including the individual faculty member. Then they think they own it.
3. They don't. The university owns all the space. Not the college, department, or faculty member.
4. Faculty members think their space is part of their academic freedom. It isn't.
5. Retired faculty members don't need space, but active faculty members do. Space for retirees should be the lowest priority, even below graduate student offices.
6. Don't make the same mistakes with new space. Keep it all for the university and let departments and faculty members use it for a specifically assigned length of time.
7. Office space matters a little, but working space is the real issue—laboratories, studios, classrooms.
8. Expect territoriality from everyone. When the topic is space, no one is your best friend.
9. New buildings will always disappoint their occupants. That's because new buildings live as fantasies for a long time before they become realities.
10. In the meantime, they get value engineered.
11. Someday everyone gets value engineered. It doesn't feel good.
12. Don't worry when business people tell you how to manage the university. If they had to manage under the university's constraints, they'd act just like you.

13. Universities do a great job of building facilities, on time and on budget. We achieve great value for the money, and we do it with everyone watching. Don't let anyone convince you differently.
14. In bad weather, everyone hates the provost.

PART SIX

FACULTY

32

ADMINISTRATORS LOVE
FACULTY, REALLY

I didn't want to write this section. In the halls of academe, the supposed battle between faculty and administration is legend. So, even though I intend to write a chapter that praises faculty members while it also criticizes them, I am afraid it will be interpreted as just another example of faculty-bashing by the administration. So, you see the difficult position that we're in—we have a mind-set that begins with an expectation that faculty and administration are really just Hatfields in pinstriped suits and McCoys in Birkenstocks.

At the core of the institution, nothing could be farther from the truth. For one thing, almost all administrators began life as faculty members and probably spent a good deal of time there, advancing through the ranks until they gathered enough quadrangle creds to risk going over to the dark side. Most administrators, therefore, revere what a university stands for and does, and we understand how the university (i.e., the faculty) does its work.

I can't speak for administrators who enter the university from some other field—business, politics, or public service. Their success or failure depends, I think, almost entirely on how willing they are to accept the culture of a university rather than trying to force their previous cultures onto us (notice I call the university "us"). If those brought in from the outside fail because they are attempting to slap the university out of its bad attitude, so be it.

Besides, faculty members know that they will outlast the administrators. Several times in my administrative career, contentious faculty members have said things to me like, "We are the university, not you," or "We'll be here long after you are gone." They were right.

But what really separates administrators from faculty is something that only experience can teach: Where you stand depends on where you sit.

As an associate professor at Virginia Tech, I got myself elected to the Faculty Senate, so I could gain some experience with and perspective on the larger university. I say that I "got myself elected," because that is the way most people end up in Faculty Senate. The list of candidates actually campaigning to be a faculty senator is generally pretty short, maybe even nonexistent. The existing senators usually have to go searching for an unsuspecting colleague to take the job off their hands. If some naïve do-gooder actually steps forward and volunteers to be a faculty senator, the nominations will close immediately.

Once in the Faculty Senate, I got myself appointed to the Reconciliation Committee, following an almost identical process to get that task. That committee performed a function that today we'd probably expect from an ombudsman—a last-ditch, informal, off-the-record attempt to resolve issues between disagreeing individuals. My experience was shocking. We didn't deal with many cases, but the few we tackled were horrible. The one I remember most is a bitter battle that had been smoldering between a faculty member and a department head for years. For a reason I don't remember, the matter had come to a head. They agreed to allow the committee to consider their case. When we tried to restrict our attention to the current issue, or even the more current issues, both the faculty member and department head refused. Eventually, we asked each of them what action would satisfy them, and they each wanted the other one fired.

The Reconciliation Committee made me realize, for the first time, that the university's concerns extended well beyond the scope of an individual faculty member's teaching, research, and service, even beyond winning football and basketball teams. The university didn't run itself, despite the nostalgic ruminations of schoolhouse philosophers, and running it was a challenge. In other words, the administrators running the university didn't sit where I sat.

In many ways, because of where they sit, administrators may revere and understand the university more deeply than individual faculty members. As administrators, and especially provosts, we see the entire range of the university's work and life on a daily basis. We tour the laboratories of NSF-supported chemists, but, if we're lucky and open to the gesture, we're given a signed copy of the latest science fiction novel by a faculty member in the creative writing program. We stand in the second row, behind the politicians and the news crews, at the crowded groundbreaking for the newest state-funded engineering building, but we may also be given the honor of cutting the ribbon for the new freshman learning commons, cheered on by the thin gathering of staff who came to celebrate its importance to students. We accompany congresspersons as they visit our special-grant-funded renewable energy projects, but we also may be invited to host the opening of the latest exhibit at the campus art museum. We allocate the funds for a high-profile new program for entrepreneurial teaching and research, but we also support an under-the-radar annual symposium on public history. Individual faculty members may spend a career on campus without ever visiting the arboretum, but we get there pretty regularly. Faculty members, even sports fan, may never see anything other than football or men's basketball games, but we accompany our wives as they toss the first pitch for a women's softball game dedicated to cancer research. We are bound by our jobs to respect and embrace scientists, medical researchers, and engineers—the ones who bring in the grants and get the patents—but also poets, horticulturists, graphic designers, political scientists, and composers. Please note that all the examples in this paragraph are real, and so I say thank you, respectively, to the writers, student affairs professionals, curators, department heads, facilities managers, and team coaches that make our university tick. I love you all.

33

FACULTY ARE THE CAPITAL OF
THE UNIVERSITY

L et me state unabashedly that I love faculty. I love them in general, and I love our faculty at NC State in particular. We have about 2,000 faculty members at NC State. If you assembled 2,000 folks to run a business, and they had the commitment, smarts, and integrity of our faculty, your business would win every honor that exists, and you would take in enough profits to make Scrooge McDuck happy. That's how good our faculty members are.

Faculty is the ultimate resource, the capital resource of the university. Buildings and grounds are important, of course, but only when the faculty uses them. Students are our raw material; graduates are one of our product lines. Previous knowledge is also the raw material of another product line—new knowledge. We're also vertically integrated; basic knowledge is a product of one university factory, while another further develops that knowledge into applied products, and a third packages and wholesales those products to service providers. We also process the raw materials of inspiration and originality into the product lines of art, music, and design. Faculty members are the machinery that converts all those raw materials into product.

The university in general has unusual relationships with its people. Students, for example, are both our raw material and our customers. That we function as well as we do with students in both camps is a tribute to both them and us. We grade their performance in class, and they grade our performance at the end of the semester. When we set our tuition, we ask our students what they think they should pay—and we pay attention. Fascinating.

Faculty, likewise, have multiple roles. They are both workers and management. They vote on who we hire and who we keep. They vote on what products the university will produce (i.e., majors and minors, research and scholarly initiatives) and what features the products will have (i.e., courses and other requirements).

A few years ago, some of our faculty members were upset because the university president kept talking about making the university more *demand driven*. That phrase came to life as part of a yearlong, statewide look at what the university should be doing, called "UNC Tomorrow." The university system held forums for North Carolina's citizens across the state, asking them what they needed from the university. As a political move, this was a brilliant piece of promotion. Asking citizens what they want is always a good thing to do, and it built substantial short-term political interest and support. As a direction-setting process, it wasn't so hot. Our citizens heard the question not so much as "What should the university—which has a very specific mission of education, research, and outreach—do for you?" but more as "What would you like to be different about the world today?" So, they said they wanted more and better jobs, a great business climate, better K–12 education, better and cheaper health care, a cleaner environment, and, of course, more affordable and accessible higher education. Not a bad roster—for the governor. Interestingly, except for one forum at which our Faculty Senate made sure there were some faculty-coached speakers, no one ever mentioned that they would like more research that would invent the next Teflon or Gatorade or more scholarship that would produce the next "Rhapsody in Blue" or *Huckleberry Finn*.

Our faculty, of course, squirmed at the very concept of asking citizens to guide the university. Of particular concern was the demand-driven concept. The idea of jumping here or there in response to short-term trends ("Vampires and Harry Potter are all the rage; let's create a new major in marketing of mythology") was contrary to the purpose of the university, which is to produce knowledge and knowledgeable people—both with long shelf lives. Preparing students to meet a particular demand in society, especially a new need, would convert us from an educational institution to a training institution (one of the cited needs was over-the-road truck driving; meeting that need, even dressed up as "logistics," is a considerable stretch). And this reaction occurred at NC State, which has an unassuming personality devoted to being useful and pragmatic. The problem, however, was that being demand-driven implied to these faculty members that the courses and curricula we offered would be decided not by them, but by outside forces. Such a situation would be intolerable.

After suffering through a few iterations of demand-driven speeches, I called a colleague at the system office and suggested that their rhetoric might lay off the *demand-driven* term, because it had the same effect on faculty as poison ivy. To their credit and my relief, I never heard it in a speech to a faculty audience again.

The multiple roles of faculty create this standoff between the expectations of those outside and those inside the university. As the productive engine, the capital, of the university, faculty members are the machinery for producing students and knowledge. Just as the workers and even line managers in a real factory don't decide that they should be making thingamajigs rather than doohickeys, one line of reasoning suggests that faculty members should produce what they're told to produce. But faculty members have other roles—they are also the leaders and higher level strategists for the business. We rely on them to know more about their products—graduates, discoveries, inventions, creative works—and the future demand for those products than our administrators, trustees, or alumni. By that line of reasoning, we should let them make the decisions about where we are going and how we will get there.

Therein lies the fundamental job of university administration and especially of the provost. The provost must negotiate the Maginot Line between what the public, legislature, trustees, and alumni say they want and what the faculty thinks it wants and support each of their rights to get it. Add to that the occasional mortar barrage from the flanks when students get excited about running the university, and you're managing a pretty lively war room.

So, let's get something clear right now. Although most of this section is about the other roles of faculty, let's start by recognizing and regaling the role of faculty members as teachers, scholars, and service providers. They are magnificent at performing this role. They've spent their entire lives, including about 10 to 15 years before reaching faculty status, becoming experts, and we all get the benefit. They work because of an inner drive to know and understand and create and share.

Faculty members work harder than any employer has a right to ask them to. A candidate for a dean's position once said in his interview that he wanted all faculty to have more time to get beyond the day-to-day, so they could think about the big picture, the long-term; he called it feet-on-the-desk time. Later in the interview, he said that a quality faculty member worked at least 70 hours per week. "Does that include," I asked him, "the feet-on-the-desk time, or is that extra?" Although he didn't answer, I know what he meant—those 70 hours were direct work time, not thinking time.

Every so often, a state legislature or some watchdog group decides to go after faculty for not working hard enough. We all know the drill. Faculty members teach three courses per term, each of which meets for three hours per week. So, by math so simple a legislator can do it, faculty work nine hours per week. I won't insult any teacher who may be reading this by attempting a rebuttal; we all recognize drivel when we see it.

Nonetheless, we have to respond to the watchdogs. We do some surveys and then write the usual reports that show faculty work on average somewhere around 55 hours per week (a figure that is replicated, plus or minus a few hours, in most studies of faculty effort that I've seen). Being warned about what the report is going to say, the critics generally forget they asked.

But that's the trivial part of the story. Most faculty members, really, are working all the time. They put in the 55 hours or 70 hours and then just keep at it. Ask their families. They take manuscripts to revise, while ostensibly watching their kids' soccer games. They fall asleep at night with a book over their face, and it isn't the latest spy novel. They grade papers all through the Thanksgiving break. They schedule vacation to coincide with a professional meeting—and the meeting gets most of their time. They may go to the beach over spring break—but the beach may be in a developing country, where they are leading a group of student volunteers to help rebuild after a disaster.

All that is even trivial compared with the real value. Having such faculty means that the university, and the state in which it resides, gets world experts on every subject under the sun. Every year of experience builds the faculty member's value. No one much cared about understanding Arabic culture or learning Arabic languages until about 2001; now those fields are in hot demand—uh, sort of like "demand driven." But where would we find the experts to fill the demand if we hadn't supported "minor language" programs along the way? There was no demand for renewable energy a few years ago, either, but I'm glad that we had experts working in the disciplines supporting renewable energy on our campus for the decades leading up to the present.

Faculty members work harder than any employer has a right to expect, but sometimes, we just have to draw the line.

"We'd like more faculty members to show up at our evening meetings," the representatives of the student groups told me at one of our informal chats. "We only get one or two, at the most."

"When you were in high school," I asked, "did your parents go to your soccer games, plays, and recitals?"

"Of course," they said.

"Did your folks maybe go to choir practice on Wednesday nights? Or to a book group on Thursdays? Or help you with your homework or take you to the mall for new sneakers?"

"Sure. Our folks were always hauling us somewhere."

"Our faculty members have kids, too," I said.

34

WHERE DOES FACULTY LEAVE OFF AND PROVOST BEGIN?

The provost is the liaison to the Faculty. I capitalize *Faculty* because the word really has two meanings. Just like politics. We talk about big-*P* "Politics," as the formal elective processes and offices, and little-*p* "politics," as the informal processes of forming and influencing opinions and individual decisions. (My word processor recognizes this as well. While I was writing, it would never let me write the phrase, "faculty are . . . ." It always underlined faculty with a squiggly green line, indicating I had made a grammatical error. To the word processor, *faculty* is a group noun that should be treated as singular. When I want to talk about individuals who make up the faculty, it wants me to write "faculty members are. . . ." No squiggly green line. So, if you are getting tired of reading "faculty members" in this book, blame Bill Gates, not me.)

In universities, faculty members are the individuals who are teachers, researchers, and service providers. Most of the faculty members don't care about managing the university. All they want is to teach, conduct research and scholarship, create art and literature, and help people live better lives. They've probably spent a career dodging the department head job or even being chair of the tenure and promotion committee. They are content to let the department head, dean, and provost manage things. Just please don't ask them to move to a different office.

We also have Faculty, capital *F* and singular. The Faculty is the set of formal offices and processes by which the faculty members share in governing the university. The Faculty in this regard is represented by an elected group, usually with a name like Faculty Senate. Faculty Senates vary greatly in their power and authority. At NC State, the Faculty Senate is advisory to the Board of Trustees, chancellor, and provost on most academic matters, but it has relatively little direct decision-making authority. At other universities, some academic matters are vested wholly in the Faculty Senate, such as decisions about the approval of courses and curricula.

The meaning of the term *shared governance*, therefore, differs from school to school. The American Association of University Professors (AAUP) provides general guidance on shared governance in their "Statement on Government of Colleges and Universities," and I recommend that all university administrators read their statements on governance, academic freedom, and other matters—and keep a copy of the Redbook on the corner of their desk, along with the strategic plan. To my reading, the AAUP statement makes clear that governing boards have the ultimate authority to make decisions, but that they should do so transparently and in consultation with the faculty. The AAUP statement then discusses separately the ways in which the governing board, president, and faculty ought to interact in terms of various aspects of institutional management (general educational policy, internal operations, and external relations); the described roles and relations differ according to the position and topic. Consequently, the question of where the Faculty leaves off and the administration begins has no universal, definitive answer. We have no compelling need to define the line between Faculty and administration precisely, though, because all we really need to know and understand is that such a line exists. Because the line exists, Faculty and administration will always spar about where it belongs.

(An interesting artifact in the AAUP document is its failure to mention the position of provost at all. The statement, endorsed by AAUP and other groups originally in 1966 or 1967, considers the president to be the chief academic officer of a university and refers generally to the president and deans as the collective academic officers.)

The provost, therefore, must be prepared that the Faculty will always feel that she or he has trampled on their rights for shared governance. The intensity of this feeling will vary, depending on several factors. First is the extent to which the provost's administration is trying to involve the Faculty. The more generous the involvement, the more understanding the response. I've found that explicitly building Faculty consultation into decision-making processes helps greatly. Through the devoted work of the provost's office staff, we developed a process for explicit Faculty Senate consultation into proposed policy changes relating to academic matters. Although the senate's role is advisory at NC State, we generally worked closely to resolve any issues until the senate voted to endorse the proposed policy changes.

We were generous in our interpretation of what policies were "academic" and, hence, should go to Faculty Senate for review. However, Faculty Senate sometimes expressed surprise when a policy revision didn't go to them, because they thought it was academic and the executive officers didn't. Changing the appeal process for staff layoffs could be interpreted as academic, the Faculty might reason, because some staff work directly for faculty members on research projects, and because many staff, like departmental assistants, process academic paperwork. Changing the spending rate from the endowment might also be viewed as academic, because some of the funds support academic matters. The business officers at the university would surely disagree in both of those examples, believing that staff personnel management and endowment management were administrative matters, not academic. Eventually, our senate asked that every policy change go to them before the executive officers took action, and

Faculty Senate would decide whether or not it was within their scope. I said no, the executive officers would decide what to send to the senate, and we would live with the occasional dispute. The second factor that modifies the tension over consultation is the overall institutional environment. During good times, the Faculty is much more willing to accept administrative decisions. Largess, after all, is easier to accept than pain. Normal situations, when established processes can travel at academic pace (taking as long . . . as it takes), don't excite much Faculty fervor; they've participated in such processes, gotten used to them, and more or less accept whose role is whose. But when we need to pick up the pace, feelings get tenser. When the legislature or governor demands a budget revision by the end of the month, administrators need to make decisions quickly—consultation becomes a luxury, not a necessity. And the Faculty doesn't like it.

The need for speedy action isn't always about money. Perhaps the armed forces realize that they are going to have a lot of returning veterans, and they ask the university to develop new degree programs for them—not in two years, but now. Perhaps football players at some university somewhere tweet unfortunate opinions about a rival, and we have to create a student-athlete social media policy—over the summer before the football season starts. Perhaps animal rights activists liberate laboratory subjects somewhere, and we have to review and change our animal care and use policies—before the NSF or National Institutes of Health (NIH) ask us how we protect animals. Consultation with Faculty in such situations is going to be truncated at best and will probably depend on the ability of Faculty leaders to attend an emergency meeting called for 5 o'clock that afternoon. If something of this ilk happens in the summer, when most faculty members aren't around, the tension becomes tauter, because questions arise about whether the timing was manipulated by the administration. The trouble is that these decisions are often significant and academic, just the kind on which the Faculty wants to be consulted.

The third factor that complicates the separation between Faculty and administration is the orientation of the faculty leaders.

Faculty leaders vary greatly in the intensity of their desire to manage the university. My experience is that the incoming Faculty leaders often begin with a big appetite for "shared governance." After a short time in office, though, they recognize how much we have to do together just to keep the existing level of sharing in operation. The normal business of Faculty Senate functions and committees, the entire suite of University Standing Committees, their role on university-level search committees and advisory groups, their role on faculty grievances and appeals, and the unrelenting calendar of ceremonial events typically convince Faculty leaders that the status quo is about all the sharing they can handle. At NC State, the provost's budget actually pays 51% of the Faculty chair for the two years he or she is in office, recognizing the substantial workload with which the chair is saddled (the 51% also allows us to define the chair as "administrative staff," enabling the chair to attend closed meetings at which we handle confidential matters). In other words, now that they are sitting in the chair next to the provost, they also begin to understand where he stands. So, after a brief immersion into the deep end of the faculty governance pool, we find that we are on the same team and then work together productively and without worrying much about whether we represent the Faculty or the administration. Some sparring will occur, to be sure, but it can be productive and will generally lead to modifications of policy or process that please both Faculty and provost.

Ah, if it were always that way. Unfortunately, some faculty leaders won't make it easy. I believe some faculty members become faculty representatives to satisfy an internal conviction that career administrators have usurped university leadership from the faculty—and it is their mission to take it back. This, then, will be a difficult time. The demands for consultation and transparency will be continual, and, most troubling, no amount of either will be sufficient—because the need for vigilance is eternal. As is often said about Mama, if the Faculty ain't happy, ain't nobody going to be happy.

35

FACULTY BARK; THE PROVOST BITES

From the time a faculty member starts graduate school, she is taught to be skeptical. Graduate committees probe to find fault with premises, experimental designs, data analyses, and conclusions; fellow scholars look for the same problems in journal and book manuscripts they are asked to review; grant proposal reviewers have to reject most of the submissions that come to them, so their approach is to look for reasons to dislike an idea or a project. Researchers and scholars in general worry obsessively about Type I error—the risk that something is false when we've asserted it to be true. In scholarship, we would rather do nothing than be wrong.

The old joke is pretty close to the truth: How many faculty members does it take to change a lightbulb? The answer: Change?

Because faculty members are born and bred to be skeptical about their work, we should expect the same when they review proposed university actions. Therefore, proposals for new courses creep through the approval process, partly because everyone needs a chance to comment, and partly because everyone needs to find something to criticize. Even if the committee doesn't know anything about the subject matter, they can check whether the proposal matches the prescribed format. They can check the grammar and punctuation. They can suggest that someone else ought to review it. Proposals for general education courses are even more susceptible. New majors and minors are virtual prisoners to the process.

In this regard, faculty members are administrative ecologists: They are quick to point out how everything is connected to everything else. Suggest a new curriculum, and the reviewers will ask if this and related curricula ought not be examined to see if there is overlap or if an umbrella curriculum ought to be created in which the new and old curricula can be concentrations. Maybe this curriculum should be offered jointly with the university down the road, which has similar interests. We ought to check our peer universities to see what they are doing about this topic. Perhaps we ought to start a graduate curriculum to accompany this undergraduate proposal, because some of the courses could be dual enrollment. This might be a great candidate for a hybrid program, with some of the courses being offered by distance education. This area of study is also a great area for research, so perhaps this could be part of a center that includes teaching, research and public service. We have several other centers related to this; perhaps they could be incorporated into an institute with those and a couple of other majors. Of course, we'll need new facilities to house this initiative; how does that figure into the space plan? Any of this will require new state funding, so we need to wait until we can get this into the university's budget request. Besides, this is going to be a large interdisciplinary program; we don't have an effective way to manage these, so perhaps we need to study our handling of interdisciplinary studies before we approve anything. So, let's put a hold on this action and recommend a task force be appointed by the provost, but with lots of faculty representation.

The foregoing is a provost's nightmare. The provost, you see, is responsible for making things happen. He's about the art of the possible, not the art of the perfect. He is not obsessed with Type I error, but more concerned with Type II error—the risk that we should have done something and we didn't do it. I will admit to being at the far end of wanting to see action, probably in the

99th percentile of provosts (hence, some might argue, that's why I am now a former provost). In general I believe that faculty members really don't want to make the decisions. They want to talk about them, they want to debate, to bark. Which side they're on isn't as important as having at least two sides. I came to realize this in an accidental way. The executive committees of the faculty senates at NC State and our sister school, the University of North Carolina at Chapel Hill, were having a joint dinner. The dinners were the idea of one of our previous faculty chairs—and a good idea at that. The provosts were pleased to host these dinners each year (twice per year in better budget times) as a chance to build academic bridges between our campuses.

At this particular dinner, each table role-played a discussion about some academic dilemma. Among the guests at my table was one of the more vocal, eloquent members of our Faculty Senate, someone who, I thought, believed our administration was a babbling brook of idiots; his combination of wit and vitriol could be particularly potent. Our name tags had a colored dot that indicated what role each participant was to play. His dot was purple, royal purple perhaps, designating him as provost for the exercise. Should be fun, I thought. In response to the issue—I don't recall it, so let's say it was the need for post-tenure review—he gave the most reasoned, logical, eloquent, and convincing argument in favor of a provost's position that I had ever heard. I wanted to write it down for my future use; never could I have stated it so well. Then the lightbulb went on. I realized that this had been a rhetorical exercise for him, and he was mighty good at it. I also realized then that when he spoke in senate meetings, he might be committed to the subject position, but he might just as well be exercising his debating chops—and his right to do so. After that, I no longer feared his rebuttals, but used them as a way to sharpen, perhaps change and improve, my own position, a useful foil for when I might hit a truly hostile audience. My respect for this faculty member expanded greatly that evening, when I realized how thoroughly he thought these matters through. He understood the decisions weren't black or white, and he cared enough to be sure we discussed a topic long enough to get the shade of gray just right.

The reluctance to make decisions isn't restricted to faculty members, of course. Few of us want to make hard decisions. We don't want to fire people, cut programs, choose which proposals go forward to the legislature and which don't, deny a student petition, or raise tuition in the midst of a recession. That, however, is the job of the university leadership, especially the provost. As the COO, the provost is the person who will be asked the hard questions. The provost is the person who is paid to bite.

This reality became clear in the last budget reduction that I oversaw. For years I had been asking budget officers—deans, vice–chancellors, and vice provosts—to make decisions that stopped doing some things, not just trimmed every program a little more. My admonition met with little success. Now, however, we were facing the largest budget reduction in anyone's memory. I was determined, and my best friend was there with me, that we would make programmatic decisions that would close down some functions. So, we began a series of consultations with our faculty committees, Faculty Senate, Staff Senate, student leadership, and anyone else we could corral into the room. The conversation generally went like this.

"We have to cut $25 million out of the budget. What things should we stop doing?" I'd ask.

"What we really need to do is look at the university's mission and define exactly what we're supposed to be doing," someone would say.

"We have a fine mission, and we're not going to change it because we have a budget problem," I'd reply. "Now, what should we stop doing?"

"What we really need to do is define the strategic priorities for the university and invest in those," came next.

"We wrote a strategic plan last year, with five focus areas and ten strategic investment priorities. You all know what they are. If we want to invest in those, we have to stop doing other things. Now, what should we stop doing?"

"Are we sure that the state budget is going to come out as bad as they say? Perhaps we should go down to the legislature and talk with them about how important our programs are," they retorted. "Our chancellor and other friends talk with the legislature every day. The only way the budget is going to change is to get worse. We have to decide now what we're going to do—and what we're not going to do. What should we cut out?"

"You know, we ought to go back to the beginning. Let's do zero-based-budgeting and make every unit justify everything that they want to do. And we'll just build back until we run out of money," was offered as an approach.

"We don't have a decade to do this," I'd say. "Besides so-called zero-based-budgeting is typically about 90%-base budgeting, which is exactly what we're asking. So, what should we stop doing?"

"In order to answer that question, we need data about who is using what services and how well the service providers are doing," would come next.

"Data are good," I'd say, "and we have lots of assessments. But you've seen them, and you know that any one of you could find a hundred reasons why a particular assessment isn't adequate as the basis for these decisions. You are all experienced members of our university community. If you don't have a well-informed idea about what we should stop doing, who does?"

At the end of each of these sessions, we'd leave with lists of questions and considerations, possible criteria, and maybe even a real suggestion or two ("we should only issue new parking stickers every two years," a suggestion we implemented that does save money). But in the end it was clear that few people were willing to bite, and virtually no one was willing to bite in front of their colleagues.

I've come to understand that faculty, staff, and students want to bark. They want the president, provost, and CFO to bite. It is as simple as that.

36

TO TENURE OR NOT
TO TENURE

No, I'm not going to discuss whether tenure is a good idea or a bad idea. I have nothing original to say on the topic. Tenure is an element of university life, but it is a weakening element. Whether or not tenure will weaken enough to eventually disappear is of little interest to me (I have it, thank goodness, and wouldn't have taken an administrative job without it). The interesting topic is how to deal with tenure now.

The provost is the ultimate arbiter of tenure in a university. Oh, I know that tenure is granted officially by the Board of Trustees, but they take the provost's recommendations; if they don't, the university has a big problem. And the decision not to grant tenure is directly in the provost's job jar. At NC State, the chancellor gets to send the successful faculty members a letter telling them they've been awarded tenure. The provost gets to send the unsuccessful ones their letters—another perquisite of being number two.

The tenure process is goofy. Faculty members are hired with specific expectations, spelled out in their letters of appointment, for which they are responsible to the department head and dean. But, when the time comes for reappointment and eventually tenure, those faculty members are reviewed primarily and most importantly by a committee of peers. The faculty member's peers may make their judgments based on the expectations in the letter of appointment, but they may not. They may just evaluate the candidate on their own expectations for her or him, sometimes based on the dossier, but sometimes based on their general impressions. Goofy.

These days, the university typically has an elaborate and explicit set of procedures, criteria, and standards—that specificity almost guarantees that some process violation is likely to occur at some point along the way, given the general cavalier approach of faculty members (and department heads) to rules. Hence, it's a good bet that almost every negative tenure decision will result in a process-related appeal. In my last round of tenure decisions, I sent a probable-negative case back for total reevaluation, because two drafts of the dossier had gotten switched at some point; the differences were trivial, the faculty committees groaned, but I wasn't going to continue a case for which I could anticipate an appeal.

The process can be goofy, I suppose, because the faculty discussions and votes are really just advice to the provost. The provost is the person who actually makes the personnel decision to deny tenure or recommend to the board that tenure be awarded. Because appeals and grievances only apply to the decision itself and the person who made the decision, the provost is in jeopardy, not the faculty. The provost gets sued, not the faculty colleagues.

Because the provost is the ultimate decision maker, the provost needs to be willing to make hard decisions. Not many hard decisions, but a few every year. At NC State, we reviewed about 100 faculty members each year for tenure or promotion. About 95 of those cases were easy—the departmental faculty and head, college faculty committee, and dean were all close to unanimous in their desire to award tenure. I admit that I spent very little time reviewing those dossiers.

The remaining few were tough. Some carried nearly unanimous negative evaluations, but these needed to be carefully reviewed. Most I accepted, but not all. One case several years ago involved a program whose standards required publication in one of a few designated journals. Unfortunately, their list hadn't kept up with the diversification of their disciplines and programs, and several junior faculty members were working in subdisciplines that the named journals didn't cover. The faculty member under review had published in the equivalent, highly selective journal in his particular field of expertise, but the review committees felt they couldn't abandon their explicit list. Every level voted to deny tenure. I overturned that decision in a heartbeat and recommended for tenure. The departmental faculty was livid and called me over to explain myself. I told them their standard was unrealistic and outdated, that they had been negligent in not changing it, and that I wasn't going to sacrifice a faculty member just to acquiesce to a nonsensical standard.

In a few cases, the previous levels of review arrived at different conclusions. Faculty votes were typically mixed with no decisive direction ("12 for, 10 against, 2 abstentions") and administrative reviews, either positive or negative, were tepid ("on one hand . . .; on the other hand . . ."). In general that advice amounted to, "We barked, you bite." That's when a face-to-face meeting with the department head and dean usually told the story. I could read in their body language what they really thought. Generally, we all agreed in the end. Sometimes the decision was yes, sometimes no.

Promotions to professor were less unanimous than tenure decisions, perhaps because senior promotions allow much more judgment on behalf of the reviewers. Tenure reviews are generally made about younger faculty, whose records are simple, tidy, hopefully pointed directly and purposefully at the primary evaluation factors. The dossiers of associate professors hoping to become professors are anything but simple and tidy ("I'm not putting my whole CV into that new format"). The candidate may have been an associate professor for a few years or a few decades; the frequency distribution of an associate professor filing for promotion is bimodal, with one mode at about 6 to 7 years and the second at about 12 to 15 years. Associate professors may have ventured far afield in their direct responsibilities, taking international assignments, working across departmental and college lines, and getting heavily involved in professional and community service. They may have had official or unofficial administrative duties sprinkled among their years. Associate professors don't have resumes; they have autobiographies. My personal view is that "promotion to full" is much less important to the university than is the tenure decision; make the hard decisions on tenure and the subsequent promotions will be easy. Others feel differently, I know, reasoning that full professor is a status that should come to only a few—meaning those who have emphasized their research and creative scholarship (i.e., grants, publications, patents, external recognition) rather than their teaching or service. As is sometimes said of any review, you just have to get all of your friends and some of your enemies to vote yes. If that occurred on a promotion to full, I voted yes, too.

At the other end of the continuum, some tenured faculty members eventually have to go. Fellow faculty members and department heads are reluctant to take the step of discharging tenured faculty. A department will typically isolate a nonperforming or troublesome faculty member for years rather than begin discharge proceedings. They are all colleagues, probably taught together or had joint research projects in the past, maybe wrote papers or books together. How can they now move to fire one of their own? If it starts with him, where will it end? Maybe I'm next? So, the difficult faculty member gets assigned fewer and fewer duties, gets removed from core teaching, and is avoided by graduate students looking for major advisors. If the department is lucky, he or she takes the hint and retires; if unlucky, the behavior worsens. Eventually, maybe, some personal or professional crisis causes the faculty member to snap, and the department has to take action.

The provost must be willing to discharge a nonperforming tenured faculty member. Deans and department heads need to know that the provost will support them in such a recommendation. If the provost is behind the action—in general and in any specific justifiable case—the department head will be able to sustain the effort; if not, the department head will accept the status quo as the better option, trying to work around the problem. In the meantime, faculty morale drops, tensions tighten whenever the faculty member is around, and staff get scared that they might end up in harm's way.

I once oversaw an academic unit with several nonperforming faculty members. One in particular was not only nonperforming, but his presence was damaging to our students. I approached the provost's office about discharging the faculty member; we discussed the case with the university's legal counsel. The attorney asked the faculty member's salary, and he scoffed when he heard how low it was (neither I nor my predecessor had given him a salary increase for years). "Put him in a corner somewhere," he said, "we're not going to risk a lawsuit for that little money."

I vowed that I would never repeat that scene. Consequently, while I was provost, we took on a number of difficult dismissal cases. In some circles, I was known as the "firing provost" rather than the hugging provost. I didn't like to fire people, but the reality is that the dismissal buck stops with the provost. And to paraphrase Truman again, if you can't stand the heat of tough personnel decisions, get out of the provost's kitchen.

37

THERE'S NO BUSINESS LIKE THE KNOW BUSINESS

People came to understand that I was a nut for Broadway musicals. I've loved them since I was a boy. I used to sit between the swing-out speakers of our console stereo, my 1950s version of the iPod, listening to *My Fair Lady* or *The Music Man*, reading the story printed inside the record jacket. I learned every word of every song of every musical I could find. Unfortunately, today I still remember them all. And I'll sing them at the drop of a phrase. You say, "We've got trouble," and I say, "Right here in River City."

So, one week when I was particularly vexed about the carping coming from the Faculty Senate about something or other, I decided to use my few minutes of remarks at the next meeting to hammer home an important point. Here, with considerable revision, is what I said.

Many of you know that I am a fan of the American musical theater. As a boy, I went to sleep each night listening to the Franklyn MacCormack show on WGN Radio in Chicago. From 10 to 11 each night, he played one complete Broadway soundtrack. While other kids were learning Elvis tunes, I learned Broadway show tunes. Not to worry, I've caught up on Elvis, you hound dog, you.

This morning at 4 a.m., when I awoke and took up again a thread I'd been considering to discuss today, a song was running through my mind. The song, from *Annie Get Your Gun* (perhaps not the best title analogy for a provost addressing Faculty Senate), is, "There's No Business Like Show Business." In that song, the characters describe their love affair with show business, with all its ups and downs, its hits and flops, its ticker tape parades, and clandestine late-night exits from hotels.

This seems like a great analogy to our life in the university, so I want to sing you a song today that I call, "There's No Business Like the Know Business." As we go through our daily routines, dealing with the ups and downs, hits and flops of the university, pretty well immersed in our own joys and miseries, we can sometimes overlook the essential qualities of our academic life. We can forget that there is no business like the know business. So, let me refresh our memories a bit.

First, let's remember we are members of one of the most respected and trusted professions in the world. Despite an occasional rebuff by a disappointed student, a hovering parent, or a campaigning legislator, we enjoy an elevated reputation in society. Survey after survey shows that after the clergy, we are tops with the regular folks. If we say something is true, people generally accept it (climate change to the contrary). People believe that we are committed to improving the world around us, that we aren't in this business for ourselves. And they should believe that, because it is true.

The trust and respect that people afford us also produces a second trait of the know business—we are trusted to pursue our work as we each, individually, best see fit. We're all expected to do scholarship, but what that scholarship is and how we go about it is pretty much up to us. The creative aspect of the Broadway show—writing the music and the words, choreographing the dances, designing the sets and costumes—these are all done as the individual specialists see them, linked together only by the most marginal of story guidance. So, too, is our work in the university the product of thousands of individual scholars, all experts in their own realm.

Another way to say this is that the concept of *boss* is pretty marginal in the university. I remember being amazed at the opening of a musical play for which I was "executive producer" back at Penn State (I also learned what executive producer meant—he's the one who supplies the money). Sharon and I were seated in the front row of the balcony, waiting for the curtain to rise. Just then, the writer and director sat down next to us. "What are you doing here?" I asked, incredulous that they weren't back stage, you know, directing. "It's up to them now," the director said. Just as the Broadway actor delivers her lines, sings her songs, and dances her steps to her own artistic drum, so we in the academy are on our own.

Second, in contrast to almost all other work environments, we operate in a truly benign administrative setting. Once a year (not once a week, month, or quarter), we send a report to our department head, who uses the information to decide on our salary increase—not to decide to fire us, demote us, or move us to another department or function or branch office in Bangalore. Once every five years or so, we actually have to explain what we've been doing and accomplishing to our peers. And they pretty much say, "Cool, go for it!"

Third, but still part of the first two characteristics, we enjoy an incredible level of job security. Here we differ from the acting guild—as the song says, "Yesterday they told you you would not go far . . . next day on your dressing room, they hung a star." And tomorrow, you are a goat again. Not in the university. Because we are trusted, and because people understand and value, deep down, that our work takes time and dedication and that we become more valuable as we learn more, we have the promise of lifelong employment. As long as we aren't evil or lazy, we will continue to enjoy our positions. Only the most extreme of circumstances will threaten that job security.

A few years ago, a financial planner talked his way into a meeting with Sharon and me. He typically advised people who worked for major corporations in the Research Triangle, so one of his first questions was how much available cash we kept in the checking or passbook savings account. When we answered, "Whatever is left at the end of the month," he blanched. He said that we needed at least six months' worth of income sitting in a passbook, ready to be used in case I lost my job. But, I explained, "I have tenure." And we still keep just whatever is left—if anything—lying around in the bank.

(Yes, I know what you are thinking. I did lose my job, and half of my income with it. But I still have my real job—faculty member—and a comfortable living salary.)

Fourth, and perhaps most important of all, we enjoy the enormous privilege of working in the "know" business. My song metaphor is all about loving show business, and we all know that actors, singers, and dancers don't do it for the money. Of course, some of them hit it big, but most struggle along, wedded to their love of the stage. And we have every reason for being wedded to our love of the "sage." We have the privilege—and responsibility—of working with young people who are just at the right age to learn. They have the basic skills to learn, the maturity to run their own lives, the curiosity to seek new ideas, and the freedom to explore. And when someone talks about the decline of any of those virtues from the time when we were students or younger faculty members, I say poppycock. Whatever the current condition of society in general, we have the best of the situation in the university, and we always will have.

Fifth, we work in a setting of beauty and grace. This past summer, while teaching in Prague (a great gig in its own right), we attended a concert in the Art Nouveau Municipal Building, housing a circa-1900 theater of breathtaking beauty. Theaters have always been works of art in themselves, apropos for the creativity that comes alive within their walls. Similar to a theater, the university campus is also a place of beauty. Although we might wish that a particular campus were more pastoral or elegant or concordant, the fact that we work on a campus is meaningful in its own right. We don't work in an office building in the midst of a city, or on one floor of a building, or in a cubicle in a sea of cubicles. We work in an environment, like a theater, that physically replicates the essence of our work—the work of thinkers. And to help us along in that work, the people of our state and nation provide libraries, laboratories, computer resources, auditoriums, theaters, studios, and chapels. All within a setting of grace and beauty.

So, please consider this job description of a faculty member at a public research university:

- Do inspiring, compelling work
- To make the world a better place
- With dedicated colleagues and students
- In a beautiful and safe setting
- For a very handsome salary
- With unparalleled job security
- And almost no supervision.

And that's why there is no business like the know business.

LESSONS ABOUT FACULTY

1. Provosts need to love faculty. If you don't love faculty, don't be a provost.
2. The faculty deserves our love. After all, they do the real work of the university, and they do it superbly, pretty much 24/7/52.
3. Most faculty members want to be left alone to do their teaching, research, scholarship, and outreach. Praise them for that.
4. Consequently, most faculty members don't have much idea what happens at the university beyond their academic horizon. So don't expect them to know what is happening in the Provost's Office or elsewhere in the administration. It's nobody's fault, it's just the way it is.
5. Expect faculty members to get grumpy when somebody wants to dumb down the place. Occasionally, they'll think the provost wants to do that.
6. In addition to faculty members, the university has the Faculty. The Faculty represents the general interests of all those disinterested faculty members.
7. Some faculty members, for inexplicable reasons, want to be representatives of the Faculty. The provost needs to love them for that, too, because someone has to do it.
8. However, some representatives of the Faculty aren't very lovable.
9. The Faculty has some authority in shared governance of the university, but that authority comes from delegation by the governing board. Check with AAUP if you don't think I'm right.
10. There's always a point where shared governance switches over to the authority of the administration; on academic matters, it switches over to the provost.
11. Consequently, there's always going to be a debate about where that point is. Sometimes the debate will be civil; sometimes it

will be hostile. No matter how nice or consultative you are, you'll eventually get some of the hostile.

12. The provost is the fulcrum between the authority of the administration and the Faculty. Balance, therefore, is important.

13. When times get tough and time itself gets short, the capacity for shared governance goes down. Consequently, the capacity for hostility grows.

14. Don't make decisions in the summer if you can avoid it. The Faculty equates that with evil intention.

15. Faculty members are paid to bark. They like to talk, debate, evaluate, consider.

16. Provosts are paid to bite. They are supposed to make decisions, especially the really hard decisions. If you don't want to make hard decisions, don't be a provost.

17. Tenure is a goofy process. The careers of junior faculty members are placed in the hands of senior faculty members, who are largely unregulated in their evaluations and votes.

18. So, the provost is the quality control on tenure processes and decisions.

19. Make sure the tenure processes are clear and explicit and that they are followed strictly, because you are going to get process appeals on negative cases.

20. Provosts have to say no on tenure sometimes.

21. Provosts also have to reverse the recommendations of faculty and deans sometimes, too, when they do something goofy. They aren't going to like it.

22. Provosts also have to discharge tenured faculty sometimes. If the provost isn't willing to do so, the institution and its Faculty will suffer.

23. Never be surprised by what faculty members might do. After all, they are human.

24. And regardless of all this fuss, never forget what a privilege it is to be part of the "know business."

PART SEVEN

PEOPLE MATTER MOST

38

POPULUS PLURIMUS
MAXIMUS ES

That's my motto. I made it up for this book. It means "people matter most." To be literal, it means "people are most important" because the web-based English-to-Latin electronic translator I used couldn't handle "people matter most."

Looking back through time, however, I like to think that could have been my motto. I have always believed that if, as leaders, we respected people, rewarded them, and gave them the tools and freedom they needed to do their jobs, they would perform like champions. We wouldn't need cumbersome processes for job descriptions, annual performance expectations, or reviews. All we would need is to check in with them now and again—and give them direction when they asked for it.

Such an approach may not work everywhere, but it certainly works in a university. People work hard at a university because they love the work, not because someone is watching. The faculty certainly operates from this paradigm, as I've discussed, but so do staff. And they will work especially hard if someone notices their efforts and successes every so often.

Hanging on the wall of my office is a small plaque that visitors always ask about. It holds a freeze-dried donut, declaring me the first and only recipient of the "Departmental Donut." When I was department head at Virginia Tech, I started a small tradition to encourage graduate students to complete their degrees, not ABD (all but dissertation), but all the way. Whenever a student completed an MS degree, I bought donuts for the graduate students; when a student finished her or his doctorate, the donuts were jelly-filled. When I left for Penn State, the graduate students held a small ceremony, with jelly-filled donuts, at which they gave me the award of which I am most proud—the departmental donut. Now, whenever someone asks my philosophy of leadership, I respond MBD, management by donuts.

Margaret Wheatley, in her seminal book *Leadership and the New Science,* recommended the fractal as the correct analogy to the organization of institutions. A fractal is a pattern in nature that repeats itself in total at smaller and larger scales. The fern frond looks just like the fern leaflet, which looks just like the smaller parts of the leaflet, and so forth. The whole pattern repeating at every scale is the analogy to every person in an organization representing the whole, operating not as a housekeeper, salesperson, or executive, but as an essential part of achieving the mission of the organization.

After reading Ms. Wheatley's book, I was captured by that analogy as being perfect for a university. We produce educated persons and the knowledge needed to feed that education. Everyone at the university is engaged in the educational process, not just faculty members. Education occurs everywhere, not just in classrooms, and the services that people perform around the university relate directly to the success of our educational endeavor. Prospective students, including those who come and those who don't, generally remark about how heavily the campus tour impacted their decision—if the landscape looked attractive, if the residence halls felt like home, if the food in the dining halls was appetizing, if staff at the bookstore were friendly and helpful, if the student tour guides seemed knowledgeable and proud about their university. A colleague recently told me about a student she interviewed who had decided to come to NC State rather than a few other higher-ranked institutions. The student said the person who made the difference was another staff member in our college who had personally organized a series of visits for her—and did it with a smile and a happy bounce in her step. Our prospective students seldom visit a class or talk to a professor on those initial visits, so the people they actually see and meet are truly fractals of the university. Our groundskeepers and cooks need to know that they are important and need to be treated as the true partners in education that they are.

The provost needs to understand and internalize this better than anyone at the university. He is the quality control/quality assurance officer for the core product of the university—education. The provost needs to appreciate and respect the work of every element of the educational factory. As I've admitted earlier, I didn't have a clue about the importance of the work of innumerable offices on campus until I became provost. I didn't know their value as a faculty member, department head, school director, or even dean. Ask a faculty member how a student actually graduates—how the grades and credit hours get captured and saved, how a student's accomplishments get recorded and compared with the requirements, how those records turn into a diploma and transcript. Ask them about tutoring—how tutors get selected and trained, how we know which students need what help, how it gets scheduled, how we monitor to make sure nothing shady is going on, how we pay for it, how we monitor and assess success. Ask about something truly scary—accreditation. Odds are, they won't have a clue.

As I'm revising this chapter, I have just finished giving a final exam, grading it, and posting the final semester grades. In so doing, I called on the assistance of instructional technology, copy center, disability services, registration and records, computer services, departmental assistants, academic advising, janitorial services, and, no doubt, several other offices that are entirely invisible to me. Bless their hearts.

39

SHOWING UP IS 95% OF LIFE

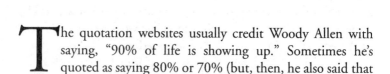

The quotation websites usually credit Woody Allen with saying, "90% of life is showing up." Sometimes he's quoted as saying 80% or 70% (but, then, he also said that "94.5% of all statistics are lies"). I prefer 95%, because the less left over for skill or intelligence, the better I am suited for the task.

In the world of provost, showing up is the biggest part of the job. The provost is the on-campus manifestation of "The University." Of course, the provost is number two, and the literal manifestation of the university is the football coach, uh, I mean the chancellor. But on a day-to-day basis around campus, Mr. Provost is Mr. University. I've come to realize that as the title and salary of the position get higher, the more the job is about showing up. As provost, I spent a lot more time sitting at luncheons and dinners than I did doing real work.

But let's not trivialize the ceremonial work, for any university administrator. About two months into my service as dean, Sharon and I were invited to take part in the opening ceremonies of the annual state finals of the Senior Olympics. Our college houses the Parks, Recreation, and Tourism Department, and one of our faculty members had been the force behind Senior Olympics since the beginning. So, when she asked if we would attend and take part in the ceremony, we were glad to say yes. We walked to the high school track and football stadium where the finals were being held, having parked some distance away in a heavily rutted field used for overflow. Over my objections, Sharon insisted that we carry a flashlight, because it would be dark on the way back to the car. The ceremony was inspiring. Just like in the big Olympics, teams representing their home lands (in this case, the 100 counties of North Carolina) paraded past the bleachers and viewing stand, yelling, for example, "Go Buncombe County!" Seventy-year-old cheerleaders turned arthritic cartwheels, while others twirled batons and others sang. When the parade ended, I spoke briefly, and so did some other officials and sponsors. Then the master of ceremonies took over for the lighting of Olympic flame. He called for the lights to be turned off, and the stadium went black. So did the speaker's platform and podium. The emcee turned around to those of us seated behind him and whispered, "I can't see my notes. Does anyone have a flashlight?" Sharon quietly slipped ours into my hand, I passed it on to him, and the ceremony proceeded without a hitch. Our faculty member leaned over, touched my arm and whispered, "You're going to be a *wonderful* dean."

The university needs a presence at all sorts of off-campus events, from the Senior Olympics to the Chamber of Commerce to funerals of political leaders. Most of those will be covered by number one. Showing up is just as important on campus, though, as it is off campus. Fortunately, the role of provost is to spend most of his or her time showing up around campus—perfect for me, and I suspect for most provosts, because we revel in the life of the university.

Many in the university begin to think of the provost as their guy or gal in the big house. They relate to the provost as being somehow closer to them than the chancellor. My proof comes from the treatment we experienced during our occasional breakfasts with faculty. About twice per semester, the chancellor and I met for breakfast with twenty or so faculty and professional staff, just to chew the fat (the fat was generally disguised as donuts). The discussions were always cordial. The faculty guests were polite and respectful, the questioning was pretty soft, and seldom were our answers challenged in a follow-up. Afterward, they always told us how much they enjoyed the meeting and appreciated us taking time from our busy schedules.

The evening before one scheduled breakfast, however, the chancellor was called to another event that required him to be off campus. So, the senior vice provost joined me for the breakfast. After a very short period of requisite politeness, the faculty guests lit into me as though this were a pig-pickin' and I were the pig. Questions cut to the quick, glib responses were rejected as bureaucratic doubletalk. They hammered us about money, space, graduate assistantships, paperwork—you name it, we heard it.

When the chancellor was present, breakfast was ceremonial; when I was there without him, breakfast was anything but ceremonial; it was down and dirty. I was the guy to whom the assembled faculty members could and would voice their concerns. They showed how much they loved us that morning, so much that they would trust us with the truth. It is an honor to be trusted like that. Nonetheless, as we stumbled out after the breakfast, I vowed that if the chancellor ever canceled again, I was canceling, too.

Showing up may be 95% of life, but you still have to do something once you get there. Even though most appearances are ceremonial, the provost's presence will be central to most of the ceremonies. As always, all eyes will be on the provost at some time during the event. On the last day of my classes, I now give the students a "little advice from Uncle Lar"; as part of that, I paraphrase Cardinal Newman, the nineteenth-century English clergyman and philosopher, as saying "A gentleman keeps his eye on all his company." So does a gentlewoman, I add.

Everyone in any room is the provost's company. I almost always looked for people I didn't know, rather than sticking close to the circle of colleagues who made me feel comfortable. The provost needs especially to make welcome those who look like they need a friend—the quiet, shy, new, international, minority, handicapped. I made a habit of joining small groups of people and introducing myself ("Hi, I'm Larry Nielsen, your provost; would you like a pencil?"). At one dinner, after we were all seated, two students came in late and ended up sitting by themselves at a round table for eight. I excused myself from the head table and sat with them during dinner. I heard about this—positively—from various sources for months.

The provost will almost certainly have to say something. The organizer will usually prepare some remarks, but I seldom used them (and I never used them verbatim). My assistants always asked for prepared remarks, however, because then the organizers had to think a bit about what role they'd like the provost to play and provide some facts that I could use. Beyond that, however, I almost always ignored the remarks. Prepared remarks, especially prepared by someone else, will sound formal and stilted, full of fancy words and overstuffed eloquence. With internal audiences, I've always found that the less formal the remarks, the better the response. Faculty, staff, students, and parents want to hear from the provost, not from the communications officer.

We all disparage Wikipedia—it isn't accurate, it isn't peer reviewed, it doesn't come in a big book with gold binding. But I gladly admit that I love Wikipedia. Wikipedia is the savior for people whose working day is punctuated by making "brief remarks." Sometimes three or four times a day. Wikipedia as a resource sure beats the heck out of those newsletters for speakers, where they teach you that the Chinese character for crisis is the combination of the Chinese characters for danger and opportunity (heard that one, have you?).

But Wikipedia is a gold mine. Giving brief remarks on November 12 (a day I just picked at random)? Wikipedia will tell you what happened on November 12 in history, who was born, who died, who took the first known photos of the Loch Ness Monster on that date in 1933. I can think of a hundred ways to use that juicy tidbit ("want another little piece of fantasy about a monster? I'm going to talk about our budget . . ."). Still stumped for material, just look up 12—Wikipedia will give you all sorts of arcane information about the number 12, like what famous athletes had their jersey number 12 retired. If you can't weave all that trivia into some theme that will wow the audience, then you don't deserve a seat at the head table. And no one cares if it is accurate. Consider:

> I know this seems like a tough time, but I'm confident we can accomplish magnificent things with the tools we have on hand. Like Warren Harding did on this very day, November 12, in 1958. No, not President Warren G. Harding, but Warren Harding, iconoclastic rock climber who spent his youth scrambling over whatever got in his way, especially in Yosemite National Park. On this day, he completed what is still considered the most miraculous climb in American history—3,400 feet up the face of El Capitan. He and his fellow climbers lived 10 days on the face of the cliff, the last three hunkered down while they waited out a blizzard. They made it with ropes, pins, and their bare hands. If they could do that, we can accomplish our mission with the wonderful tools we have . . . now stick your boring bureaucratic message here. . . . On a final note, also on this very day in 1840, August Rodin, the French sculptor was born. So Warren Harding conquered rock in one way, August Rodin conquered it in another. So, get out there and climb to the top of your rock and sculpt it into something beautiful!

40

TRANSPARENCY IS ALIVE, BUT PRIVACY IS DEAD

The university is complex. And as H. L. Mencken said, "For every complex problem there is an answer that is clear, simple, and wrong" (check Wikipedia if you don't think Mencken said that). That would be a fine motto for a university, especially if the web translator could put it in Latin. An institution with the characteristics that we've discussed in this book is going to have lots of footnotes to its life story.

The provost is one of three people, along with the chancellor and CFO, who knows those footnotes better than anyone else. The provost may know it better than the other two, actually, because of his or her central role in accomplishing the real work of the university. Consequently, the provost has an enormous capability to either clarify or muddy any situation.

I recommend clarity, otherwise known as transparency. The more honestly, openly, and directly we communicate, the more successful we will be and the happier the university will be. We worked relentlessly on this at NC State (although some local readers will scoff at this assertion), especially regarding planning and budgeting. Two years before I became provost, we formed a University Budget Advisory Committee; later, as provost, I chaired the group. That committee, composed of faculty, staff, and administration, became the formal conduit for considering broad university input into budgetary matters. We developed and published "budget principles" that we would use to both expand and contract budgets. The CFO and I went to the committee with the preliminary stages of budget cuts to gauge their view. We trusted the committee members with information that formerly we would have kept under wraps, not because it was confidential but because we were uncomfortable with lots of people having access and possibly misrepresenting the numbers, either innocently or purposefully. But the committee members respected their special access, and we were all wiser for the effort.

As we gained confidence, we went further. The Faculty and Staff Senates began cosponsoring semiannual budget forums, at which the CFO and provost presented information about the status of the budget and how it got that way. Miraculously, some people even attended—and stayed awake. Eventually, that information found its way onto the web and evolved into "budget central," where we put virtually everything that had to do with the budget—more than any rational human being would ever wish to know. I actually began to worry that we had so much information out there that an interested faculty or staff member wouldn't be able to sort through it all to find what she or he really wanted to know. When the state chapter of the AAUP listed us as a role model for the transparency of our planning and budgeting, I knew we were on the right track.

But misrepresentation will always parasitize the commitment to be transparent. That is the nature of life in the contemporary public university. People are watching. Lots of people are watching, and they may have motives that have nothing to do with improving the efficiency or effectiveness of the university in an informed, constructive way. We are as vulnerable as fish in a barrel, as visible as fish in a fishbowl.

I learned the hard way that whatever the provost says is potential news. Soon into my term as provost, I attended the summer meeting of the University of North Carolina system program regarding diversity. During the summer, the system held (maybe still holds, but I haven't been back) a two-day symposium and workshop on some diversity topic. All schools were requested to send a team of five or so to the workshop, and they asked that the provost lead the school's delegation. So, during the summer of 2006, I attended along with our team. I was the only provost to attend and, unfortunately, was the highest-ranking university person present. The organizers, therefore, asked if I would summarize the proceedings at the end of the first day.

The day's topic was how to make the university more accessible to our growing Hispanic/Latino population. Speaker after speaker recited the need to allow undocumented children to attend the university at in-state tuition rates and with the availability of financial aid. Under UNC policy, undocumented students could attend, but they had to pay out-of-state tuition and couldn't qualify for any federal or state financial aid. I still personally believe that such conditions are folly—these students came here along with their parents and had no say in whether they were documented or not; they have gone to public schools for as many as 13 years, studying, playing, and socializing with the rest of our public school students. At the time, a majority of state senators were cosponsoring a bill to allow undocumented students to attend college at in-state rates, as long as the student had gone to high school in North Carolina for four years and was applying for citizenship. So, in summarizing the meeting, I said that we needed to get the law changed. Thunderous applause reverberated through the meeting room.

I didn't canvass the room for the presence of reporters—never occurred to me that one might be present. One was present, however, and my statement was reported the next morning in a regional newspaper. Panic ensued. Talk radio had a heyday, all the way up to national shows. The legislature was irked at the unwanted attention and at the gall that a university official would publically recommend a change in state law and policy. The bill lost its sponsors and disappeared from the calendar. Legislators favorable to NC State were especially irate—"We could understand something like that coming out of Carolina, but not out of *our school.*" The university president took me to task (through the chancellor), the first strike in my at-bat in the provost's league. My bosses required that I appeared on local television that evening, definitively stating that my remarks represented my own opinion, not NC State's and certainly not the system's.

The concepts of *transparency* and *no privacy* go hand in hand, of course, because the goal of transparency is to get rid of privacy. But together the concepts could be the two Chinese characters that add up to crisis. How can university administrators, grappling with complex and difficult conditions and decisions, embrace transparency, when everything we say is subject to immediate reinterpretation by those who don't have the full context? When the situation surrounding my hiring of First Lady Easley was being covered by the newspaper, the paper eventually got access to all materials related to the hiring. Included in the materials were all the pages from my daily planner that had anything to do with the first lady. At my first meeting with the first lady, I had scratched notes about what roles she might have if and when she joined us at NC State. I had written a side note that read, "wise?" The newspaper reported that notation, without comment as to its meaning. You might conclude that I was wondering if hiring the first lady was wise. In fact, my notation referred to the campus program called "Women in Science and Engineering," or WISE, and I was wondering if she might serve a role in that organization to support young women in their professional development.

How could I have managed my relation with the press better? Certainly I needed more caution. The provost must always keep in mind that whatever she says will be repeated, whatever she sends in an e-mail will be forwarded (unless, of course, she actually *wanted* it to be forwarded). I have always been cautious about the words I use publically and in correspondence, striving for civility, clarity, and decorum. But I've never been cautious about voicing ideas—about considering them or discarding them. Nonetheless, what the provost says matters, and listeners will extrapolate from the actual words to their own situations and interpretations. As I gained experience as provost, whenever I was about to voice an opinion, I always asked if a reporter were present. I don't know if professional ethics require reporters to fess up that they are present, but at least everyone else knew that what came next was not intended for widespread distribution.

I have learned one lesson about the press: Avoid being quotable. I've found it a useful quality to seem dull to the press, especially in official situations. Earlier in my career, I wasn't so cautious. I craved being quoted, seeing my name in the paper. Once at another university, I was being interviewed about an arboretum that we were planning. When asked what an arboretum was, I rambled for a while and then said, "It's a zoo for plants." Now that was quotable, and I could see the excitement in the reporter's eyes. "Zoo for plants" was the dropped out headline in the story in the next day's newspaper. The quote was innocent enough, but the director of the arboretum burst into my office the next morning, chastising me for trivializing the project—his project—so cavalierly.

I've learned in the intervening years to avoid the memorable quote. I like nothing more than watching the reporters scramble to get the sound bite from someone else—most likely a student or faculty member who made a definitive and extreme statement. In my last years as provost, reporters would have long interviews with me, in which my answers always began something like this: "Well, that is a complex question with many facets; let's start at the beginning . . ." Then I rambled around the complexity for a bit—being both intellectually and practically honest and transparent—but never got to the zoo-for-plants big finish. And I seldom got quoted.

When it comes to the press, be particularly cautious about the campus newspaper. Of course the provost has to talk with the campus paper whenever it asks. But, just like with other campus student functions, the reporters and editors turn over regularly. Consequently, the newspaper doesn't develop a deep understanding of the university, and your discussion with an individual reporter may be the first time he or she has ever encountered the topic. If a student reporter is covering proposed tuition increases, you can't assume that they will understand the difference between tuition and fees, resident versus nonresident tuition, special fees for professional or graduate programs, or the effect of financial aid on what students actually pay. They are unlikely to understand faculty tenure, and they probably have little concept of academic freedom or shared governance. So, when being interviewed for the student newspaper, always end by saying, slowly, "We have a great university with great students, and we're working hard every day to make it even better." That quote will never get you into trouble.

41

NOT EVERYONE IS LIKE ME

No, I didn't write "not everyone likes me," which is also true. Read the chapter title again: "Not everyone is like me." They shouldn't be, and we shouldn't expect them to be. Ah, here we go—the chapter about diversity. I don't need a chapter about diversity, you are thinking; I've been through it over and over. Well, yes, you do need a chapter about diversity, because it is a much more pervasive issue than we generally acknowledge.

For example, one of the core hiring problems in universities is our unwavering commitment to merit. Nothing wrong with merit, as long as we recognize that, like a smorgasbord, it offers a wide variety of choices. In universities, we tend to see merit implicitly in terms of a simple template: How much is this person like me? We've all been to seminars about embedded bias, the subconscious or just barely conscious views that we hold and that affect how we judge others. And we've tsk-tsked about people so blind as to miss those biases, smug that we don't have them.

Fitting that I just used the word *blind*, because blindness is what first caused me to really understand embedded bias. One of my doctoral students was legally blind. He could see somewhat using his peripheral vision, and he could read, but only when the text was greatly magnified. The university provided a computer that projected text on the monitor at a size he could read—a few words filled the entire screen. He was a remarkably capable person who had learned to accommodate his blindness through a variety of strategies. When he began to write his dissertation, however, the literature review became a significant obstacle. His first drafts weren't acceptable to me or his other committee members. His drafts were basically individual paragraphs in which he summarized and discussed the content of a relevant paper. What we expected, I explained, was a comprehensive integration of the literature—he could do this verbally, but he wasn't producing it on paper. Then I thought about how a fully sighted person produced a comprehensive synthesis of the literature, as I did for the end of this book. We spread out papers all over the table in front of us, sticky notes covering all available surfaces, jumping from one to the next, turning pages forward and back, finding our notes from previous readings scribbled in the margin. We can synthesize in this way, because we have the gift of sight. A blind student would have needed years to get all the information synthesized to meet our conventional expectations. My expectation for "what a literature review is like when I write it" represents an embedded bias against his blindness. His intelligence, persistence, or even his merit had nothing to do with his inability to produce a literature review in my preferred style; no, it was just that he wasn't like me.

Let's talk about women in the workplace. Most faculty members and many administrators tend to think that we've solved the issues relating to women faculty and staff. Their numbers keep growing, albeit slowly. We watch the salary differential between men and women, and we fix it every few years when raise money is a bit more available. Hey, if the problem is solved, how come we have to fix it every few years?

No, women's issues in the university are not solved. Tenure is still less likely for women candidates than for men. Women still end up on the nontenure track more frequently than men. Women still feel less accepted in faculty circles than men; men still have strategy sessions while lined up at the urinals. Personnel policies still exact a price from women who are bearing or rearing children, especially if they are doing it by themselves. Lactation rooms are rare. Women in general feel less satisfied with their work and their role in the university than men; women who are associate professors are especially unlikely to be satisfied.

The reality about women's issues is also the reality for all other forms of diversity at the university. Diversifying the academic staff of the university is a journey, not a destination. The provost must plan the itinerary, herd everyone aboard the train, and help them enjoy the ride; and, if necessary, shovel coal into the boiler.

To do this, the provost must walk the walk. Whenever we were forming a committee for a dean, vice provost, or vice-chancellor search, our senior staff and I would get together around the whiteboard. We would work through the diversity needed on the committee. First, diversity in types of positions and roles—administrators, tenure-track faculty, nontenure-track faculty, extension/outreach faculty, technical staff, office staff, undergraduate students, graduate students, external stakeholders. Then, diversity in subunits, making sure all major disciplinary parts of the unit were represented. Then, diversity in rank—assistant, associate, and full professors, distinguished faculty. Then, diversity related to gender, race, and ethnicity. We didn't stop until we felt that the committee represented the university on all its dimensions. This process usually took hours, with constant reference to the university's website, calls to department heads, and various other consultations.

I also never let reviewers rank candidates until the very end of the recruitment process. Ranking along the way leads to an artificial assessment based on only partial information and gives embedded biases their rein. At every preliminary review stage, I only gave reviewers two choices. At the first stage, the choice was "the candidate is qualified for the position, or not." At the next stage, the choice was "get letters on this candidate, or not"; at the third, "interview this candidate, or not." Only then, when we had conducted the interviews, would I allow three options: "This candidate is unacceptable, this candidate is acceptable, this candidate is best." By keeping all surviving candidates in one unranked pool, the embedded biases associated with "this candidate is like me" can be kept under control.

Merit is also the enemy of another essential tool of diversity at a university—opportunity. I have been criticized for using the "opportunity hire" too much. Part of the criticism of my hiring of the first lady, for example, was that I created a new position for her and hired her into it without the typical search. But I contend that if the provost isn't using opportunity hiring as a routine strategy to recruit the best faculty and staff to the university, he or she isn't doing the job. We use opportunity hires for a questionable purpose—when we want to hire one pair of a couple and end up hiring both—so why shouldn't we use it for the best purpose—strengthening and diversifying the university's faculty capacity? When we had a chance to hire a Pulitzer prize–winning poet, I jumped at the opportunity; she never would have responded to a posted job offering. In another case, we negotiated down to the fine print—where his parking space would be—with one of the top Native American scholars in the country, who would never have applied to a typical advertised job. Unfortunately, we landed neither. These failures further prove the point—because competition for the most talented faculty is so intense, we will have to try many times for every candidate we successfully hire. The legislature in North Carolina even created a special fund for targeted recruitment and retention of faculty. If the legislature understands opportunity hiring, surely our faculty colleagues can.

We have another, but unexpected, diversity challenge creeping up on the university—our incoming faculty will not be like us. Kathy Brower of Harvard University gives a fascinating seminar about the changes in the generations, from post–World War II traditionalists to baby boomers to Gen X, and now to the "Millennials." Millennials are folks born in 1984 or later, and they have begun moving into the age range for starting faculty.

These new faculty members are not like us, the administrators and senior faculty members who will mentor, supervise, and evaluate them. Those of us in the baby boom generation have envisioned our careers as ladders we're supposed to climb. Get on the bottom rung and keep working our way up, rung over rung, and no detours. We read the job description and accept it. We produce what the job description says, and we're satisfied with an annual review by the boss. We expect to be given the base resources to succeed, but then we reckon it is up to us to do the work.

Millennials aren't like us at all. They don't imagine a career ladder, but rather a lattice. They move up, over, down; they step out for a while, if it suits them, to try something else. If they encounter a work environment that is too stressful or unrewarding, they'll get out. They don't expect to be one place, doing one thing, for a long career. They expect constant reinforcement regarding their job performance; if the boss doesn't come to them, they'll go to the boss. They expect a voice in deciding what the work expectations are and how to run the place, from their first day on the job. They expect to work where they want, when they want, and as much as they want—and they are willing to be in constant communication, electronically, of course. They mix business and personal matters in a patchwork that defies traditional accountability. Somewhat contradictorily, since they seem to be pretty self-absorbed, they also want to contribute to the community around them, also from day one.

We better be ready, then, for making massive changes in the way we manage faculty when the Millennials join us en masse. Do we need a different, more flexible approach to the concept of tenure? You bet. Will the advice to hunker down and concentrate on your research until you get tenure ring true? Nope. Will large investments in start-up funds and laboratory renovation pay off with faculty loyalty? Probably not. Will they want opportunities to do international work or service-learning? Yes (interestingly, at my last new faculty orientation as provost, the most common question to me was not about getting tenure but about how to get involved in service-learning). Will we finally have to figure out how to recognize and reward work across disciplinary boundaries— not occasionally, but as a routine matter? Absolutely.

Think we need to love people who aren't like us? Absolutely. Think that the provost is the person who needs to love them the most? Absolutely squared.

42

LEAVE YOUR PHONE AT
THE DOOR

I f people matter most, why are they all looking at their phones when I'm talking to them?

IMHO, the quickest way to convince someone that I don't care about them is to ask them to wait while I take someone else's call. This used to be an occasional nuisance, because it could only occur when sitting in the office. Not anymore. Along with the ability to be contacted electronically anywhere, anytime has come the ability to insult people anywhere, anytime.

Things were bad enough when only telephone calls threatened to distract us. Today the biggest culprit is e-mail, accompanied by its posse of text messages, tweets, Internet browsing, angry birds, and whatever will come next. BTW, administrators have a dual addiction. First, we have to read the message right now, and I mean *right now* right now. Second, we have to respond right now, so we can keep our inboxes empty. Like cleanliness, an empty inbox is close to godliness.

At a special meeting of our executive team with new members of the UNC Board of Governors, I was appalled to look down the row on our side of the conference table and see four executive officers sitting side-by-side, each absorbed in their personal digital assistants. I wondered what the governors were thinking as they watched our leadership, heads down and hands in their laps, silently but not unobtrusively clicking away? Perhaps they didn't mind, but I did. I was speaking at the time. LOL. My point, again, is simple. If people matter most—and they do—then pay attention to them.

We created a special way for anyone at the university—or outside it, for that matter—to communicate with the provost. In a moment of whimsy occasioned by my amusement with the Staples "Easy" Button, I started talking about the provost's YES button. I could see the eyes light up on listeners every time I started to describe the YES button—because they thought I meant they would get the answer "Yes" if they asked me a question. No, I explained, the YES button stood for Your Effectiveness and Efficiency Suggestions. Our enterprising staff in the provost's office actually made up lapel buttons in red and white that said "Provost's YES button." We passed them out to advanced audiences that already had pencils.

We also put a YES button area on the provost's office web page. One had simply to roll the cursor over the YES button and click, and a blank e-mail automatically popped up, pre-addressed to the provost. I ended most presentations with an invitation for folks to send me their thoughts through the YES button. As you can expect, the public relations value was terrific. Providing a specific, direct communication channel to the provost was a welcome symbol of accessibility and transparency. Most contacts were easily handled and answered; some, of course, could only be acknowledged. As you might not expect, the traffic was light. For most people, having the opportunity for access was more important than actually using it.

Perhaps the greatest honor a provost can pay someone is to give them time. I recommend being generous with your time to individual faculty members, staff, and students. Screen the need first, but then invite them in. Like with the YES button, relatively few people will actually seek a personal meeting; those who actually do so will be profoundly appreciative of the opportunity. Most are also respectful of the provost's time and, especially, authority, and they are invariably so nervous that they can hardly speak. For them to come to the provost's office, however, means they have a serious issue.

So, be nice. Listen to their message. Don't ever let on how busy the day has been or will be. Don't tell them how tough the provost has it. Promise to consult the dean or vice provost or vice-chancellor who is in charge of their world. Promise to report back to them.

Most importantly, leave your phone in its holster, at the door.

43

IN THE PRESENCE OF GREATNESS

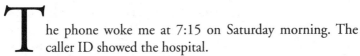

The phone woke me at 7:15 on Saturday morning. The caller ID showed the hospital.

"Hello," I said, fear in my voice.

"Hello, Larry." I recognized the voice immediately. "I wanted you to know that Coach Yow passed away a few minutes ago. Will you please handle the university matters for her?"

Kay Yow, longtime women's basketball coach at NC State, died early on the morning of January 24, 2009, after what the world would acknowledge as a heroic battle against breast cancer. As the years went by, we could all tell that the disease was taking more and more from Kay. But she never focused on that. She'd tell us about some side effect of the disease—sore throat, numb fingertips, perpetual tiredness—but it was always about how she couldn't spend as much time as she liked with her team when they needed her. Never about Kay, always about others.

People use the phrase "in the presence of greatness" pretty casually, but I will use it only in reference to this wonderful woman. Every time I was with Coach Yow, I knew I was in the presence of greatness.

She was a great coach, of course. The banners flying in Reynolds Coliseum, the home arena of the NC State women's basketball team, attest to her coaching milestones—500 wins, 600 wins, 700 wins, numerous ACC championships and NCAA appearances, coach of the 1988 gold medal Olympic team. The statistics and championships, however, say little about the true greatness of her coaching.

I knew she was a different kind of coach from the first time I met her. In my first year as dean, I was called by the provost to a meeting with our football, men's basketball and women's basketball coaches. They wanted to talk about NC State adding a physical education major, like many other Division-I sports universities had. Because our college houses the parks, recreation, and tourism program, we were the likely home of a PE major, should one be formed.

The three coaches put up a formidable offense. Herb Sendek, our intellectual men's basketball coach, led the meeting, working methodically down his logical list of reasons why we needed more majors suitable for athletes, just as his teams worked the ball methodically around the perimeter before taking a shot. Every so often, Chuck Amato, our effervescent football coach, would interject a rah-rah statement about doing this for the spirit of the Wolfpack—Go Wolfpack! Then back to Sendek for more logic. Kay Yow would enter the conversation to talk about "her girls," how much she cared about them and their success, and how they would benefit from additional opportunities for career paths. Sendek was all logic, Amato was all spirit, Yow was all love.

Kay's love for her players showed all the time. One evening, after a university event in the early fall, Kay stopped to talk with Sharon and me as we were making our way toward the door. We asked how the team was looking. Any other coach, even the best of them, would have told us about the offense or defense, where the weaknesses and strengths were, maybe even something about team chemistry. Kay never said a word about those matters. She told us that the team was coming together as a family, the seniors were providing great leadership and friendship for the new girls, the new girls seemed like nice young women who were adjusting well to college life. Her eyes radiated affection and concern for the players, not as players who might bring her a championship, but as young women she would have the chance to mentor. She smiled and said, "I think they are going to be just fine." She coached basketball, of course, but what she really coached was life.

She was a great advocate for breast cancer research and treatment. We walked that path together, as my wife's cancer and treatment coincided with the return of Kay's. I cried in the basketball stands on the night of the first Hoops for Hope game, when during halftime cancer survivors were welcomed onto the court. Carrying signs showing the number of years they had survived walked hundreds of women; behind the sign for 1 to 5 years walked my wife. Kay beamed during that ceremony, recognizing, I think, that these women represented the promise for all women who had or would have breast cancer. Today, because of her commitment, Hoops for Hope is a national phenomenon, with millions of dollars directed toward a cure for breast cancer.

It seems trite to say that Kay Yow was an inspiration to the rest of us. But she was. She knew what lasted, what was ephemeral. Her funeral was a national event, with well over a thousand there to pay homage. And, of course, being Kay, she had prepared for the funeral—she had left a videotaped message for us. The message wasn't about her life on earth, but about her new life, and mostly it was about us and what our lives could be like if we accepted Jesus as she had. Always thinking about others.

Her funeral was a big show, but her interment in her home town of Gibsonville was much more like Kay—down home, soft spoken, unassuming, attended by a small gathering of family and friends. The team and coaches came in a bus, on the way to a game that evening after the service. We asked one of her players to describe how it felt to be truly in the inner circle of Kay's influence. She hesitated to answer at first, but then told us what we already knew but hadn't said: Kay didn't have an inner circle or an outer circle—once you knew her at all, you were part of her and she was part of you.

Although no one else I know ever reached the kind of greatness of Kay Yow, the university is filled with people who get pretty close. Most of us do our jobs well, but others can't stop at that point. I teach my class just before a class taught by a colleague in another department. Some students are in both classes, because both have a sustainability element. When I talk to them, they are prone to say, "I like your class a lot." When I ask them about the other teacher, they say, "We love him." Oh, they like his class a lot, too, but they love *him*.

I could go on for pages about the special people I've known in the university. Advisors who won't let a student fail, staff that won't go home until their work is right and then some, teachers who follow their former student's careers for decades, providing advice and encouragement. But let me just mention Margaret Henning. Margaret was one of our college's housekeepers for thirty years. We loved the job she did, but more than that we loved her. She cared about each one of us, knew about our kids and grandkids. After I'd become provost and would make a visit back to the college, Margaret would always ask me how my daughter in Texas was doing—and then how the other one in Maryland was doing. When Margaret retired, more of us showed up for her reception than we typically do for a faculty member or dean. At the party, Margaret went around the room, asking each of us about how our lives were going. I know it is trite to describe the dedication of this or that housekeeper—but it isn't trite that we loved Margaret, and she loved us.

Kay Yow and Margaret Henning knew what mattered most.

LESSONS ABOUT PEOPLE MATTERING MOST

1. Simply said, people matter most. (I know I wrote earlier that money is way ahead of whatever is in second place, but you know what I meant there—and what I mean here.)
2. Each person at the university personifies the mission and work of the entire university. Respect each one for the important work that they contribute.
3. Faculty work depends on the work of lots of staff, academic and otherwise. Don't forget that, and don't let the faculty forget it.
4. The provost needs to show up all over campus, all the time.
5. When the provost shows up, he needs to speak from his heart and mind, not from remarks someone else prepared.
6. Wikipedia is a great resource when you have to give "brief remarks" all the time. I don't care if it isn't peer-reviewed; neither do the listeners.
7. Transparency is a great idea. Be clear, be honest, be complete.
8. Everything that you are transparent about (and everything else) is public. Everything you say, everything you do, every key you stroke.
9. What you say is susceptible to being misquoted and misrepresented. And there is nothing you can do about it.
10. Reporters are not your friends, no matter what they might tell you. No reporter will be your friend if the story leads them to an unfriendly place.
11. Try not to get quoted. Bad for the ego, maybe, but good for longevity.
12. Diversity is still a top priority for the university, and it always will be. You don't get done with diversity.

13. Since most provosts aren't diverse themselves, it requires extra effort to keep true to the cause.

14. Uncompromising commitment to merit, which sounds really good, isn't. It is a red herring that will keep your university bogged down in the quagmire of embedded bias.

15. The opportunity hire is an essential tool of leadership. Use it often and without apology.

16. Special attention to the issues of women faculty and staff will always be needed.

17. Millennial faculty members are going to be very different from baby boomer faculty members. Get prepared for a revolution.

18. Give people your time and attention, without interruption. They'll love you for it.

19. Put down the phone and don't pick it up until you are alone.

20. Kay Yow was a great human being.

PART EIGHT

EXPERIENCE IS A GREAT TEACHER

44

FIRST REPORTS FROM
THE FRONT

General Henry Hugh Shelton, retired chairman of the Joint
Chiefs of Staff and a loyal alumnus of NC State, is the
kind of man you want running your country's defense.
He projects the quiet confidence of John Wayne or Sean Connery,
but he's not acting. He is soft spoken and gentle in demeanor,
but you sense he'd send in a missile strike without blinking if he
thought it was needed. He is a true leader, committed now especially to providing leadership experiences for young people.

He once told me the most valuable piece of administrative
advice I ever received. I was, no doubt, boring him with my frustra-
tions of this or that faculty member or vice provost clamoring about
their latest crisis, which they asserted I must solve now, right now.
"Larry," he said, "first reports from the front are always wrong."
The situation may be worse than first reported, he explained, or it
may be better, but it is never exactly like first reported.

General Shelton was speaking from his long and varied experience as a line officer, especially during wartime. We want experience
like that in our military leaders, because we believe the experience will keep them from doing something rash or tragic.

The same is true of the provost. Experience, especially front
line experience, seems almost essential in the provost's position. Without having lived in the administrative trenches of the

university, the provost won't have the perspective to make decisions correctly. And she certainly won't have the perspective to understand that "first reports from the front are always wrong."

"Hello, this is Larry Nielsen," I said, picking up the telephone.

"Are you the provost? The person responsible for professors?" she asked.

"Yes, I am."

"I can't believe what my son's teacher did," came next.

"Try me," I answered, "because I've heard a lot of things you wouldn't believe."

The parent would then launch into one of a familiar set of routines. "The teacher wouldn't accept a paper late, when my son had asked him for help several times." "The teacher didn't show up for an appointment that my daughter had set up to take the test late." "The teacher made our kid buy hundreds of dollars' worth of books and never once used them."

We all have a penchant for telling stories from our own perspective—and first reports from students to their parents regarding the student–faculty front are naturally one-sided. So when confronted by an angry parent, I always said that I would check on their issue and get back to them shortly. I would run the trapline down—to dean, department head, and finally to faculty member. Almost invariably first reports from the student front were wrong.

The teacher didn't accept the paper because the student hadn't shown up for several office appointments to discuss earlier drafts that were dreadful. The daughter had shown up the day after the appointed time to take the make-up test. The books were recommended, not required, and the faculty member held several extra class meetings at which the books were discussed—but the student had never come.

I never had a parent call back after I reported the additional information from the front.

But here is the classic. "My son had a 59.6% in his class, and the teacher gave him an F. According to what I learned about rounding, the teacher should have rounded the grade to the next highest whole number. That would have given my son a 60 average, which, according to NC State grading scales, is a D–, and then he would have passed. I want you to change his grade to a D–."

My answer was no, exactly how teachers calculated grades was the teachers' prerogative.

The answer I wanted to give was that she should duck, because my friend General Shelton was calling in an air strike.

45

WHAT IS A DEPARTMENT HEAD, ANYWAY?

I've written earlier that department heads have the toughest job in the university. Let me repeat, department heads have the toughest job in the university, bar none. Consequently, experience as a department head is the best experience anyone can have for becoming effective at any other role in the university. To understand the university, listen to a department head.

Exactly what is a department head? Tough question. Department heads are the university's Minotaur, part human and part another animal. The analogy I'm after here is that the department head is of two parts, but you can stretch it if you like to the actual composition of the Minotaur—body of a human and head of a bull. Department heads walk the line between faculty and administration. Universities have all sorts of trouble figuring out how to categorize them. Are they instructional or administrative? Are they middle-management or something lower or higher? Is it different for headcount versus FTE? Can they consult on university time, like faculty, or do they have to take leave, like deans? Department heads at NC State can serve on Faculty Senate, but they can't hold office (good rule, given they have the heads of bulls). *The Chronicle of Higher Education* hasn't figured it out, either. In its annual review of salaries, *The Chronicle* has extensive salary data for faculty (all ranks, all kinds) and for administrators (deans and above, staff positions of all kinds), but they have no salary data for department heads.

The difficulty in categorizing department heads is understandable, perhaps, because departments come in such a wide range of sizes. At the universities where I've worked, departments have been as small as 10 faculty members and as large as 100 or more. Clearly the jobs of running departments with 10 and 100 faculty members are quite different. At the low end, the department head is part time, with the expectation of having major teaching, research, or outreach responsibilities similar to other faculty members. At the high end, the department head administers a major organizational unit, with little or no hope of continuing a typical faculty role. A very large department will have assistant department heads, along with full-time accountants, personnel specialists, research administrators, undergraduate and graduate coordinators, and, perhaps, communications and development specialists. In some cases, a small college at a university may be smaller than the largest departments.

Department heads live in an administrative wilderness all by themselves. We have a faculty senate, staff senate, and student senate; we have a dean's council and an administrative council composed of deans, executive officers, and a few others. But we don't have a department head anything. When I was a department head, I complained loudly about our lack of access to and representation of the university. Although department heads are the managers who control the university's production—teaching, research, and outreach—they are without an official voice.

Because of my previous experience, as provost I understood what department heads wanted, and I sympathized with them. They wanted an official role in university decision making, and they deserved one. I just didn't need another constituency. I met with formalized groupings of the faculty, deans, vice provosts, standing committees, executive officers, student leaders, trustees, athletic administrators, and others. "Others" even included the Association of Retired Faculty (they were a hoot: "we want a retired faculty center, but it has to be on the first floor with parking right next to it, because we don't get around so good anymore, and a fireplace, because we get cold").

Eventually, the NC State department heads got sufficiently tired of nonrepresentation that they formed their own group, not officially recognized by the university. In good representative style, they elected some leaders, formed an executive committee with one member from every college, staffed some largely nonfunctional committees, sent each other and me some memos and reports. So, without making any promises about our obligation to include the department heads' group in any official processes, we assigned a formal liaison to them from the provost's office. I started meeting with them every semester, and we asked their advice when we needed a department head assigned to a committee or other function. The senior vice provost and I also started meeting with small groups of department heads twice a semester for breakfast, just like the chancellor and I did with the faculty. I was pretty darn effective at not creating a new constituency, wasn't I?

Their argument for representation was compelling. The policies, procedures, and other administrivia that we created at the executive level ended up being implemented by them—so shouldn't we ask them if some brilliant construct of the administration was a good idea or even a possible one before we told them to implement it? I know it stretches the imagination, but sometimes the provost's office and others had bad ideas. For example, in rewriting faculty hiring procedures, my office was trying to include faculty governance as fully as possible—the Faculty is a formal constituency—so, at the Faculty Senate's urging, we decided that all nontenure-track appointments had to be approved by the entire faculty of a department, both tenure-track and nontenure-track. This plan didn't bother most department heads much, including the departments in which the provost and staff had had their appointments, because we only had a few nontenure-track faculty members in the department; seemed like the right faculty-governance-respecting kind of thing to do. But several departments with large service teaching functions—English, mathematics, biological sciences, business management—were incredulous that we could be so stupid. They hired dozens of nontenure-track faculty members every year, sometimes every semester, sometimes at a moment's notice, often over the summer when the rest of the faculty was flung to the four winds. Department heads did most of that hiring, maybe with advice from a small group, but certainly not with the input and vote of every faculty member. Score one for the Minotaur! Not being bullheaded ourselves, we changed our minds and abandoned the policy.

We also instituted a clever device to ensure that department heads' views had a better chance to surface. When we sent a proposed action to deans for consideration at an upcoming Council of Deans meeting, we also sent the materials directly to our 60+ department heads. We asked them to review the action and get their views, if any, back to their deans in time for the scheduled review meeting. Our previous practice had been to send the materials to the deans with the expectation that the deans would get department head input; some did, some didn't. With the new process, input from department heads skyrocketed, the deans were more prepared for the discussions, and we started making better decisions. Score another for the Minotaur!

Throughout this book, I have used the term *department head*, rather than *department chair*. Most readers will have noticed this and thought that, like my general practice of alternating she and he or his and hers, I should have alternated head and chair, or used "head or chair" every time I mentioned the position. Some might even have wished that I just used the term *chair*, because they object to the idea of a head. I've used the term *head* all the way through for a reason.

I don't believe in department chairs. The chair position remains popular in various disciplines, primarily those in the liberal arts. The term *chair* implies that a member of the faculty performs this function for a few years and then rotates back to the faculty; then the next unfortunate soul has to take over. In this model, the chair is viewed as someone who mostly presides over participatory meetings of the faculty (whose membership is defined in some way or other, but not necessarily the same way in every department, of course), which is the universal decision-making body in the department. That concept of departmental leadership should have disappeared long ago, along with the practice of teaching in robes. The department chair is a quaint, nostalgic view of departmental business that has no place in the modern public university.

The department is the fundamental business unit of the university. Most of the university's resources—personnel, space, money—are managed inside departments. Most of the problems—from student conduct to animal care to sexual harassment to insufficient seats and sections—manifest themselves in departments. Departments need to raise funds, manage grants, serve the community, run personnel processes, and retain and protect records and do all of it in a dauntingly public and legalistic context. Overseeing and conducting these and a hundred other tasks is the job for a person who wants to be an administrator and has the skills to do so—not the person who sighs and agrees to take an administrative bullet for his or her colleagues.

"Has the skills to do so." Interesting point. Department heads need extensive care and feeding, to which they are highly resistant (they don't mind actual feeding). Department heads, in general, don't want to be trained. Training is insulting. They are, after all, highly educated and experienced academics who have handled complex management situations—research laboratories, student orchestras, design studios, statewide outreach programs, classes with hundreds of students and cadres of graduate assistants—successfully for many years. They have fundamental faith that logic, their own intelligence, and common sense and the collegial spirit of goodwill are enough to guide their departments. That is also a quaint and nostalgic view of departmental business. Sure, for most of the daily business of a department, logic, common sense, and collegiality will suffice.

But when the trouble comes—and it will come—none of those are sufficient. Goodwill doesn't prevail when a faculty member needs to be dismissed; every step in the process will be examined in detail by the faculty member and perhaps a phalanx of lawyers, schoolhouse and real. Common sense doesn't handle the mess when safety inspectors find cabinets full of out-of-date and unlabeled chemical wastes in faculty labs; of course we were going to get rid of all that stuff at the end of the academic year, notwithstanding that there is a decade's worth in the cabinets; the Environmental Protection Agency (EPA) will still issue fines and restrictions. Logic is irrelevant when a conservative faculty member claims he was prevented from running the departmental seminar because of his politically incorrect views on U.S. policies about illegal immigration.

I wish I could say how department head training should be done. But I can't; I don't have the faintest idea how to do it right. The tendency in the university is to create a continuing series of training events to which department heads are invited or perhaps required to attend (I also don't know how to require department heads to do anything like this). The central staff of the university generally likes this approach, because they have a legitimate responsibility to make sure department heads do all sorts of things right—recruiting, hiring, evaluating, and dismissing faculty and staff are the most obvious. But the list keeps going—assessing student learning, reviewing curricula, handling harassment, implementing federal export controls, managing volunteers, upholding university graphics standards—literally dozens of possible situations that the department head might encounter. This is called "just-in-case" training. We'll run you through this situation just in case you ever need to know how to handle it.

Department heads hate this; so do I. An astounding amount of time could be taken up in training about situations that won't ever happen or that will happen so far in the future that the rules will have changed by then. I am in favor of being prepared, but the jump from sublime to ridiculous is a small one. For example, we spent countless hours preparing for the bird flu—it was coming, and we needed to be prepared. We devised plans for when the first case hit anywhere in North America, when it appeared within 500 miles, when it arrived on campus. We all realized, though, that none of our planning would really matter, because state and federal officials, who hadn't even begun to plan, would overrule all of our plans if an epidemic actually occurred. Which, not surprisingly, it hasn't.

So, we're now trying to do training that is "just in time." That means we have some resource available—online or in person—for just when the head needs the help. Of course, to ensure that the department heads know that it is available and how to recognize the situation as it's developing, they have to do a little online tutorial, which we need to produce, make available, keep updating, have registration records for—so we better add several staff to several offices. Like I said, I have no solution. Whether just-in-time or just-in-case, department head training is just-a-pain.

The training I always wanted as a department head and school director was about how to stay sane, healthy, and happily married while I had this wonderful awful job to do. I never got it.

46

BEING A DEAN HELPS

I don't want to make my dean buddies angry, so let me say that experience as a dean is also highly valuable on the way to becoming provost. But, as I wrote earlier, if department head is the hardest job in the university, dean is the best job. I think what deans learn most as deans is that they landed in a great place—and they want to stay there.

Deans acquire three major sources of additional valuable experience. First, having a broader scope of authority means that the dean will encounter a broader set of situations than will a department head. A department head may never dismiss a tenured faculty member during her term, but the collection of a college's departments will almost certainly do so during a dean's term. The same is true for any specific event, positive or negative, that can occur in a university—discrimination charge, research misconduct, budget deficit, facility disaster, opportunity hire, honorary doctorate recipient, construction of a new building, major gift, new degree initiation. The dean sees almost all of what can happen at a university—except the need to fire a coach.

Consider the College of Natural Resources at NC State. The college's foundation owns and operates about 80,000 acres of forests. The college manages some of the forestland for educational purposes, including a summer camp for our undergraduates to gain field experience; so, the college operates a dining hall and dormitories, just like the university. The purpose for most of the forest, though, is to make money, just like it is for industrial or private forest landowners. Consequently, our staff members plant, fertilize, thin, and harvest thousands of acres every year—running, in essence, a moderately sized business venture. The college employs forest management professionals, contracts with local logging companies, has a fleet of trucks and heavy construction vehicles (and people say we've never had to make a payroll). We have the usual problems with trespass, vandalism, erosion control, bankrupt contractors, and, tragically, accidents and sometimes accidental deaths. Sales of harvested trees provide funds to operate the college, but, more importantly, the funds support student scholarships and research innovations. So, the dean is in the middle of functions that an individual department head would probably never see.

Second, the dean learns to allocate resources strategically. The university's resources come from the central administration to the colleges. These may be resources directly, as in the continuing base budget, or they may be opportunities to request resources when new funds become available (or they may be negative resources when the budget gets chopped). The dean gets to decide how to manage these resources. At the departmental level, most resource allocations are egalitarian—divide the travel budget by the number of faculty, and everyone gets the same amount (let's see, nothing divided by anything is—nothing). At the college level, resource allocations have to be strategic. The provost won't give the college new resources if it didn't ask in terms of the university's strategic plan (at least I hope not), and consequently those resources don't get to be spread equally among the departments and other programs. So, the dean gains the experience of making strategic allocations. She also must deal with the question of centralization versus decentralization, another allocation issue.

Third, as king or queen of the college kingdom, the dean replicates, on a smaller scale, most of the functions of the chancellor or president. The college typically has an external advisory board; operates a development function; communicates through a magazine, newsletter, and websites; staffs an alumni group; employs a substantial IT staff; may house a specialized library, museum, or other collections; may have off-campus facilities; and may operate a significant human resources function. At NC State, most of the colleges have a private box at the football stadium, just like the chancellor. Few of these functions occur in a department, unless it's a mega-department, like some in engineering or life sciences—and then it is interesting to watch the power struggle between the dean and the department head.

All this experience helps prepare a dean for the university-wide functions that occur in the provost's office—library, admissions, financial aid, international programs, diversity. In many ways, however, the broader experiences of deans leapfrog right over the provost. The provost doesn't have an alumni group or an external advisory board, and he certainly doesn't have his own luxury box at the football stadium!

Experience as dean also provides one additional perspective that one doesn't get as a department head. Department heads, remember, are part bull. And the bull-most part tends to be their unfettered devotion to their department. In other words, department heads typically only wear one hat—advocacy for their department. Department heads tend to evaluate a situation in terms of "Will this be good for my department?" Whereas deans, provosts, and even faculty members may talk about the value of interdisciplinary programs, department heads will typically ask questions about who is going to get credit for the work. They track their departmental statistics about numbers of student majors, credit hours produced, research grants, and overhead returns, and they want to know how any bright new ideas from the administration are going to affect "their programs."

Deans gain a different perspective. Because they are the first level at which the base administrative units (departments) get bundled together for additional administration, deans are the first to have to oversee a world with levels of consideration—the individual departments and the collective college. He is forced to wear two hats and will try to convince the department heads to wear two hats, too (good luck with that).

The need to consider decisions in two different contexts is an essential tool for a dean. As I've written earlier, deans are valuable to the university only if they can switch effectively between their roles as college advocates and university officers. Becoming facile and comfortable with these multiple perspectives within their own colleges prepares deans to be effective in a university decision-making context.

The benefit of experience for a provost also goes in the other direction. Experience helps prepare a provost to do her job, of course—nothing new to surprise her once she hits the big leagues. But the most important benefit may be that a provost who has come up through the ranks understands the jobs of department head and dean. She can then make decisions in the context of departmental and college realities and aspirations, rather than just thinking at the university level. A provost who has "paid her dues" has a better chance of generating support and acceptance of her decisions than one without that experience—not to mention a better chance of making good decisions.

47

IT'S A CLINGY ENVIRONMENT

About a year after becoming provost, the student organization in my old home—fisheries and wildlife—asked me to speak to one of their meetings. They wanted me to talk about what it was like being provost. Of course I accepted the invitation (remember what 95% of life is?).

I chose as the theme the difference between being a dean and provost, using an analogy these students might appreciate. Being a dean, I said, was like living in the air, as a bird or terrestrial mammal does. Air is a thin medium, easy to move around in. By analogy, the dean's job is one of substantial authority and independence; I hope that deans consult widely before making decisions, but in the end, their college-level decisions are pretty much their own. Most of what they decide is internal to the operation of the college, so it doesn't need extensive review outside the college.

In contrast, I said, being the provost was like living in water. Water is a dense environment, hard to move around in; an aquatic animal is in intimate and constant contact with the water. By analogy, the job of provost requires intensive and extensive consultation before a decision can be made. Because the decisions of the provost have ramifications for many other parts of the university, the provost can't be nearly as independent and autonomous as a dean. Just like fish living in the water, the provost lives in a clingy environment.

I was surprised early in my tenure as interim provost about how clingy it was. Coming from the dean's role, especially the dean of a small college that flew mostly under the university's radar, I enjoyed our autonomy. Moving in as provost, as number two, as the COO, I expected that I would have even more autonomy.

Not so. I had less autonomy, and for months it chafed. It seemed as though every time I wanted to do something, a parade of people who had heard about the possible action would march through my office to tell me why it was a bad idea. Whenever the provost spoke, it seemed, a whole team of oxen was going to be gored.

Through experience, I've come to understand the necessity of the clinginess. Like an octopus (which lives in the water!), the decisions made by the provost have multiple tentacles winding sneakily throughout the institution. Consider tuition increases. In my opinion, NC State's tuition is too low—too low by a long shot. Our in-state undergraduate tuition ranks 15 out of 16 among our peers; only the University of Florida's tuition is lower (and they'll probably surpass us fairly soon, given their large planned increases). Graduate and out-of-state undergraduate tuitions are a little closer to the average, but not much.

So, I believed that tuition ought to be increased, and I thought I'd just find out how to do it—and do it. Not so fast, Nielsen. We have a tuition advisory committee, cochaired by the provost and the student body president, that meets in the fall to discuss and vote on recommended tuition rates to be forwarded to the chancellor. The committee is pretty well stacked so that a well-regarded administrative position will carry, but the students have tremendous influence. In fairness to the students, I was impressed by how seriously they took their work. The seriousness varied by year, of course, and the more seriously they took it, the more seriously the whole committee considered their viewpoint. One year, the student body president told me that he would never vote for any increase while he was in office; consequently, his voice didn't have much influence on the committee's opinion—and our tuition increased anyhow. A more recent student body president and his staff came to the critical meeting equipped with enough statistical analyses to make all of us plead uncle, and they recommended a tuition increase equal to the increases in the Higher Education Price Index, an amount about half what I had been working toward. Their analysis was so professional, objective, reasonable, and compelling that the committee voted unanimously for their proposal over mine.

Now comes the clingy part. Let's say we're recommending an increase in undergraduate tuition. We have a parallel committee that looks at proposed fee increases—what are they thinking, and what will be the combined effect of tuition and fee increases? Financial aid needs to know how we're going to offset the extra expense for students on financial aid—will we cover all their needs from the expected tuition increase, or just part of it, or not at all? Will we cover the fee increases for students with financial aid out of tuition income? Distance education needs to know whether we're applying the increase to off-campus courses or just those on campus. Summer school wants to know if we want to prorate as we've done in the past, or do a straight dollar add-on. Athletics and development want to know what this will mean for them in terms of the costs of the scholarships they pay for. Students want to know exactly what the new tuition dollars are going to be used for—telling them that it's up to the "provost's discretion" rings hollow.

All those considerations are just about undergraduate tuition. Graduate student tuition is the real dilemma. Raising the graduate school tuition means that every grant will have to pay more and that our state-funded tuition rebate for teaching assistants will need an infusion from the tuition receipts, if we're going to keep up. Those costs skyrocket for out-of-state students, especially international students. Graduate tuition increases are almost entirely a matter of taking money out of several of our university pockets to put it into another pocket. But if we don't raise graduate tuition at least a bit, the legislature will start asking questions, and our peers will think that we are so desperate for graduate students that we're putting the university on sale.

Now come the political questions. What is Chapel Hill going to do? We can't look too different from them. What is the president thinking? The president at that time was a self-avowed "low-tuition man"; what would he accept this year? Do we try to anticipate what he'd like to see (you bet) or challenge him by presenting what we need (most assuredly not)? Is the legislature going to accept a campus-based tuition increase, or are they going to raise tuition themselves for the entire UNC system to help close the state's budget gap?

And all I wanted was to increase the tuition by $200 per year. About $17 per month or $4 a week, the cost of one happy meal.

While the provost needs to consider the clinginess at most times, he also needs to ignore it sometimes, shaking it off like static cling. The tendency to overthink is a permanent condition in the university—because, as I've said, we live in fear of Type I error, of doing something when we shouldn't have.

I defied the clinginess with one major organizational change I made as provost. I decentralized summer school. If I had asked for advice, I would have heard all sorts of reasons why we couldn't do this and how it would mess things up. Everyone knew that summer school was suboptimal as we ran it, but I knew it would take a revolution, not an evolution, to change it. So, I revolted. Now, summer school is in the control of colleges and deans, enrollments are up, tuition is flowing to where it is needed, we reduced the administrative staff from about a dozen to two, and everyone is happy.

48

DANCING WITH A GORILLA

The old saw goes something like this: When you ask a gorilla to dance, you dance with the gorilla until the gorilla gets tired of dancing. For a public university, that means a decision, once made, will continue to have possible repercussions for as long as the public—in the form of the press, legislature, electronic media, and your neighbors—wishes to continue talking about it. You, as the decision maker, have little power to make it go away.

Early in my time as provost, a person who sometimes taught a course or two for NC State made a racially provocative comment at a conference (I am purposefully understating the nature of the comment). The comment was videotaped and then streamed on the Internet. The media picked it up and reported that the speaker was a faculty member at NC State. The speaker wasn't teaching for us at the time, but had been a part-time instructor at various times in the recent past (this was fortunate for me, or else my tenure as provost might have been very short indeed). I issued a carefully crafted statement that said the speaker wasn't on our faculty and that we deplored the statement—we put it on our website and sent it in response to the flood of e-mails we received. Eventually, the e-mails stopped, and we took the statement down from the website. Case closed? No such luck. For the next several years, at irregular intervals, some news service or website would find the video and play it again, causing a new stream of how-could-you e-mails. That gorilla danced for a long time.

The problem is, of course, that many dance partners don't seem like gorillas when you ask them to the floor. They seem like perfect gentlemen and ladies. When I nominated a prominent Native American attorney for an honorary doctorate, I was proud of our university. But when the award was announced in the newspaper a few days before graduation, I received a call from a representative of another group of Native Americans who threatened to picket graduation, because they thought our recipient was undeserving (actually a lot worse than undeserving, but let's leave it at that). Fortunately, they were just bluffing, and that gorilla wasn't much of a dancer.

We created a GLBT (Gay, Lesbian, Bisexual, and Transgender) center when I was provost, with co-funding from the provost's office and the vice-chancellor for student affairs. The media reported it as a routine news item, but we still got an immediate negative backlash. A prominent donor came to visit me with another alumnus in tow who was also a donor. The second visitor was clearly upset about the center and, I guess, had convinced the major donor to bring him in to see me. They sat across the table from me in my office, and the lesser donor pushed a copy of the newspaper article over to my side. Tapping the article with his index finger, he said, "Larry, NC State will never get another dollar from me."

We had recently completed celebration of the fiftieth anniversary of the first admission of African American students into the university. Citing that celebration, I said, "I'm sure that fifty years ago, someone pushed an article across the table about the admission of African Americans to the university and said something similar."

As far as I was concerned, that gorilla could dance as long as it wanted.

49

THE GORILLA THAT GOT ME

I often suggested to the chancellor that he involve me more in the political aspects of the university, like visiting with legislators. I did much more politicking as dean than I ever did as provost. I thought it was important that the legislative leaders know the provost, because if anything ever happened to the chancellor, I would have to step into his role with the legislature. He always said no, that he wanted me to remain separate from such things, be his pure academic guy.

Ironic, because politics is the gorilla that got me.

As I reported on the first page of this book, I resigned because of the intense scrutiny over my hiring of the first lady of North Carolina as a special faculty member. The questions about her hiring came nearly four years after she joined the university, during which she had performed well and had been praised as a great addition to our faculty. She was regularly asked to participate in conferences and workshops on campus, to open meetings that the university was sponsoring, to lecture in others' classes. In simple terms, her hiring was a strategic success for the university. So how did this all unravel?

When I hired the first lady, I gave her a three-year contract, which is pretty standard for someone we want to employ because of their special skills or other characteristics but to whom we do not wish to extend tenure. I hired her using the waiver-of-recruitment process, which allows us to hire an individual without the usual advance position description, advertising, search, and interview process (as I discussed in an earlier chapter). We hired the first lady as she was completing her most recent contract at another UNC institution, North Carolina Central University, where she was a member of the law school faculty. Central was highly satisfied with her work and had offered her a subsequent contract. In fact, the speed with which we handled her appointment at NC State was occasioned by the need to act quickly, so she could let Central know that she would not be returning. Also, she had been teaching some special courses for NC State for years, as part of a training program for law-enforcement officials—so she had been on our payroll for many years as a part-time faculty member.

I hired the first lady to do one major job—create and implement a new university speakers' program. She also had some teaching responsibilities in our public administration program, but her major task—the one we would really judge her performance against—was to create what would become known as the Millennium Seminars. As a university, we wanted to elevate our profile among the nation's leaders. The Millennium Seminars was one strategy to do so, a strategy that I had outlined in a memo some time before the first lady entered the picture. A world-class lecture series would bring important people to campus to see us and learn more about us—as well as inspiring our faculty, students, staff, and the Raleigh community. I had suggested that our Board of Visitors (not Board of Trustees, but another group of supporters) might be the right group to sponsor such a seminar series, because their mandate was to enhance the university's reputation and recognition. But when I learned from the chancellor that the first lady was interested in working at NC State, I knew we had a match.

She made the Millennium Seminars a total success. With her broad personal and professional network, she attracted speakers who would never have given NC State a second thought without her. Senator Lindsay Graham of South Carolina came to speak about the treatment of political prisoners; the surgeon general came to announce a new national program to discourage underage drinking. TV host Charlie Rose led a panel of national experts on green architecture. Former Senator Bill Bradley spoke about the reemerging importance of Russia. University of Miami President Donna Shalala spoke about the medical treatment of wounded warriors, just as she was completing her role of cochair of a federal investigatory panel on the subject. NCAA President Miles Brand made one of his last public presentations here. Former President Bill Clinton came to speak about our global future. We filled in the gaps with a few folks on speaking tours and local or regional business leaders and scientists, holding a total of four seminars annually. Seminar attendance grew regularly, from several hundred at the beginning of the series to well over a thousand in later seminars and more than 5,000 for President Clinton's presentation. Some speakers charged fees, but others, including President Clinton and Charlie Rose, came for free, because of their relationship with the first lady. With a co-invitation from her as first lady and our chancellor, the Dalai Lama accepted our request to present a Millennium Seminar, one that would have attracted 60,000 or more attendees. We were in initial stages of inviting the UN secretary general. Our faculty and students loved the seminars, and they loved the person who led them.

As her first three-year term was ending in the spring of 2008, she was also approaching the end of her time as first lady; her husband's term would end in January 2009. I was eager to re-sign her to a new contract, and, as it turned out, she was just as eager to remain with the university. However, she said, she hoped to do more for the university as the demands of her first lady role dwindled and eventually disappeared, and she would require a different salary to go along with more work. We talked about her capacity to perform more work, which she assured me would be about double what she had been able to do when she was first lady. So, we developed a new job description that doubled her responsibilities, mostly in the form of establishing a center for research and training of first responders. We signed a new five-year contract, which approximately doubled her salary.

Despite the fact that the contract was for nine months each year, she went right to work on the new programming for first responders. She developed collaborations, wrote proposals, and began attracting grant money, again using her network of law enforcement leaders and agencies across the state and nation.

Now, I'm afraid, I must interject a technical detail. NC State had always interpreted giving a subsequent contract to a nontenure-track faculty member as being an entirely new work arrangement. In this case, the old contract, including its responsibilities and salary, ended on May 15, and the subsequent contract, with its responsibilities and salary, would begin on August 15. Technically there was no raise, but rather a new salary for a new set of responsibilities.

However, nine-month salaries are always paid over a twelve-month schedule, ending not on May 15, but on June 30. And, if an employee were to begin a subsequent appointment on August 15, the pay began on July 1. Of course we would do it this way, so that the employee didn't suffer a gap in benefits or pay and so that we didn't create any additional work for our human relations staff.

These technical details didn't matter when a reporter called the university on July 1 to get some background information about the first lady for a story unrelated to her employment. Reporters know that our privacy laws allow them to ask for current salary and the most recent previous salary. Had he called on June 30, there would have been nothing interesting to report. But he called on July 1. The university reported truthfully that her current salary was 88% higher than her previous salary. The next day, the newspaper reported that the first lady had received an 88% raise.

The gorilla had just gotten up to dance.

I took the blame, and I deserved it. I had negotiated the new contract, with the new duties and new salary. In my characteristic drive to get the job done, and my concern that the first lady might look elsewhere for better opportunities, I wanted to close the deal immediately—and I did. I had not considered the negative risks of the arrangement and had not given my senior staff or the chancellor an opportunity to weigh in on the plan. I made the agreement with the first lady, based on an instinctive sense of what she and the job were worth. My instincts weren't good.

Public reaction was immediate and hateful. Letters, e-mails, and calls flooded the chancellor's office. Citizens wrote to the state auditor's hotline, demanding an investigation. The Auditor's Office began investigating almost immediately and continued for several months. Eventually, the Auditor's Office would not even issue a report, because the only things wrong were my instincts.

More importantly, the UNC system wanted to know how we had given someone an 88% raise without their approval. University regulations required that raises beyond 15% and $10,000 had to be approved by the UNC Board of Governors. We explained that in eight years of giving faculty and staff subsequent contracts, we had never submitted any to the system office as though they were raises—because our interpretation was that subsequent contracts were not raises, but new salaries for new responsibilities.

The UNC system rejected that argument, saying it was nonsensical—the money was what mattered, not the dates, job description, or other technicalities. Consequently, NC State's human resources personnel spent the next two months combing through eight years of personnel actions to find all that would have required approval under the interpretation that a subsequent contract at a different salary did constitute a raise.

Because the first lady's contract had not received UNC Board of Governors approval but should have, under their interpretation of the salary increase, the university system declared that it was void. The university president set me on the task of generating a detailed report that would justify the new duties and salary of the first lady, for his review and presentation to the Board of Governors. Using my report and some changes to the contract (basically, we made it a 12-month contract and substituted some private funds for state funds), the university president argued publicly and forcefully at the September 2008 Board of Governors' meeting in favor of the new 5-year contract for the first lady at the salary I had given her initially. He said that the job was an important one, she was the right person for the job, and the salary was appropriate, given the job and the person. The 34-member UNC Board of Governors asked some questions and voiced some differing opinions, but approved the contract unanimously.

The first lady had continued working throughout this time, and, with the new contract in place, we all breathed a sigh of relief and got back to work ourselves. But the gorilla was just warming up.

When the governor left office in January 2009, the local newspaper began reporting on a wide range of matters relating to his personal and official life. The newspaper raised issues regarding campaign finances, land purchases and sales, and other forms of influence that might be considered inappropriate, publishing a multipart series they called "Executive Privilege."

The newspaper also included my hiring of the first lady in their coverage. Stories also appeared about how I had been hired as provost, raising a doubt that my hiring might have been improper. At this point, I could no longer remain in the job. I had offered to resign several times since the 88% raise had been reported, but the chancellor had always wanted me to continue. By now, though, the university had suffered too badly over this matter, and so had my family and I. The situation was eroding the chancellor's confidence in me—I could feel it in every interaction—and I was determined to leave on my own accord. I had told the chancellor again in March that I wished to resign, and he finally accepted. However, he wanted to wait to make the announcement until the CFO and I had completed our budget-cutting work, presumably until sometime in the summer. I had hoped that I could announce a resignation for one year hence, so that we could conduct an orderly search and transition. That strategy became impossible when questions surfaced about how I was hired. I resigned within a few days, giving about one week's notice.

But the gorilla was still dancing.

One afternoon, two federal agents showed up at my office. They issued a subpoena for me to appear as a witness before the Grand Jury that would be investigating matters relating to the governor. They questioned me that day in my office for two hours, during which I explained the story I've just related.

Soon after I resigned, we took a week's vacation at the beach. I called back to the provost's office on Monday morning, just to see how the staff members were doing. That's when I learned the chancellor had resigned. In preparing to give information to the federal investigators, the university discovered a set of e-mails between the chancellor and representatives of the governor's office, discussing a job for the first lady. The set of e-mails was a surprise to me. I had no knowledge of them before reading the newspaper that day.

The chair of our Board of Trustees was also involved in the e-mail exchanges, and, as a consequence, he also was forced to resign. Eventually, to my great surprise and disappointment, the university also dismissed the former first lady. Her dismissal was the least fair of the bunch, as she had done nothing except accept a job and perform excellently in her required duties. But the dancing gorilla can be clumsy, stepping on lots of toes.

Based on advice of the university's legal staff, I hired a criminal defense attorney. A criminal defense attorney! How could a situation have ever developed in which I would need a criminal defense attorney? I'm just a guy who gets up and goes to work every day. What was happening to my life?

Thank goodness I hired him. He helped me understand what was going to happen at the Grand Jury. He was the perfect combination of scare tactics, to make me take the situation as seriously as it was, and reassurance that nothing bad would happen to me. He sat with my wife while I testified. He got us into and out of the federal courthouse with a minimum of contact with the press, who were following us across the sidewalk with cameras rolling— the "perp walk," as they say.

I testified before the Grand Jury for two days. The first afternoon was one of the worst days of my life. Afterward, as Sharon drove us home, I collapsed sobbing into my hands.

The following morning was better, and then it was over. In fact, there was never any question that I had done anything wrong. I was there as a witness, to explain my role and actions in the hiring and supervision of the first lady. But testifying before the Grand Jury is an experience that I never want to have again, not ever.

The Grand Jury investigation into the governor's affairs continued for some time, along with a state-based investigation as well. All that time, I had to wait for whatever finding they might arrive at before we could call the matter closed and move on. More than a year passed before the investigations finished. At the end, the governor accepted one felony charge for a campaign violation; the state and federal attorneys announced then that all other investigations were closed.

The gorilla finally got off the dance floor.

50

WHAT I LEARNED FROM THE DANCING GORILLA

The story of my resignation and the events surrounding it is intensely personal. More than three years have passed, and hardly a day goes by without me thinking about the events, how we handled them, how I could have been so stupid and so naïve, how I let people down. In addition, however, I believe it holds several important lessons for universities and their leaders.

The first lesson is that this could happen to you, to any university, and any university leader. The institutions that we manage are so large, so diverse, and so decentralized that hundreds of potentially damaging activities are going on at all times. Faculty and staff members are being hired and dismissed regularly, somewhere on campus, by someone who may not know or care about the rules. Students and faculty members are interacting in intense situations that may cross the line into hostility or intimacy; either can flash wrong in an instant. Researchers are working with dangerous materials, some of which can injure or kill, some of which are living and can escape (my department once had a group of captive black bears; one escaped and roamed a neighboring rural town for a few weeks until it was killed). Scholars are producing opinions, artwork, and literature that may offend or contradict community standards. Hundreds of students and dozens of faculty are flung across the globe in situations that can turn hostile or dangerous without warning. Students on campus are experimenting with new ideas and lifestyles, some of which may be heading them and others into harm's way.

Despite everyone's best efforts, university leaders cannot be watching all these activities to be sure they are under control. Things will go wrong. On the day I wrote the first draft of this chapter, NC State reported a leak in our experimental nuclear reactor. Whether or not this is an event that would develop into a major calamity depends on many factors, most of which are well beyond the ability of the university to control (fortunately, it did not develop into a major issue).

My advice for provosts, therefore, is to be prepared. Use good judgment at all times, of course, but be prepared to find yourself sitting in a chair over a trapdoor. It can open any time.

The second lesson is related to the first. No matter how much the institution likes and values you, it will sacrifice you if it feels that the institution is under threat. Throughout my career, faculty, staff, and postdoctoral fellows have come to me many times, asking my advice on a particular dilemma. For example, they may have received an offer from another school, one at which they always hoped to work, or is near their family home, or where they get to work with a famous colleague, or some other logical reason for going; but, they say, they promised to stay here for the whole fellowship or for at least three years or some other condition. My advice was always simple: They had no dilemma. They owed no loyalty to the institution, so they should go where their heart and mind were telling them to go. The institution, I said, would desert you in an instant if it needed to, so you are free to do the same.

I knew this lesson theoretically before; now I know it from personal experience. As I wrote earlier, people have treated me wonderfully since my resignation—just as wonderfully and supportively as they did before I resigned. I had received consistently positive feedback during my tenure as provost, and I believe I could have remained provost as long as I wanted. But when the university was threatened by this event, the leadership was willing—perhaps grudgingly for many of them—to let me take the fall for the university. Had I held on, I know that eventually I would have been asked to resign, and if I resisted, I would have been relieved of my position.

I experienced this lesson most clearly when the university chose to release to the public the terms of my return to the faculty. That document is classified as personnel information and is not subject to public disclosure. Although members of the Board of Trustees had told me repeatedly that they would do anything for me, anything at all, after my resignation, they nevertheless decided to make my appointment letter public, under a legal exception that allows release if the Board deems it necessary for the good of the institution. In order to prove that I didn't get a sweetheart deal on my return to the faculty, the board chose to release my initial appointment letter as provost and my subsequent appointment to return to the faculty. Once again, I was front-page news.

The third lesson is to always consider the downside risk of decisions and actions. I feel like a traitor to my personality by saying this, because I am a true believer—I like new things, to try new things, not to be hounded into inaction by the threat of failure.

When we hired the first lady, no one considered that we might have a political liability on our hands in four years when she and her husband moved out of the Governor's Mansion. From my perspective, having the first lady on our faculty seemed like a coup, an appointment that would elevate our status and reputation in the state and well beyond. No one talked about what might happen when the governor left office, even though there had been previous dustups about aspects of his business dealings before this time.

I hadn't given anyone much chance to tell me this was a bad idea. I believe my enthusiasm washed the doubts right out of the provost's staff, and I didn't discuss the decision outside my office, for fear of it leaking before we and the governor's office were ready to announce the appointment. I should have discussed it more.

When we started to consider this hire, the chancellor, lobbyist, CFO (as a good conservative thinker), and I should have huddled about it for honest, no-holds-barred discussion. I'm not sure we would have changed our mind, but I might have structured the job differently, and I certainly would have been more careful the second time around.

That approach should be used for all major decisions and for any decision that takes the university out of its comfort zone. We need to always ask the question: What is the downside risk if we . . .

- Take a major gift from this person, company, or foundation?
- Give an honorary doctorate or other award to this person?
- Allow this person or group to use university facilities?
- Hire this high-profile faculty member, administrator, or coach?
- Create a new program in partnership with this organization?
- Allow our students to visit or study at this location?
- Name this facility after this person?
- Accept this athlete or performer as a student?

The list could be much longer, but I think the point is clear. Especially as senior administrators, we have to be optimists, can-do people. But we also always need to temper our enthusiasm with reality, honestly sought and honestly considered.

The first three lessons are pretty obvious. The fourth is perhaps just as obvious, but needs a bit more development. I believe the university handled this situation appallingly. I believe, had we been more proactive and courageous, we all could still be in our positions—the chancellor, chair of the board, provost, and former first lady—with the university having hardly skipped a beat in its progress.

When communications consultants give advice about how to work with the media in times of trouble, the fundamental admonition is to get all the bad news out at once. The news media, they say, can smell a story that isn't finished, and they will keep coming until they find out everything. So, you should tell the whole story, on your terms, so that there is no new story tomorrow or next week.

NC State did the opposite. The university kept as silent as possible. Of course, it complied with all requests for information under the right-to-know laws, but those responses were reactive, not proactive.

The university's failure to be proactive is particularly unfortunate in this case because *no one did anything wrong.* The chancellor had some conversations with the chair of our board and others about the availability of the first lady to work at the university. This is totally appropriate. Individuals, including public officials, talk to university leaders all the time about prospective faculty, staff, and students—especially students—who they think should be admitted or hired. If the chancellor weren't hearing this, he wouldn't be doing his job. I was hired as provost through the normal channels; the hiring was done publicly and strictly according to standard processes. The university could have, and should have, said so. My hiring of the first lady was also done strictly according to the rules, through a procedure we used more than a hundred times a year. My subsequent hiring of her for a second term was, eventually, unanimously and publicly approved by the UNC Board of Governors.

In my opinion, the university should have called a press conference early in the unfolding of this situation. It should have said all the things in the previous paragraph, accompanied by the documents that proved the veracity of the statements. I believe that strategy would have controlled the situation and that the university would have been stronger for it.

So, the obvious lesson is to deal with crises openly, fully, and courageously. Because, if you cringe in the corner, you will be eaten alive.

LESSONS FROM EXPERIENCE

1. First reports from the front are always wrong. General Shelton said it, so you can believe it.
2. So, never act rashly when someone reports a crisis. Take a few deep breaths and get more information. Consult colleagues who have a cool head and the experience to help guide your thinking.
3. This is particularly true when someone tells you what a faculty member has done. Usually, it isn't true, or at least not the way initially reported.
4. Department heads have the toughest job in the university, so being one is great training for the prospective dean or provost.
5. Department heads have to make the place produce. So listen to them when they say you are about to step in it.
6. Remember, though, that department heads always advocate for their own departments. They seldom take off their departmental hats in exchange for college or university hats.
7. Department heads hate being trained. Too bad, because they need to be trained. I only wish I knew how to do it.
8. The department *chair* is an old-fashioned, obsolete concept. Ban it from your vocabulary and your administration.
9. Deans do wear two hats—as college advocates and university officers. Being a dean is almost a prerequisite to becoming a provost.
10. Colleges are miniature universities (and sometimes not very miniature). So, deans experience most of what the provost does.
11. The provost's world is "clingy." Decisions made by the provost ripple throughout the university, so they need to be carefully considered. It's a pain.
12. Political decisions will get you into trouble. Maybe not now, but probably sometime. So be careful.
13. More decisions are political than you think. So be careful.

14. A great academic decision could turn out to be politically disastrous. So be careful.
15. Calculate the downside risk of every decision, explicitly and openly. In other words, be careful.
16. Something risky is occurring every day at the university, and you don't know about it. But it could go sour any time, and the provost will probably be blamed for it.
17. The institution will sacrifice the provost, immediately, if it thinks it must. The institution might regret doing it because it likes you, but it will do it anyhow.
18. Be courageous about what you did, why you did it, and how you did it. That's the only way to survive—and thrive—as provost.

PART NINE

WHO OWNS THE UNIVERSITY?

51

NO ONE COULD DO A BETTER JOB THAN YOU

Buried in the files of many professors is tongue-in-cheek advice about how to write letters of recommendation that disguise the truth about a candidate in clever language. Among my favorites is "No one could do a better job than this candidate." Unfortunately that's the way many people feel about all university administrators—"no one" would be better than the one we have.

Being provost is a wonderful job, the best job that I've ever had. The joy and honor of making good things happen at a university, not just in your own area of disciplinary expertise, but for the institution as a whole; the reflected pride that comes from successful students, faculty members, and staff; the excitement of having opportunities, events, and programs flow in so fast that it takes your breath away; the magic of being at the center of all that is happening; all these make the job of provost a daily upper. Most days, sometime during the day—maybe over breakfast, at lunch, or at the end of a banquet, concert, or basketball game—I'd say to Sharon, "I love my job."

Nonetheless, the job is far from easy for a kaleidoscope of reasons. Every one of the opportunities comes with choices—difficult choices, not about good and bad, but about which good to keep and which good to discard. Remember, we have all the resources we need to do the most important work, but we have to decide among many worthy candidates which is the most important.

Also, with more than 2,000 faculty, 5,000 staff, and 30,000 students, somebody's problem is going to become your problem, pretty much every day. And only the toughest problems get to the provost's desk. The needs always surpass the capacity to meet them. The expectations of those outside the university are generally unrealistic and simplistic.

One reality for me in this controversy is the eagerness that some people have shown to characterize university administrators as overpaid, underworked royalty. I suppose that need to judge is part of a general rush to judge anyone on the public payroll, especially those who are at the top and make un-public-servant-like salaries. The vitriol may not be personal, but it sure tastes that way.

So why is it that most people feel universities need to be better managed? Many explanations are possible. First, most of us, especially those who feel entitled to offer opinions loudly, have been subjects of the university at some time or other, either as students or parents of students. From that experience, we remember the faculty members who taught poorly and seemed to do so with impunity. We also remember that we were always looking for ways to beat the system—not buy the textbook, let alone read it, cut classes, avoid seeing an advisor, never attend the extra "recommended" activities—and usually managed to do so without immediate or obvious consequences. We may remember, with a mixture of glee and dismay, that the situations we experienced outside class were much more meaningful to us then (and maybe still) than what happened in class. And we may believe that we didn't learn much of value—"I've never used calculus in my life after I left calculus class." Hence, folks may decide that college is pretty much a frivolous enterprise, and, therefore, the people who lead such nonsense must be pretty frivolous themselves.

Second, many equate the work of a faculty member and the university as a whole to teaching classes. Then they ask how many hours per week we spend in class, as though that were the only time that it takes to teach. When they hear that the average faculty member spends 3, 6, 9, or even 12 hours per week in class, they are incredulous. Given the explanation that we have to prepare for class, grade papers, advise on careers, do research, write books and papers, perform community service, and keep the university running, these critics are apt to start playing the air violin of mock sympathy.

Third, no one likes how much money faculty members make, especially given the low workload they seem to have. When the average full professor makes a cool hundred grand, our complaints that we are poorly paid relative to our peers fall on deaf ears (perhaps deservedly). The average state employee in North Carolina makes about half that, which itself is more than the average North Carolina family makes in a year. Add that faculty members can consult during normal work hours and that they get royalties for books and inventions they produce while on the job—and the average taxpayer is miffed.

The list could go on for some time. Football coaches make millions. Buildings sit empty for three months every summer. The professor who lives down the street is home cutting his grass every Friday afternoon. Faculty members get a year of paid vacation every seven years. Tuition goes up every year, and still my kid can't get any of the courses she needs to graduate. The library is full of kids playing computer games, for heaven's sake. And why do we have to pay some pointy-headed academic to be an expert on seventeenth century French poetry, when real people are out of work?

All of this, however, is as true today as it was fifty and a hundred years ago (all except coaches' salaries and playing computer games in the library). The rancor may seem to have kicked up a notch, but I suspect that is just an artifact of the rancor increasing on everything. Twenty-four-hour news stations and the Internet make information accessible, and e-mail makes us accessible. I'll resist the temptation to declare that we are in a crisis of imminent danger. Everyone always wants to say that their time is *the* time.

What I would like to explore, however, is what I've come to believe is the crux of the problem—the ownership issue. The fundamental question is, "Who owns the university?" And the troublesome, but correct, answer is, "All of us."

In some sense, the same question and answer could be applied to any public resource, but not with the same meaning as for universities. Certainly our public parks are owned by all of us. The public has a lot to say about parks, but they do it either casually—please fill out our user survey—or from a distance—please attend a public meeting about campground improvements. And the employees don't pretend to "own" the parks; in fact, the former practice of the National Park Service to move park employees to different parks every few years was designed specifically to keep them from "going native," that is, becoming too attached to any specific park.

The state mental health hospital belongs to all of us, as well. But health professionals run those facilities, led by various boards and with the employees certified to perform their functions through other external boards, sometimes public, but also sometimes private. And no one expects the patients to be determining the policies (please resist the temptation to make the obvious comparison to universities).

52

A MESSY BOTTOM LINE

The public university has many goals and many constituencies. I've referred to most through this book in my examples—undergraduate students, graduate students, faculty, staff, alumni, donors, trustees, legislators, sports fans, contracting businesses, agricultural communities, economic developers, schoolteachers, research sponsors, state agencies, elder-hostel attendees, public watchdog groups, media. Within each of those, the subsets divide up in many other ways—in-state versus out-of-state, domestic versus international, Black versus White, Christian versus Judaic, conservatives versus liberals, men's sports versus women's sports, vocational versus liberal arts. The mix is so complex that universities have been called organized anarchies, and rightly so.

What is the ultimate currency by which universities are judged? There are many, but not just one, not even just an obvious one with a host of asterisked footnotes. We have a messy bottom line, maybe no bottom line at all. I feel confident in saying that no institution in existence is as complex in its organization, aspirations, or responsibilities as the modern public research university.

Each one of those constituencies owns a part of the university. Unfortunately, each one also believes they own a much larger share than they actually do. Or at least than I think they own. The ownership proposition has never been defined or apportioned, of course, so no one really knows. Wouldn't it be wonderful if we were all shareholders in the institution? Business leaders often look at our operations with disdain, claiming that we ought to run the university like a business. Let's not argue that point now, but just recognize the first thing we'd have to do is figure out who owned the business. Let's see, every faculty member gets one share for each year they are employed; staff members get a share for every three years; every student gets one share when they enroll, then one each time they pass 30 hours, and another share upon graduation; donors get one share for every $25,000 donation; and so on. Imagine trying to get that through the Faculty Senate!

All fantasy aside, we are never going to assign formal voting shares to the university's owners. We come closest to representing how we feel about this when we create a search committee or a university standing committee. On search committees, we put faculty, students, administrators, staff, and maybe an alumnus or advisory board member; the largest proportion is typically faculty members (we generally tried to appoint more than half of a search committee from faculty ranks), which makes it clear that faculty is the majority owner of this function. The same is true for most standing committees, except for those that are clearly operational (such as the insurance committee—wait, we have an insurance committee?). On standing committees, we often let the colleges choose their members, implying that the university is really a federation of pretty autonomous college-states. But remember that these committees are usually advisory, not decision-making.

That leaves us still negotiating our way through the organized anarchy we've created. Most of the time, there are only three big constituencies that we have to worry about for the major affairs of the university—students, political officeholders, and faculty. Alumni and donors are another constituency, but they tend to rule over a limited part of the school, like their home department or college, or athletics. Generally, however, what alumni and donors want is also what the major constituencies of students and politicians want—keep their degree programs, don't raise tuition, make the place beautiful, get rid of the bum who can't win an ACC championship, and replace him or her with a better, higher-paid bum-in-waiting.

Students are a unique constituency. They wear several figurative hats, which is appropriate, because most of the time they wear literal hats (even in class, to the constant irritation of a set of old cranky faculty members). Students are our clients, the people to whom we sell our unique core service—teaching. If they don't come, and if their patrons don't pay for them to come, we don't have a university. So, we listen to what they want, and we try to accommodate their wishes. We tend to include them in most advisory functions that we create, from curriculum planning to bookstore operations; but we usually make sure they are in a minority so they can't out-vote the more permanent members. We formally institutionalize their voice as owners in many ways, making them members of the Board of Trustees (in NC State's case, a voting member, but in many universities the students are non-voting) and appropriators of various funds (e.g., the student activities board typically passes out funds to student groups, with only a little oversight to make sure they aren't breaking any laws). We have allowed and nurture a full student government on campus, with student body president, cabinet, senate, and staff. We might even compensate the student body president, from fees the students pay. Student government, aided by student media, has a powerful bully pulpit, and they use it.

At the same time, however, they are our charges, unfinished minds and personalities who have come to us to be transformed into professionals and thoughtful citizens. Their parents have entrusted their care to us. We take them through their paces, at the same time testing their preparation, diligence, memory, and aptitude. If all is going well, we keep them around, giving them more responsibility and expecting them to jump higher every time around the corral. We discard many of them along the way. We do it lovingly, of course, but we make firm judgments, deciding that many of them are not worthy of receiving the benefits of our imprimatur.

These twin roles for a major constituency make strange bedfellows, ones that wouldn't sleep together in the business world we're often told to emulate. Imagine that the university were a restaurant. To act like a university, the restaurant contacts a collection of residents from the local area, asking them what they would like to have the restaurant serve, with what ambiance, and for what price. After compiling the results, the restaurant designs a menu, decor, and atmosphere to meet those needs, and then advertises widely that they are open for business. An individual calls for a reservation and, after being questioned thoroughly to determine that the caller is really hungry, the restaurant accepts the reservation. The guest comes to the restaurant and orders a meal. Still unsure of the guest's seriousness about getting all the way through to dessert, the waiter asks him to pay for the salad now. After the salad course, the waiter announces that the guest is no longer welcome, because the guest has eaten his salad with the wrong fork, spilled onto the tablecloth, and left crumbs in the water glass. Consequently, the restaurant has no confidence that the guest could complete the rest of the meal to the staff's satisfaction. So, he is escorted to the door and told to try the sandwich shop down the street if he is still hungry and, if he improves his manners, he might call again for a reservation in a year or so.

Students negotiate between these two roles adroitly, well aware that they have both roles—as raw materials molded through the machinery of production and as owners of the machinery. We often would prefer that they forget about the ownership role, but the students don't. When challenged by the inability to register for a class that is already full, an aggressive student might blurt out, "Aren't I paying to be able to take the classes I need?" At the end of a recent semester, a student wrote in his or her evaluation of me, "He taught a really good course, but I think it is ridiculous how much money he makes for doing this."

Fortunately, because most students remain more worried about their grades and recommendations, their forays into ownership are generally mild and targeted away from academics. They want to influence decisions about textbook prices, timing of spring break, registration practices, and where the student section will be for basketball games. They don't ordinarily get involved with faculty salaries, building priorities, or departmental consolidation.

Political officeholders, the second major constituency, are the nominal and official owners of the university. Clearly, the governor and state legislature are the ultimate trustees of the university, acting as representatives of the true owners (you and me). They and their predecessors have passed laws that allow a decision-making body to be appointed or elected, usually called a Board of Trustees. The board then has the authority to create policies and other instruments that allow the university to function. In the shareholder analogy, the Board of Trustees owns at least 51% of the voting stock of the university. What they say goes, goes.

I am confident that the average faculty member, staff member, or student has no conception about how important the Board of Trustees is to the life of their university. The board has enormous power and scope of influence. That's why section LB2341 has shelves of books about boards and controlling them. A sensible board will respect the traditions of the university, most importantly the traditional ways in which it conducts its business, but the board does have the authority to change virtually anything that a university does. For example, NC State has a well-reasoned faculty-dominated process for recommending honorary degree candidates to the Board of Trustees, but the board has the authority to decide without consultation to give (or deny) an honorary degree to whomever they want. That's a trivial example, but they have the same authority regarding curricula, faculty appointments, and student conduct. What they say goes, goes.

I only put these paragraphs about the Board of Trustees in at this point to make the description complete. All readers of this book understand the formal processes that underlie the official decisions at a university. But I have now described two of the three major ownership categories of the university, leaving the interesting one to last, the one that is the provost's responsibility—the faculty.

53

THE FACULTY'S PROPERTY INTEREST

A few years into my time as provost, I was tabbed to chair a committee for the university system to revise the faculty discharge policy. Lucky me. I considered the appointment an honor, however, because this task would only be entrusted to someone whom others believed was naïve enough not to have a preconceived agenda. Boy, were they naïve.

This task was never going to be easy. The University of North Carolina system then included 16 institutions, ranging from research-intensive, world-famous universities, like UNC at Chapel Hill, to minority-serving institutions, with a few thousand students, mostly from the surrounding counties. The needs and perspectives of these institutions might be as far apart on the topic of faculty dismissal as Western Carolina University and UNC–Wilmington (that's about 600 miles). The still relatively new president of the system was also more actively engaging the UNC system Faculty Assembly, a combination of representatives from the faculty governance bodies of all 16 schools. Hence, "ownership" was becoming more real with that group, as well.

I also had a preconceived agenda. From my perspective and the general perspective of the provosts as a whole, the faculty discharge process didn't give enough latitude for dismissal based on unsatisfactory performance—I wanted to see that changed, and I'd trade almost anything else in the policy rewrite to accomplish that goal.

The committee membership itself was instructive. It included several provosts, several faculty members, including chair of the Faculty Assembly, and several institutional and system lawyers; in this case, faculty members were not the majority. We sloughed our way through the deliberations, made recommendations that went back to the individual campuses, appeared before the Faculty Assembly, and eventually negotiated an agreement that went to the Board of Governors for approval. It was approved. The major outcome, from my perspective, was an explicit statement that unsatisfactory performance, sustained over time and with plenty of notice and opportunity for improvement, is cause for dismissal.

But that's not why I mention it. It took a committee of this magnitude, at this high a level, dealing with significant issues in a legal and purposeful way, for me to first hear that a faculty member had a "property interest" in his or her position.

As we were deliberating, we started stumbling over the language of "reappointment" versus "subsequent appointment." This is administrivia that only a provost and legal counsel could brook. We reached the understanding that tenure-track faculty members came to the university with a four-year initial appointment and then could be *reappointed* for three more years before they either received or didn't receive a tenured appointment. Nontenure-track faculty members, however, were appointed for a specific term, let's say three years. If we wanted to keep them, they did not get reappointed; instead they were given a *subsequent appointment*. The existing policies, however, and the ordinary conversation about faculty status used the term *reappointment* indiscriminately, meaning either situation.

We changed the policy language to be precise, and I became obsessive about the use of these terms in speech because of the difference in property interest that they carry with them. Tenured faculty, you see, have a property interest in their positions, and faculty on the tenure track but not yet tenured have a property interest as well. The use of the term *reappointment* implies that they have a legitimate expectation of continuing in the position. Therefore, say our legal experts, they have a property interest.

Nontenure-track faculty members in our system, however, have no legal expectation of an appointment that would continue at the end of their current contract. Their contract letters explicitly state this. Consequently, to avoid unintentionally granting a property interest to a nontenure-track faculty member by casually referring to their reappointment, we became scrupulous in our description of any new work they might be offered as a new appointment or a subsequent appointment.

All the legal gobbledygook is immaterial except that it explained the university to me in a startling new way. As a natural resource professional, I have encountered the concept of property rights and "takings" throughout my career. Laws and regulations to protect the environment and natural resources have been debated for decades regarding whether or not they were "taking" an individual's property. The concept is clear if the government takes your property away entirely to build a road or a school; the government has to compensate you for the loss of your property.

The concept is less clear for taking of value that amounts to less than totally taking your deed away. If the government makes a law that says you can't plow up your land because the slope is too steep and the resulting erosion would impact the adjacent stream, do you have a right to compensation because your ability to farm is impaired? Maybe, maybe not. If the Food and Drug Administration changes its rule on how much of a pesticide can be in a product and that law makes it more expensive to produce the food, do you have a right to compensation because your profit is reduced? Probably not, but a hungry lawyer might be willing to argue the case. The legal battle over "takings" and their compensation continues, and it won't ever be totally resolved.

University ownership is directly analogous to public resource ownership. Faculty members have an ownership stake in the university—that's what our legal staff said, so it must be true. Any proposed changes to a faculty member's position or their ability to perform their position's responsibilities can be seen as "taking" part or all of the faculty member's property. When is an action actually a taking, and when isn't it? I don't know, but the faculty definitely has an interest in considering the question for every action the university contemplates.

The old saw that "faculty politics are so mean because there is so little at stake" becomes nonsensical when one realizes that the battles are about who owns the university and every part of it. Faculty members care about decisions, explicitly or implicitly, because their property interest might be at stake.

Tenure gives a faculty member a considerable property interest in the university—that is easy to understand. So, naturally, they have deep concerns about understanding the tenure process and negotiating successfully through it. The provost is well served, therefore, to make the tenure process as explicit and recipe-driven as possible.

Both before and after tenure, however, faculty members are also sensitive to any other decisions that might affect their ability to continue their success. Faculty members are trained to think about how one thing connects to everything else, so it is natural again for them to associate any university decision with how the decision affects their ability to succeed. When the department head asks a senior professor to share her laboratory with a starting assistant professor, she isn't just being asked to show kindness to her colleague, she is also being asked to cede part of the real property that she owns, or at least presumes she owns, as a tenured faculty member at the university. Should the department head attempt to force the sharing, sparks will fly, and someone, probably the department head, may get burned.

Asking a tenured faculty member to give up teaching an upper-division course in order to cover an introductory course is akin to asking him to give up a portion of his future salary. Asking him to drop his ongoing research to work with a team of others on a proposal for a major grant is just as threatening. In both these examples, if the faculty member takes time away from his specialized work to help the larger institution, the change might reduce the pace or direction of his research, hence reputation and ability to do more and better things. Even if his current work may seem stalled, the investment in it to date is a real part of his perceived property interest.

Thinking of faculty decisions in terms of property interest also explains why the faculty in general is so conservative about the university's management, so committed to the status quo. The status quo represents the established distribution of property interests, perhaps not explicit but at least implicitly agreed to in practice. Any action to change the status quo has the potential to shift the relative distribution of property interests among the owners. Remember how many faculty members it takes to change a lightbulb?

The same reluctance to change also rules faculty reaction to group actions. Making tough decisions on a colleague's post-tenure review only invites similar action on your review in coming years, a threat to your property interest. Agreeing to give up space or positions as a department because of a budget cut is a direct assault on the ability of the department to succeed—better for all to suffer a little than to take a big hit somewhere.

Changes in policy are likewise subject to the same commitment to the status quo. I was amazed at the intense reaction that Faculty Senate had to switching from paper-and-pencil course evaluation forms to an online version. Faculty members have railed about the failings of student evaluations of their courses since the first forms were invented. I figured that they might be appreciative if we at least got the process out of their classrooms and could get the Internet-generated results back to them while they still remembered which class they had just taught. And as a supposed leader in STEM fields, our university ought to be on the leading edge of such technological innovations. When we introduced the online system, faculty members went ballistic. Even though it had been recommended by a faculty-dominated standing committee and had been approved unanimously by the Council of Deans, the faculty's representatives were still angry.

Their basic concern was that significant decisions might be made about a faculty member's teaching based on a new system that had not been validated and that could not be compared accurately to the results from the previous paper form. At the time of the debate, I couldn't understand the importance of this, mostly because I have faith that no competent administrator ever makes significant judgments based on small or isolated variations in student evaluations. Now I understand. The faculty was heavily invested in the paper-and-pencil system, having come to some implicit understanding of how the data would be used and how to manage how the data were collected and analyzed. By implementing a new system, the administration was "taking" their property interest in the existing system.

54

THE PROVOST'S JOB

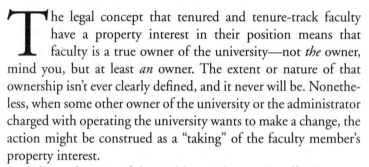

The legal concept that tenured and tenure-track faculty have a property interest in their position means that faculty is a true owner of the university—not *the* owner, mind you, but at least *an* owner. The extent or nature of that ownership isn't ever clearly defined, and it never will be. Nonetheless, when some other owner of the university or the administrator charged with operating the university wants to make a change, the action might be construed as a "taking" of the faculty member's property interest.

This is the crux of the problem. Whereas the official owners of the university own the university in trust for the public, the faculty members own their part of the university for their individual benefit. Consequently, managing the university within the context of that property interest is always going to be negotiating a contest among the owners—faculty, students, and political officers—about where public interest ends and personal interest starts.

The relative positions and interests of the university's owners doesn't generally become a subject of direct confrontation. As long as the university sits in a stable position, life can go on quite peacefully. Students, as I've said, generally concern themselves with the matters of immediate interest to them, mostly not involving faculty. Students have concerns about amenities and representation, which typically put them into conversation with the administrative leadership at the university, not with the faculty. As long as the official political leadership concerns itself with the larger questions at the university—political and donor friend-making, athletics, administrative policies—the faculty, board, and legislature also can coexist readily.

However, when the stresses put on the university begin to drive at the core mission and its execution, the furnace of joint ownership gets hot. Budget reductions and demands for increasing enrollment make challenges to the ownership treaty; when these occur together, the heat goes higher. In North Carolina, the idea that the university should rearrange its programs and priorities to respond to the stated needs of North Carolinians met with immediate resistance by the faculty. The use of the term *demand-driven* by the university president was like waving a red flag in front of a bull; after he stopped using that language, faculty quit breathing through their noses and pawing the ground.

Nonetheless, stress has continued. The Board of Governors decided that degrees were proliferating, especially doctoral degrees, so they required the system's administrative staff to develop new guidelines to manage the creation of new degrees. The new guidelines required consideration of the demand for graduates within North Carolina. NC State's desire to implement a new doctoral degree in public history was held hostage to this process for several years. Our desire to have a doctoral degree stemmed from faculty interest to move beyond our master's degrees in history, particularly in an area—public history—where we have a national reputation and, hence, would have instant status as a national program. The degree is not uniquely relevant to employment needs within North Carolina, but would help achieve strategic priorities of NC State to expand social science graduate programs and attract the best faculty and graduate students into our history department—good for the state in principle, but not a stimulus to anyone's local economy. So, the faculty's interests remained in limbo, waiting for an eventual decision by the official leadership. Along the way, the history faculty, which had committed to do the hard work of developing the proposals and to direct their resources toward this end, felt that their role—their ownership—in the academic process was being ignored. Their trust in the administration crashed (both the chancellor and I had pledged our commitment to getting this degree implemented), along with their willingness to commit time and energy to an initiative like this again. (I am happy to report that the degree has now been approved.)

The provost's job is to manage this negotiation. As the administrative officer who is explicitly responsible for faculty and academic matters at a university, the provost sits at the intersection of the faculty's personal interests and the university's academic interests, as expressed by students and the official leadership. Because the faculty role as owner is real—it is a legally extant property interest—and because faculty opinion is afforded great deference in the ordinary operation of the university, these issues fall squarely into the provost's lap.

So, my fundamental message is that managing the interaction among faculty and other university constituents is *the* essential element of the provost's job, not an add-on or a nuisance that has to be borne. Provosts spend a significant amount of time working with and through the line organization of the university—deans and departments, vice provosts, and their staffs—but we need to spend quality time, and lots of it, working with the faculty directly. The extent to which the faculty knows, likes, and trusts the provost is the extent to which the provost will succeed in moving the broader university agenda forward on behalf of the other university owners.

Relationship counselors tell us that time spent with spouse and children is akin to making deposits in the family's emotional savings account, building up a positive balance for when hard times come along. Investing in the relationship with faculty has the same effect for the provost. In this way, the provost makes investments in faculty collaboration when she spends time attending Faculty Senate, visiting individual college and even departmental faculty meetings, hosting informal faculty events, recognizing faculty achievements with an e-mail or note, opening faculty-led conferences and workshops, or presiding at award ceremonies. People remember how they are treated. So, as I end this chapter, let me focus again on the importance of working well with people. Perhaps the single most important lesson that I have learned from my time as provost, and especially from the tortured end of my term as provost, is that a career built on ethical performance and respectful treatment of others does count. In the weeks immediately following my resignation, I received hundreds of e-mails, cards, calls, visits, and hugs from people expressing their dismay at my resignation and their unshaken belief in my integrity and commitment to the university. Some of these contacts have been from people I have had to discipline or release from their positions, from people whose programs I closed and from people whose decisions I have reversed. I will be forever grateful for their kindness and support, to both Sharon and me, during the trying times before and since my resignation.

The provost's job is difficult, to be sure, but it has limitless rewards. Gary San Julian, a lifelong friend and colleague, and I had a mutual support slogan when we were both administrators at Penn State, paraphrased from the James Taylor song—"don't let them take your soul." We are each guardians of our own souls. But the provost has another important and wonderful role: He is guardian of the soul of the university.

LESSONS ABOUT WHO OWNS
THE UNIVERSITY

1. Everybody thinks they could run the university better than we run it. Don't take it personally.
2. People love their universities and, therefore, love to criticize them.
3. Universities are messy places. We'd run them like businesses if they were businesses. But they aren't.
4. The university has no single bottom line, like a business, or even the so-called triple bottom line of a green and community-oriented business. It is just a complex, wonderful mess.
5. The university has many owners, but we don't know how much each of them actually owns. Try that in business.
6. Students and their parents are owners. Fortunately, they care mostly about tuition, the operating hours of the gym, and when spring break will be.
7. The public is an owner, whose interest is managed by elected officials and trustees. Fortunately, they care mostly about budgets, buildings, and basketball.
8. The Board of Trustees is a lot more important than most people, both inside and outside the university, think.
9. Faculty members are owners, too. As tenured or tenure-track faculty members, they have a legal "property interest" in their jobs and, hence, the university.
10. Whereas others have a public trustee ownership, faculty members have personal interest. Unfortunately, their personal interest often butts heads with the academic interests of the university.
11. The provost is the arbiter between the faculty's personal interest and the institution's academic interests. That's the provost's most important job.

12. Building trust with the faculty, therefore, is essential for the success of the provost and the institution.

13. The provost is the guardian of the academic soul of the university.

PART TEN

BEING THE EX

55

STARTING OVER

B urt Reynolds starred in the 1979 movie *Starting Over*. He played a middle-aged man, a writer, whose life had fallen apart—so he was starting over. With the help of friends, he landed a job as an English instructor at a local college. As he nervously met his first class one morning, the scene showed Reynolds standing behind an ancient desk, the blackboard behind him, and a clock visible above the board. The bell rang; the clock read 9:00.

Reynolds began the usual first-day conversation, and the scene panned to the students, suggesting the passage of time. Then Reynolds closed his book and said, "Well, class, I think that will be all for today." The scene widened to show the clock—now reading 9:05.

My first day back on the faculty was eerily similar.

Sharon and I had emptied my possessions from the provost's office over the weekend and moved the relevant items to my new office. The office was equipped with the leftover furniture from the previous occupant—neither he nor I believed in buying new furniture with university money. Besides, the furniture in the office was pure faculty—an oak desk, an oak table, and an oak chair, made by the prison system in the distant past. A few more modern bookshelves and a couple of filing cabinets completed the suite.

Hanging on the bulletin board was a copy of a poster I had commissioned for the college's 75th anniversary celebration when I had been dean. It was signed by many of the departmental faculty and staff, with welcome-back messages. Yeah, you're right, I cried.

On that Monday morning, I was to begin my six-month study leave. In my case, however, I didn't dare actually take a study "leave." I wasn't going to succumb to the idea that I had the freedom to think, study, and prepare, in whatever manner I deemed best and on whatever schedule in whatever place. Too many people might be watching, and I didn't dare risk the possible publicity that someone would report they saw me at the pool during working hours. Besides, I had a date coming up with the Grand Jury.

So, fearing that reporters might be waiting outside my door at 8 a.m. to make sure I was back at work, I arrived a few minutes before eight. No one was there. My homecoming wasn't as newsworthy as I thought.

I unlocked the door, turned on the light, fired up the computer. Then, at 8:05, I called Sharon. "Now what do I do?" I asked.

The contrast between this world and the provost's world was startling. In the provost's office on any day, when I arrived, at least one assistant was already at her desk and handed me a few messages as I walked through the door. She was also likely to say, "The chancellor wants to see you," or one of the other type-A early birds might have left the same message. A meeting was most likely scheduled for 8:30, so folks were beginning to arrive in the outside office. The message light would be blinking on the telephone, and the e-mail would have stacked up to a depth of 50 or so overnight. And I loved it!

My faculty world was empty. No calls, no e-mails, no mail, no blue "immediate action required" folders, no files slipped under the door, no best friend peeking through the door for a quick consultation—no nothing.

And so my first re-revelation was how self-directed the faculty world is and how institutionally driven the provost's world is.

Admittedly, I had no real reason to expect a big workload sitting on my desk—I wasn't supposed to have one. I was on a study leave, to prepare for reentry into the professorate. And I obviously needed one, because I was in shock!

The shock has worn off in the intervening three years, and I am enjoying several parts of being a faculty member again. Perhaps most pleasant is that I actually have time to do work. As provost I mostly directed other people's work or just nodded my head when they told me what they were doing. That's the job of a senior administrator. Ten hours of meetings per day doesn't leave a lot of time for researching the next lecture.

But as a faculty member, I have time—time to work. If I need to take a day to research and prepare tomorrow's lecture, I take it. Little is on my agenda that can't be put off so that I can devote myself to some specific time-consuming task. If an advisee needs to talk about career goals (many need to do so) or internship possibilities (they all need to), I can spend the time with her or him.

All of us got into this racket because we groove on learning things and sharing what we've learned. It takes time to learn and even more time to prepare thoughtfully to share. One joy of being a faculty member is the gift of time.

I admit that the relaxed nature of my workday might ring hollow to the harried assistant professor who is up to her armpits in academic alligators—teaching, submitting grant proposals, managing the grants she has, writing papers for the looming tenure decision, advising current graduate students, and recruiting the next batch. In contrast, I am a senior faculty member who used to be everyone's boss—so other folks pretty much steer around me. What's more, no one in their right mind would give me a grant to do research, so I'm not looking for one. I'll be retired in a few years, so no one wants me to join their research or seminar group or build a partnership around me. For all these reasons, my colleagues mostly let me fossilize at my own pace.

But even considering the difference between other faculty members and me, it is still true that all faculty members—new ones and old ones—are making their own choices about how they will spend their time. When they are not actively teaching the core courses of the curriculum, they have the opportunity to work when and where they wish. So, when I started back to my faculty job in late May, most faculty members had opted to do their work elsewhere.

The main administration building for the university, though, was still hopping busy. As I've mentioned earlier, the rhythm of the academic year gets out-shouted by the rhythm of bureaucracy in the halls of administration, so much so that the cloistered vice-chancellors often don't know whether school is in or out of session. The expensive cars are still lined up in the expensive parking lot well before 8 a.m., and the suits are still being worn by "the suits."

Over in the faculty world, however, common sense has resurfaced. The inexpensive faculty cars are sparse in the inexpensive parking lot, and no student cars are filling in the vacant spaces, willing to risk a parking ticket in order to make class on time. So, we never have a worry about finding a space, even at 10 a.m. on a Monday, Wednesday, or Friday. The faculty dress however they want, mostly sporting T-shirts, shorts, and sandals. The lights are off in the hallways, keeping the building cool and suppressing any latent compulsion to act pedantically.

Each summer, at least for a while in the summer, faculty members get to do what Burt Reynolds and I were doing. We all get to start over. We all get to spend some time concentrating on the reason we came to the university in the first place—our love of learning, knowing, and sharing. And that keeps us coming back for more.

56

THE HALF-LIFE OF AN
EX-PROVOST

The first university event we attended after I was the ex-provost was at the beginning of fall semester. Just before classes start, the university has a service day. For several years, our student affairs staff had organized a meal-packing event. Thousands of students assembled for the morning or afternoon to repack wholesale quantities of dried foodstuffs into family-sized quantities for hunger-relief efforts run by the group Stop Hunger Now. Student and staff groups formed teams. It was an exciting time—the organization of the process was intricate, and the pace was blistering; we packed hundreds of thousands of meals in a morning shift.

We joined a group from creative services who kindly asked Sharon and me to participate. The event started with everyone in the student center ballroom, getting some background on the activity and some lessons on how to do it. Toward the end of the introductory program, the leader said, "And now please help me welcome our provost who has some words of encouragement."

I almost got up from my seat to head for the stage. But someone was already there ahead of me—the interim provost. He said some words, but I heard none of them. I was devastated. I belonged up there, I was the provost, these were my students and staff and faculty gathered for this wonderful purpose.

I had not been prepared for my reaction. I grabbed Sharon's hand for something to hold on to, she looked over and asked me if I was okay.

I answered "No."

But I got over it for the moment, and we went on to have a rewarding day filling plastic bags with dried rice, vitamin tablets, and soy powder.

I still have emotional reactions at times when the university passes by and I'm not in the parade. I was recently helping a student who needed some career advice, and we looked together at the advising center's website. The sidebar of the main page scrolled automatically through a series of photos of their work and staff. As we were looking at the site, the sidebar scrolled to a picture of me, as provost, giving an award to an advisor. I don't know why it was still up there—probably because no one had had time to change the website for a couple of years—but it caught me by surprise. Yep, I thought, I'm still the provost in some places.

But in fact, I'm not the provost anymore.

And I'm not going to be one ever again. For a while, I harbored the belief that maybe I could get another provost's job. After a few months to let the fuss die down, Sharon and I decided that I should give it a try. I called several search firms who were leading searches for schools I thought might consider me—mostly smaller state schools who might appreciate the chance to have an experienced provost from a land grant university. I made it pretty far in several of the searches, usually getting at least an airport interview.

Twice I made it all the way to the final interviews. In one I was told I was the runaway favorite. In the other, I was the only candidate called back for a second visit—and eventually a third visit. The chair of their board of trustees told me that I was a once-in-a-lifetime find, like a McDonalds' All American who decided to transfer to their school after one year at Duke.

Neither offered me the job. My conclusion is that they just couldn't make themselves hire a provost with an asterisk next to his name. If there is another good candidate—and all these schools would have other good candidates—why take a chance? During a meeting at one school, the search committee asked me if I would hire myself if I were in their shoes. I answered that if I didn't know me, I wouldn't—how could I be sure that something similar wouldn't happen again? But because I know me and know the full story of the circumstances of my resignation, I sure would hire me. So, of course, they didn't hire me.

I remember a time when a retired university president was called back to serve as an interim provost at his former school. When asked if he or others might not feel awkward with him in this different lower position, he replied no, that anonymity came quickly to a former administrator.

I agree. The half-life of a former administrator is pretty short. Most of the students I teach don't remember that I was the provost (actually, most of them couldn't name the provost if their grade depended on it). Occasionally, they discover the history themselves and get pretty excited. A student came up to me after class recently and said that she had attended a meeting in the college's main conference room. During the meeting she had looked up at the portraits on the wall and, seeing mine, blurted out, "That's my teacher!"

New faculty members arrive every year with no knowledge of who went before, and staff members turn over often enough that name recognition doesn't last long. When I call an office on campus now and say, "Hi, this is Larry Nielsen," I usually pause, waiting for the recognition. Most of the time, the answer comes back with a flat, "How can I help you?"

The interim provost told me he'd be calling regularly to get my advice. I told him that I appreciated the gesture but that he wouldn't actually call; and he never did. I had told other previous provosts that I would do the same things when I became provost, and I never did. For a while when I would see a dean or vice-chancellor, they would say we should get together for lunch or dinner, but that has happened only a couple of times and then very early after my resignation.

I don't blame them—they need another work-related social obligation about as much as they need a new revision of the travel policy. And my old best friend is now sidling up to someone new, purring "Good morning, Mr. Provost" into his receptive ear (let me be fair—I've shared more post-provost lunches with him than with anyone else).

"The king is dead," the loyal subjects lament, followed immediately by, "Long live the king." A new king always follows an old king, and a new provost always follows the old provost. So, it is true, as you'll read in the literature review section, that "provost" is a temporary title of position, not a permanent title of rank.

There is a big lesson to be learned from the half-life of a decaying ex-provost. You better not identify too closely with the position. The position is a job that belongs to the university, not a knighthood that belongs to the individual. If you put all your identity into the job, you might have nothing to hold you up when the job is withdrawn. When I first came to NC State to be dean, the outgoing dean told me the most important task was developing a set of friends beyond the university. They, he asserted, would remain friends long after the acquaintances of university position had disappeared. He was right, and our nonuniversity friends have remained constant and invaluable through the transitions.

A corollary is not to get a big head about how wonderful and powerful you are. That is temporary, too. Sharon and I really like sports, and the complimentary box seats that we had for bowl games, ACC championships, PGA golf tournaments, and Stanley Cup finals were great. We seldom missed an opportunity to attend, and I'm glad we didn't miss many. Because we aren't getting any invitations now.

In preparing to write this book, I looked back through five years of my planners to see if I had forgotten anything that absolutely needed to be mentioned. I was amazed to see how many things I had worked on that we just couldn't get accomplished. The list will be long for any provost and university; my list includes a judicial research center, forensics institute, national copyright center, semipro football league, research ethics program, state aquarium, and performing arts center, among others. So many great plans and aspirations; so many things that might have been. But even more distressing are the projects that we implemented and that now have been canceled or changed. The textbook adoption incentive is gone, along with the Millennium seminars, the Korean campus (and possible Italian, French, and Dubai campuses) and the precollege recruitment program for minority kids. Many decisions that you make as a provost will be reversed by the next team, partly because you made some bad decisions, but also just because it is their turn to decide.

And one of the things they are sure to decide is that they don't want to hear from you.

57

WE DON'T KNOW
ANYTHING—AND WE DON'T
REALLY CARE

I had lunch with my former best friend, the CFO. Mexican, just like always. At the end of the meal (not wanting to make him angry early), I told him that, as a faculty member, I had no idea what the administration was doing. I didn't know the condition of the budget, what buildings were being planned or requested, what our programmatic priorities were for the legislature, who was leaving or coming in major positions. I had just learned through the grapevine that the chief counsel had retired—but I hadn't seen it announced anywhere.

I knew this would make him mad, and it did.

"It's all on the web," he said. I replied that I knew it was out there in cyberspace somewhere and that I could probably even find it, because I knew where to look. Spend enough time noodling around on the web, and you find out all sorts of things. But, I explained, the typical faculty member doesn't know where to look and isn't interested enough to go find out.

"So, how do we fix that?"

We don't, I explained. That's just the way it is. The worlds of the faculty member and the senior administration are pretty much in different orbits, maybe in different galaxies.

I've been back in the classroom for three years now, and little that the senior administration has done seems to have any direct impact on me. I teach my classes, which means I need a classroom to teach in—the classrooms I've used have been there for at least 50 years. I need the Internet and the software on my computer to research and produce class materials, and I know very well that some smart people make sure they work, thankfully—but that's not the work of the senior administration.

Certainly the work of the administration has impact in the big picture. We get a budget each year, and a bunch of people in the administration make sure that happens. We have a building or two under construction at all times, and the folks in suits are making that happen. Regulations governing how we hire and fire, how our retirement and health insurance work—all these things are overseen by the senior administration. New degree programs eventually have to get approved by the provost, chancellor, and Board of Trustees.

But on a day-to-day working level, the connection between our two worlds is minimal. I've written earlier that many people working in the administration building probably don't know much about the academic calendar—when spring break or finals or the first day of class are. I recently called a friend in the legal office to have lunch; he said not today because the Board of Trustees was meeting. As provost, I would have known that; my work aimed toward that meeting for the two weeks leading up to it; in fact, the entire senior administration was a ganglion of raw nerves in anticipation of each board meeting. As a faculty member, I had no idea the board was meeting that day. And my ignorance had no consequence.

The provost needs to know that the typical faculty member doesn't have a clue about the provost's world—same with the work of other senior administrators. The life of the faculty member is about classrooms, labs, graduate assistants, grant administration, and hiring practices. How well these things work is what matters most to a faculty member. The classroom where I teach is old, and I discovered my first winter, the heating system was awful. Once the heat went on, the room had to be at least 85, maybe 90 degrees. Add 225 students, and it was a convection oven. I want the campus to be beautiful and environmentally sustainable, meeting some lofty 2050 goals for carbon neutrality, but I really want my classroom to be habitable—fixing the heat was my top priority (I'm pleased to report that the heat has been fixed). For the past two years, I've asked for a clock on the wall where I can see it while I'm teaching, but it isn't there yet. I know it sounds trivial, but that clock is much more important to me than whether the course approval policy gets revised.

We have an online travel authorization system. We used to be able to travel on our own judgment and authority, and the signature of our supervisor on the travel reimbursement was acknowledgment of approval. The auditors didn't like that, so now we have an online system for travel, created by people in IT, with advice from others in the administration. I was filling out the page for a trip I was taking to plan a doctoral seminar course I'd be teaching in the upcoming summer. The form asks us for the purpose of the trip, selecting from a drop-down menu. The menu includes research, presentation, workshop, athletic recruiting, fund-raising, business matters, and "other university business." It doesn't list teaching. How could anyone make a list of university activities and fail to put teaching on the first line? Well, it happens.

A senior administrator came to our college faculty meeting one recent spring, part of the great idea for senior administrators to get out to the troops, so to condescendingly speak. He began by apologizing for being substantially late and saying that he would only talk a few minutes and then wanted to engage in a discussion; 45 minutes later, he stopped talking. He spoke the whole time about the issues on his agenda, mostly the budget. Of course, his perspective about the budget is all about what is happening in the legislature, with tax revenues, reserve funds, and the like. Our interest in the budget is whether we're going to have money for a clock in the classroom and whether we're going to get to fill the faculty vacancy when Joe retires this summer. I watched the faculty and staff as they listened; they were trying hard to be friendly, but their faces were stony, various combinations of boredom and disappointment.

I don't suppose there is any deep lesson here—just the simple reality that faculty are from Mars and administrators are from Venus. And when you go to Mars, it's a good idea to speak Martian.

58

LEARNING TO LOVE AGAIN

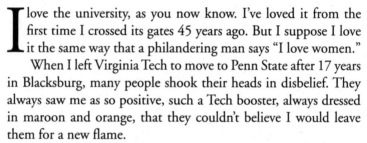

I love the university, as you now know. I've loved it from the first time I crossed its gates 45 years ago. But I suppose I love it the same way that a philandering man says "I love women."

When I left Virginia Tech to move to Penn State after 17 years in Blacksburg, many people shook their heads in disbelief. They always saw me as so positive, such a Tech booster, always dressed in maroon and orange, that they couldn't believe I would leave them for a new flame.

But, you see, I love the university in general. And following the advice of Stephen Sills, I love the one I'm with. I loved Virginia Tech as a place to be an assistant professor in the 1970s and 1980s, when it was young and hungry to be a big-time school, and we were all trying our hardest to make the A-list. It wasn't so good a bit later as a department head, when the gap between our ambition and our budget became too wide to straddle—and it was my job to do the straddling.

So, then I fell in love with Penn State as a great place to be as a school director. Penn State gave me the opportunity to stretch my administrative wings in an institution that had great capacity and reputation. If you could convince Penn State that your idea was a good one, Penn State would get it done. Penn State was a complete university, with everything from engineering to the arts, and that suited my eclectic personality. We lived just off campus, in a neighborhood known as "deans' row," and I could walk to my office. Besides, I look better in blue and white than I do in maroon and orange.

But Penn State became confining after a while. It is a huge institution that had been huge for a long time—trying to get something new implemented was a stretch. Our School of Forest Resources was a small tree in a big wood. Strategic decisions were made at levels well above a school director, and we weren't going to get noticed much or often.

I left Penn State for my new love—NC State. I won't dwell on why I came to love NC State so much, because you have read it many times in earlier chapters. But NC State is a place where, as I often said, every person can make a difference. As dean and later as provost, my love was constantly fanned with every accomplishment or event that came first to the college and later to the university.

But then my love turned her back on me, told me she didn't love me anymore. Oh, for sure, she said, I still want to be friends; we can still hang out together; let's do lunch.

Now I am struggling to stay in love. I still love the idea of the university, and I still love my colleagues and our students and the work that I do. Like an old married couple, the university and I still value what each brings to our relationship—I teach and advise students; the university pays me.

It isn't easy, though, to continue loving all the parts of the university that don't belong to me anymore. I have stayed away from all the public forums that the chancellor and provost have held over the past three years about budgets and reorganization. I don't think they would have appreciated seeing me in the audience. I went to a couple of basketball games as a guest in the athletic director's box, but the looks coming from the chancellor's adjacent box seemed to say, what's he doing here?

But just as with the end of any love affair, it creates the opportunity for a new beginning. I'm now like the retiree who finds new joy by returning to her "avocation" after giving up her "vocation." I've given up being the ex-provost (pretty much) and am now concentrating on being a current faculty member. The benefits are many.

Teaching is an absolute delight. Faculty members tend to get grumpy and crusty as they age, certain in their opinion that students are lazier and less competent than they used to be. But I find that students are alive with interest and curiosity and the desire to change the world—just like we were. Admit it, as students most of us spent most of our time on other things than making the world a better place—in college, my pool game got pretty sharp, I could finesse a bridge hand pretty well, and I spent a lot of time in the pub (working as a bartender, but the effect on world peace is the same on either side of the bar). I'm more impressed with today's students than I am with the memory of me and my friends. After almost every class, a student comes up to ask me questions or tell me their experience related to today's topics. Their eyes are glowing, and their horizons are limitless. We have so much to offer to them, and they have so much to offer to the future.

Advising is wonderful, also. If faculty members sometimes get grumpy about teaching, they can get downright hostile about advising. Students don't seem to want to do any of the preparatory work, they say, having been spoon-fed by hovering parents their whole lives. Poppycock! The world of the university is as foreign to incoming students as the dark side of the moon. We get the chance to be their surrogate uncles and aunts. We get to know them, and then we can love them, too.

But perhaps the best thing to love about being a faculty member is that your time is your own. As provost, every minute of every day belonged to someone else—to thousands of someone elses. My electronic calendar as provost throbbed in Technicolor with overlapping appointments. Now, my calendar lists mostly two things: "class" and "prepare for class."

My time is my own. And given that the clock is approaching noon, perhaps you'll forgive me for ending now, because I'm going to lunch with Sharon.

LESSONS ABOUT BEING THE EX-PROVOST

1. You aren't the provost anymore. Accept it and get over yourself.
2. The provost's job belongs to the university, not to you. So get over yourself.
3. Better not invest too heavily in the fact that you're the provost. You aren't; you just sit in the provost's chair. You'll sit there just for a while, probably less time than you anticipated.
4. Many of your initiatives as provost will be stopped or changed by the next provost. Enjoy knowing that the ones remaining were the good ones.
5. Faculty members work on Mars, administrators work on Venus. Admit it, your jobs don't have a lot in common.
6. Faculty members don't know what's going on in the university administration. But that's okay, because they don't really care.
7. Not much that the provost does makes much difference to the daily work of the faculty.
8. So, when you go to meet the faculty, keep your mouth shut about what your problems are. Instead, listen to theirs.
9. Being a faculty member is a great job. They get to do real work. Provosts just get to watch work being done by others.
10. If you love being provost, then you can probably learn to love being a faculty member again.

PART ELEVEN

THE LITERATURE OF
THE PROVOST

59

WHAT IS A PROVOST?

In 1943, the Board of Trustees of Cornell University considered a proposal to change the name of the position of "provost" to that of "vice president." In the proceedings of their meeting of October 15, the Board wrote the following:

> The President and several other members of the Committee expressed themselves as opposed to the title of vice president as this title implies "a second-string" man. . . . It was held that one of the great virtues of the title of provost is its ambiguity. It is not a second-rate title; it is coordinate with that of the President and this position needs a title that will cover that conception of its status. (Cornell University, 2011)

That day Cornell wisely retained the title of provost for their second in command. Their decision encapsulates what most have written about the position of provost: Ambiguity reigns supreme!

Universities didn't always staff themselves with provosts. The journey is actually quite interesting. James Martin and James Samels (1997) present a brief and cogent review of the evolution of the position. When universities were young and small, they say, the president did everything, including leading the academic program of the institution. As the institutions became larger and more complex, the job of running the internal processes was given over to a second in command. This was the birth of the provost, but he (and he was typically a he) wasn't called provost—he was called the dean. Universities and colleges started out with just a single dean, in charge of the administration of the institution and, especially, the academic program. Even then the job titles weren't uniform, as academic dean, dean of the faculty, and dean of the college sprouted up in a range of universities.

The next phase occurred, mostly after World War II, as universities grew much larger and the advent of pre-professional specialties began to split the faculty into colleges. *The* dean gave way to many deans, one for each college and a few others for growing functions like undergraduate affairs, the graduate school, and the library. Needing another title for the position that oversaw the entire institution and its academics, universities began adopting the title "provost" en masse. Since the 1970s, most universities have created a provost, although now the titles have spread back out. The other common titles are chief academic officer (a genuflection to corporate style) and vice president for academic affairs; in community colleges, according to Peggy Teague (2000), chief academic officer is the most common title.

None of that, however, tells what a provost is—and, surprisingly, no one particularly cares. Authors of works about CAOs or provosts seem to think that attempting to define the job precisely is a fool's errand. In 1984, David Brown wrote, "The position of CAO is defined by its occupant" (p. 1). Twenty-five years later, Herman Berliner (2009), reflecting on the American Council on Education (ACE) Census of CAOs, stated, "I am convinced that there really are no average CAOs" (p. 3). Martin and Samels (1997, p. 3) state that in contrast to the increasing clarification of the roles of president and faculty over recent decades, "the role and status of the chief academic officer has remained a blur at many colleges and universities." Ann Ferren and Wilbur Stanton (2004) spend an entire chapter examining the job description of the provost, with the same result as chewing a piece of tough meat: With each chomp, it grows bigger and harder to digest. The job descriptions that universities write are daunting, they say, and those lead to situations of role conflict—and a really tough job. Ferren and Stanton write:

> Chief academic officers recognize that, other than the football or basketball coach, theirs is the most difficult position on a campus because of the high expectations of diverse constituencies and the number of persons affected by their actions. (p. 3)

In other words, the provost lives in a clingy environment. Robert Wolverton (1984) compares the provost to Argus, a mythical Greek giant said to have one hundred eyes that looked in all directions, allowing him to protect the sacred heifer Io. So, says Wolverton, the provost must be capable of looking at the institution from myriad perspectives, up, down, laterally, and obliquely. He also notes that only a couple of those eyes are supposed to be closed at any time, so as to protect against danger creeping toward the sacred heifer under cover of darkness, fog, or any other camouflage. Paula Hooper Mayhew (1997) also refers to the unique capacity the provost must have for oversight; not oversight in the supervisory sense, but the ability to "see over" the entire institution.

This characteristic—a comprehensive view of the institution—seems to me at the heart of the provost's job. As I have written earlier, the provost is one of three people—CEO, CAO, and CFO—whose job is clearly institution-wide; among these, the provost's may be the most important, because the provost's frame of reference is the academic core of the institution.

So, the provost's job is daunting, ambiguous, a blur, and it requires a hundred eyes, always scanning for danger. No sweat. In reading these various studies and reflections about the provost, I believe they are all saying that the provost's job has only the following two big elements. All of the rest reads as "other duties as assigned."

First, the provost's job can be summed up simply as leading the academic program of the institution. Joan Lorden (2009, p. 5), provost of UNC-Charlotte, expressed her attraction to the job as "the opportunity to develop and execute an academic plan, encourage faculty interaction at the interface of disciplines, and help create the context for successful faculty and student careers." She could have stopped after the first phrase, in my opinion (but it is her statement, not mine, and when Joan speaks, I always listen). Ferren and Stanton (2004, p. 24) expressed the idea similarly, in stating that the CAO has the responsibility for providing the "forward momentum of a campus," especially in terms of the strategic academic plan.

Second, the provost's job is to balance, using all one hundred eyes, the competing constituencies of the institution. The job of provost, it seems, is to balance a large series of couplets joined by the word *but*:

- Increase the quality of the student body BUT retain accessibility to unrepresented populations.
- Make the curriculum relevant to tomorrow's needs BUT respect the essential role of the faculty in curricular matters.
- Encourage innovation BUT retain our historic strengths.
- Address the professional preparation of students BUT encourage broad appreciation of the humanities and arts.
- Infuse the campus with modern technology BUT maintain the personal touch that students love and parents expect.
- Become a global university BUT advance the state's economic development.

The couplet will change from day to day, maybe from hour to hour, but the reality is the same: The institution is a "loosely coupled system" (Ferren & Stanton 2004, p. 7, quoting Karl Weick from 1983)—and the provost's job is to keep it that way, coupled and loose.

60

WHO GETS TO BE A PROVOST?

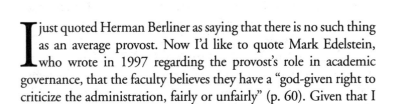

I just quoted Herman Berliner as saying that there is no such thing as an average provost. Now I'd like to quote Mark Edelstein, who wrote in 1997 regarding the provost's role in academic governance, that the faculty believes they have a "god-given right to criticize the administration, fairly or unfairly" (p. 60). Given that I am now a faculty member, I shall proceed to prove Provost Berliner wrong by describing the average provost!

The new CAO Census (Eckel et al., 2009) provides the most recent and comprehensive data on average provosts, collected in 2008. The CAO Census covered a large sample of provosts from the entire range of four-year institutions. For the most part, I'll quote only their data for provosts of public doctoral universities, the largest and most comprehensive type of university or college—because that is the experience I've recounted in this book. Unless stated otherwise, all the data I provide are from the Eckel et al. (2009) study, and I will refer to it as the CAO Census.

In addition to this new census, however, a few writers have developed more limited data for the population of provosts in the last few decades. Harold Hartley and Eric Godin (2010) extracted data from the CAO Census to characterize provosts of independent colleges. Karen Walton and Sharon McDade (2001) provided demographics of women provosts. Peggy Teague (2000) produced data on community college provosts and summarized earlier studies of community colleges. The most remarkable aspect of these various studies is that the data have changed so little over the last 40 years or so. There might not be an average provost, but the non-average ones haven't changed much over the years.

Today's public doctoral university provost is Caucasian, 60 years old, tenured (probably in a STEM-based discipline), and will last about 4.4 years in the position (Eckel et al., 2009). About 60% are men, 40% women. Let me say that I am Caucasian, was 60 years old when I left the provost's job, am tenured in a STEM discipline, and lasted 4 years and 4.5 months in the job (I believe that is 4.375 years, more or less); oh, and I am a man, but a sensitive one. If readers had any doubts before whether or not my experience was representative, let these data put that worry to rest. I am dead average.

In the interest of unbiased reporting, however, I must also cite Walton and McDade (2001), who quote a 1984 essay by Louise Allen, an experienced CAO herself. They say that Ms. Allen describes the typical CAO as a Caucasian male in his late 40s or early 50s, articulate, well-read, and "usually rather good looking." I regret to say that I am not dead on her average. I'm half a generation older, am prone to "asides" when I speak, read mostly from the Kindle sale catalogue, and have ruined thousands of photographs in my time.

These demographic data have changed relatively little over the years. The proportion of women in the position has gradually increased from about 30% in 1988 (a figure reported by Martin & Samels, 1997) to about 40% now; the proportion of women is lowest in public doctoral universities compared with other categories. Average tenure has crept up a bit also, from about 3.9 years in 1988 to 4.4 years two decades later; yes, about half of us are getting an extra year now. As with all senior administrative posts, persons of color are still rather rare; only about 9% of public doctoral provosts are persons of color.

Perhaps the most interesting change in demographics is the increasing age of provosts. Whereas the typical provost two decades ago was Louise Allen's good-looker in his 40s or 50s, today's provosts are about ten years older, averaging around 60. This has disturbed some observers who note that provosts are the most likely source for presidents (more about that later) and, consequently, we may have a depauperate population from which to choose presidents in the future (Eckel et al., 2009; Smyer, 2009).

The overwhelming majority of provosts come from the step just below them. Deans provide about 50%, and other academic officers, such as vice provosts, provide about 30% of the individuals who become provosts. So, half of provosts give up the best administrative job on campus—dean—for what the literature suggests is the hardest. A small number skip a rung or two on the ladder, coming from the ranks of faculty, department chairs or heads, and nonacademic officers; that group totals about 10%. To the great credit of search committees, only 2% of provosts come into the job from outside the academy (ah, if those selecting presidents were only as wise as those selecting provosts). The remaining 8% had served as provosts at another institution, a phenomenon I would have guessed was much rarer than this; my guess is that these are provosts moving from smaller institutions to larger ones.

According to the CAO Census, about half of provosts rise from lower positions at the same institution, the other half move from another school. This proportion shows a much higher acceptance of internal candidates than we would expect from other positions, like department heads or deans (at NC State, our current dean population is 20% internal, 80% external). I believe it reflects the recognized need for the provost to know and understand an institution well in order to manage it well. Given that the provost serves as the "inside face" of the university, hiring someone who already knows the institution from the inside makes good sense. And the high proportion of provosts coming from the ranks of deans and vice provosts similarly demonstrates that experience in the line or staff of academic administration is almost a prerequisite for selection and success as a provost.

Teague (2000) reports from her survey and from earlier surveys that a high proportion of community college chief academic officers come from blue-collar backgrounds. They told her that they thought a blue-collar background helped them understand and appreciate their university and their job so they could perform respectfully and conscientiously. I find this particularly interesting, having come from a blue-collar background myself, where I was taught that education was the most important attribute for success and that teachers were always right (not usually right, always right). I wonder also if a blue-collar background might make the provost more willing to do the routine tasks of managing the university, rather than being more interested in the star-power executive role of the president.

61

HOW DO PROVOSTS SPEND
THEIR TIME?

A s I summarized earlier, most writers have concluded that there is no universal job description for a provost and that every provost and her or his job is different. Dig below that a bit, however, and you'll discover that the conception of the provost's job is pretty similar through time and across observers.

The most obvious commonality is that the provost and the president are the two faces of the institution. Eighty-six percent of provosts at public doctoral universities report that they are the number two official of the institution, acting as president in the president's absence and as his or her alter ego at all times. As reported in the CAO Census, provosts scored their relationship with the president as best (40% mentioned this) among all others at the university (deans were second at 33%). But perfect agreement between president and provost perhaps isn't optimal. Wolverton (1984) suggested that the perfect relationship for the institution exists when the president and provost agree on 80% to 85% of issues; more than that makes the provost a yes-person; less makes for internal strife.

The president and provost, however, do entirely different things. Like the two-faced Janus of mythology, one, the president, faces outward, and one, the provost, faces inward. Virtually everyone agrees that this is the case (Ferren & Stanton, 2004;

Walton & McDade, 2001; Wolverton, 1984). Risa Palm (2009), provost of the SUNY system, suggested that the jobs were so different that the job of college dean is actually more like that of president than is the job of provost. This separation of duties, which I have characterized earlier as the provost being the university's stay-at-home parent, should not surprise anyone. The provost position was invented explicitly to allow the president to be involved more in external affairs, leaving the administration of the institution to the provost (Martin & Samels, 1997). The purpose of what was created as the dean of the faculty and would become the provost and executive vice-chancellor at North Carolina State University was clear: "The purpose of the Dean of the Faculty position is to strengthen and coordinate educational policies and to aid the chancellor in academic planning for the future" (Winstead, 1999, p. 1). In other words, stay at home and get the job done.

As the university has evolved as an institution, the role of the "inside guy" has evolved also—from scholar to administrator. Martin and Samels (1997) contrast the rather quaint and nostalgic views of the provost as a true academic, leading by example the educational mission and standards of the institution, with the more corporate reality of today's provost as a bureaucrat and career administrator. The idea that provosts should continue to teach, they wrote, is doomed to making either the teaching or the administration poor (or, I would add, making both poor).

As the institution gets more complex, the provost gets more administrative. Teague (2000) reported that the major function of community college CAOs was curriculum planning. But for four-year institutions and beyond, curricular and academic leadership didn't get near the top of the list of duties. For public doctoral universities, only 31% of provosts listed curricular and academic leadership as one of their top three duties, the lowest of any of the university types surveyed in the 2008 CAO Census.

If big-school provosts aren't teaching, performing research, or personally guiding the curricula and academic standards, what are they doing? The CAO Census asked provosts to name their top three duties. The top three entries for public doctoral institutions were personnel management, strategic planning, and budgeting and financial management, in order from most mentioned to least. No surprises there.

The typical provost is up to her elbows in strategic planning. Kenneth Mortimer and Annette Caruso quipped that as they were writing in 1984, ". . . the national higher education community is in the midst of a love affair with strategic planning" (p. 45). Amazingly, the volume in which their work appears (Brown, 1984) devoted an entire chapter to reprinting all 39 recommendations of the University of Notre Dame strategic plan. It is a fine plan, but totally routine in its form, content, and level of strategy, from Recommendation 1 (form a university curriculum committee) to Recommendation 38 (re-evaluate how much they will rely on the main-frame computer versus distributed systems). Recommendation 39 sums it all up: "It is recommended that current efforts in the area of planning be extended and that long-range plans ultimately become an integral part of the annual budget process, involving all units of the university" (O'Meara, 1984, p. 96).

Since then the love affair has become an obsessive-compulsive disorder. Legislatures, governors, boards of trustees, and internal constituencies demand strategic planning today—and, perhaps most importantly, so do accrediting organizations. Ferren and Stanton (2004) devoted their second chapter to strategic planning, the first specific topic following an introductory chapter on collaboration in general; I interpret this placement to represent the central importance of strategic planning in a collaborative leadership environment. Strategic planning turned up second on the list of the top three duties for provosts in the CAO Census. However, when asked what their *most important* three duties were, the provosts listed ensuring academic quality (53%), developing an academic vision (51%), and leading change (33%). All three of these, it seems to me, are euphemistic sub-terms for strategic planning. So, I think we can conclude that provosts, whether they use the words or not, are the strategic planning leaders for their institutions.

The most frequently mentioned "top three duties" in the CAO Census, finishing just a few percentage points above strategic planning, was personnel management. Sixty percent of provosts mentioned this, and I am surprised that it wasn't unanimous. Dealing with personnel problems themselves takes a big bite out of the provost's week, but personnel management also includes faculty and staff recruitment, evaluation, development, and compensation, along with direct supervision of some people (I had about 25 direct reports). Interestingly, the literature on provosts is mute on this job element. Where the subject is covered at all, it is done so obliquely, disguised as topics such as faculty development (Austensen, 1997; Glickman, 1984; Hynes, 1984) and faculty leadership (Oppelt, 1984). Ferren and Stanton (2004) differ from the others by addressing topics of faculty workload and compensation, and, as with all the topics in their book, they deal with it in a practical, straightforward manner. Austensen (1997) notes that post-tenure review is one of the most dramatic changes coming (then) in higher education, an example of an additional layer of personnel work that has been added to the provost's job in recent decades.

While most commentators have neglected personnel management as a topic, they have written voluminously on another aspect of personnel: Faculty. Virtually every work on the provost's position emphasizes that working with faculty is key to success, of the provost and of the institution. And here the writers do not mean working with the individual faculty member (which is personnel management) but with the collective faculty, *the capital F faculty*, as I have termed it. This theme is covered in the previous sections of this book, in which I concluded that the essence of the provost's position—the defining characteristic, if one were to be so bold as to list one—is to work with the Faculty to govern and manage the university.

Martin and Samels (1997, p. 8) went so far as to call their edited volume, *First Among Equals*. The intent of that title seems obvious—the provost is the convener of conversations and decision processes in which the faculty, and perhaps other constituents, like students and trustees, provide the content and, by their consensus, the direction. Their message is more subtle, however, recognizing that being first among equals requires providing such leadership "in a climate of changing faculty priorities, declining institutional resources, fickle student consumer preferences and eroding public confidence." Mark Edelstein (1997, p. 64), calling on the overworked "herding cats" analogy, noted that universities are "organized anarchies," and that understanding and respecting the role of faculty in academic governance, especially through faculty senates, was crucial to a provost's success. Similarly, Ferren and Stanton's (2004) volume on the CAO is entitled *Leadership Through Collaboration*, emphasizing the need for partnerships between the provost and other segments of the institution's administration as the core of the provost's success.

Kenneth Mortimer and Annette Caruso (1984) linked the duties of faculty collaboration and strategic planning. The 1980s were and would be a time for "painful choices," and the need to be strategic about those choices would conflict with the tradition of faculty governance. Consequently, they wrote, the proper and informed balance between strategic choices and faculty governance could only be achieved with early and ongoing participatory leadership and freely available information.

And it isn't easy. In the CAO Census, provosts were asked with whom they had the best and most challenging working relationships. Only 6% reported that their best relationship was with the faculty (the lowest of any category listed), and 25% reported that working with the faculty was their most challenging relationship (only one other most challenging relationship outranked faculty, that being the relationships with executive officers other than the president or CFO). Ferren and Stanton (2004) explain part of the reasons for these difficult relationships. First, because faculty members have been trained to do research, they require a higher level of problem definition, data availability, and analysis than is typical for administrative decisions. Second, although the faculty has long been considered a legitimate partner in governing the academic aspects of a university, they are now asking for a greater share of governance in all aspects of the institution. Both features "muddy up the waters" about what is the faculty's role and what is the administrator's role. Austensen (1997, p. 22) summed up the situation succinctly, quoting from William Berquist: the relationship between faculty and provost is "intricate—almost baroque."

The third biggest job of provosts, as they reported in the CAO Census, is dealing with budget and financial matters. They also reported that their biggest frustration is not enough money (61%); no other topic gets more than about half as much mention. As early as 1984, Mortimer and Caruso noted that 79% of provosts reported being engaged in "significant reallocation" (p. 44). Big surprise. I'm confident that 100% of provosts are so engaged today.

The unsurprising conclusion most have reached is that being provost is hard. Walton and McDade (2001, p. 87) wrote that the "literature on the CAO position reinforces its reputation as the toughest job in any college or university." Martin and Samels (1997, pp. 17–20), based on many conversations with individual provosts, presented their top 10 characteristics of the "new" chief academic officer:

1. An expert with ambiguity
2. A champion of new technologies
3. An institutional entrepreneur
4. A student affairs advocate
5. A savvy fund-raiser
6. A supporter of selected excellence
7. A legal interpreter
8. A public intellectual
9. A shaper of the new consensus
10. A visionary pragmatist

In other words, provosts do it all. Remember what Ferren and Stanton (2004, p. 3) concluded: "Chief academic officers recognize that, other than the football or basketball coach, theirs is the most difficult position on a campus. . . ."

62

IS THERE LIFE AFTER BEING PROVOST?

I don't need the literature to answer this one. You bet there is life after provost; a good life, too. That's why former provosts don't write books. They are too busy enjoying themselves, no matter what they are doing.

They are doing a variety of things. The CAO Census asked sitting provosts where their predecessors had gone. For public doctoral universities, 35% had become presidents, 20% had returned to the faculty, 20% had retired, 9% took another administrative job other than CAO or president, 7% became a CAO someplace else, and the rest did "other" things. I'm surprised by only one statistic—the proportion that move to other provost positions—because I've not known anyone personally who has done that.

Public doctoral universities graduate more than a third of their provosts into university presidents. This proportion is highest among all the other categories of universities, by a considerable margin (the closest is 27%, for private doctoral universities; Hartley & Godin, 2010). The provost position is also the biggest single source of presidents for public doctoral universities, providing 58% (Hartley & Godin, 2010); again, this is the highest single source of presidents for any category of university or college. Also, the proportion of provosts becoming presidents is more than twice as high as the next largest source, which is other academic officers (28%).

This means that big public universities like to recruit their presidents from the ranks of the provosts. This reality has baffled some observers, because the jobs of president and provost are so different. As discussed in the previous section, the president is external and the provost is internal. Walton and McDade (2001) noted that the CAO position has tended to be divorced from fund-raising activities, which is a major task for presidents. My own experience in presidential searches has been that the consultants and committees invariably asked, "What was the biggest gift you have ever solicited and received, with you as the lead?" (obviously my answer was not large enough). The CAO Census asked provosts in what three areas they most needed more proficiency on their way to becoming a president. The top three were economic development (44%), board relationships (42%), and government relationships (36%). I suspect fund-raising didn't make the top of the list because most had been deans at one time, a position in which they did lots of fund-raising. Economic development, board relationships, and government relationships, however, are largely university, not college, matters. From my own observations, I would judge that those three areas, along with intercollegiate athletics and fund-raising, made up the bulk of the topics on which the NC State chancellor spent significant time. I spent almost no time on those areas. Berliner (2009) and Lorden (2009) both noted that the discrepancy between the experience of CAOs and expectations of future presidents in fund-raising, external relations, board governance, and other areas was a problem that needed to be addressed in order to prepare CAOs better for their next career step.

But what about that next career step? Provosts are at best ambivalent about becoming presidents. More provosts go back to the faculty or retire (40%) than go on to be presidents (35%). Why don't they want to be presidents? The top reason, according to the CAO Census, is they consider the nature of the work to be unappealing (76%). This reason again points out the fundamental gulf between the positions of provost and president; despite how corporate the administrative role of the provost might be, she is still focusing that administration on the fundamental mission of the institution—academics. The next two reasons for not wanting to be a president are that provosts don't want to live in a fishbowl (29%), and they anticipate the demands of the position will be too great (24%). As busy as the provost's job was, I always found that there was refuge for me at home—nobody disturbed me there. But this wasn't the way it was for the chancellor. Students might march to his house at 3 a.m. to protest shortened library hours, an athlete might get arrested (or worse yet, a coach), and a trustee, after a bit too much wine at dinner, might decide he just has to talk to the chancellor right now. As I wrote earlier, the provost is a little bit famous; the chancellor is a lot famous, maybe too famous for most provosts' tastes.

Provosts also like the jobs they have. This may be surprising, given a literature that emphasizes the challenge of defining and implementing "academic leadership on a campus in a climate of changing faculty priorities, declining institutional resources, fickle student consumer preferences and eroding public confidence," to quote Martin and Samels (1997, p. 8) again. The CAO Census found that 63% of provosts responding were very satisfied with their job, and 31% were somewhat satisfied—a whopping 94% that were pretty happy with their work. Not bad for the hardest job on campus, needing one hundred eyes that must be open all the time, wrought with ambiguity, and operating in an organized anarchy.

But the job of provost is temporary. As the CAO Census reported, the average provost remained in his or her position for about four and one-half years—a "short happy tenure," to quote Jacqueline King, one of the report's authors, from a web-based presentation. The temporary nature of the job was confirmed by the Protocol School of Washington, in a blog post by Robert Hickey. He had been asked whether the proper way to address a provost was as "Dear Dr. Wilson" or "Dear Provost Wilson." Hickey answered this way:

One of the basics of formal forms of address is "address by rank" and "identify by office." When "Dr." is one's permanent personal rank and the "office of provost" is a temporary position you address as "Dr." and identify them as "Provost." (Hickey, 2011)

Thus, the address would read, "Dr. Wilson, Provost of We-Are-a-Great-University," and the letter would open, "Dear Dr. Wilson." The provost doesn't own the title; he just borrows it for a while.

Which brings me to the best advice I found in the literature of the provost. Glenn Brooks (1984), then dean of Colorado College, asked thirteen colleague provosts and deans what advice they might give others. He compiled 36 aphorisms and maxims, some trite, some original, some practical, some aspirational. But one, the last one, was exceptional:

36. Don't give up your tenure.

LESSONS FROM THE LITERATURE

1. My experience and the literature are in almost perfect agreement; where we differ, I'm right.
2. When college presidents couldn't handle the work themselves anymore, they created provosts to do the hard bits.
3. Provosts were called deans until that title became too common. Now many are also called chief academic officers.
4. The provost position has always been ambiguous, and it always will be. The provost is in charge of whatever needs to be done academically, so don't worry about the PD.
5. The provost's job is to advance the academic interests of the university.
6. The provost's job is also to balance among the competing academic interests of the university.
7. The average provost is still old and White, but could be a man or a woman.
8. The average provost lasts in the job for 4 to 5 years.
9. Most provosts were deans just before becoming provost. Others were vice provosts first.
10. The provost is the inside face for the university. So, about half of provosts got promoted to the job internally.
11. Provosts spend most of their time on personnel, strategy, and financial matters, but they think that academic leadership is the most important part of the job.
12. The provost's fundamental task is to work with the faculty on collaborative leadership and governance of the university's academic affairs.
13. Unfortunately, provosts and faculties have very challenging relationships.

14. A lot of provosts become presidents. And more presidents come from provosts than any other source.
15. In order to succeed as presidents, provosts need more experience with board, economic, and governmental relationships.
16. Provosts like their jobs, but they don't stay in them very long. About 5 years of happiness is all they can take.
17. Then most of them retire or go back to the faculty.
18. So, don't give up your tenure.

PART TWELVE

SO YOU WANT TO BE A PROVOST

63

A CITIZEN OF THE UNIVERSITY

If you've read this far into the book, you might still be interested in pursuing the life of a university administrator. Many people would question your judgment, but not me. I agree with you—the life of a provost (or dean or department head) is worth pursuing.

The next few chapters contain my advice about how to prepare for the job of a university administrator. If you are far into an administrative career already, some of the advice is too late (but it might be reassuring). If you are still early in your career, but are reading this book, you probably don't need the advice, because you've figured it out already—that's why you are reading the book! Nonetheless, since my current job as a faculty member includes being an advisor and writing books, here comes some written advice.

The current chair of our Faculty Senate, Hans Kelner, spoke to our yearly college faculty meeting recently. He mentioned that university governance is undertaken by a "coalition of the willing," quoting a phrase that President George W. Bush used regularly (or so Hans tells me). Hans estimates that the coalition of the willing-to-get-involved is only about 15% of the faculty. If you wish to become a university administrator, you must first join the coalition of the willing.

Another way to say this is that you must work with your head up, rather than with your head down. The culture of faculty is that we each have an individual mission (rather than a collective one), and that mission is to become expert at a particular topic, to know more and more about less and less, as the sarcastic axiom describes us. Publish in your field, get more and better grants, get to know peers around the world, supervise a "lab" of clannish postdocs and students. This is a great strategy for a faculty member, but not for an aspiring university leader.

Rather, you must become a university citizen, a leading member of the coalition of the willing. The term *willing* is accurately descriptive, because trying to engage an unwilling faculty member in university leadership is like getting a two-year-old to eat lima beans—it ain't gonna happen. Apart from the minimal expectations that we all will attend to a modicum of community duties, generally in our home departments, the university doesn't force the unwilling faculty member to eat any administrative lima beans. The plate remains full, therefore, for the aspiring administrator to eat up all the experience that she or he wants.

Working with your head up means that you devote some time to becoming a generalist in the life of the university. Just as one of the joys of being provost is that the entire university passes across your desk regularly, one of the joys of becoming a university citizen is that you get to know and love the university a bit at a time.

Essential to this transition is accepting that you work for the university. You don't work for the department or college, and even more importantly, you don't work for the field of mathematics, art history, or ceramics engineering. A common saying among faculty in my field of fisheries and wildlife is that "we work for the resource," our manifestation of the Lorax speaking for the trees. But that isn't true—we work for the university. Once you get your head wrapped around the idea that you do, indeed, work for the university, the rest comes pretty naturally. Here's how to do it.

First, start working on behalf of the whole university. Teach an honors seminar open to the entire student body, or even better, teach an interdisciplinary general education course. Serve as advisor to a campus-wide student group, one not in your field of study. Organize some event on behalf of the university.

When I was working for Penn State (notice I wasn't working for the School of Forest Resources at Penn State), the human population of the Earth was approaching six billion people. The idea of the "Day of Six Billion" was catching hold, designated by the United Nations to be October 12, 1999. About a year before, national environmental and human-development organizations began gearing up for programming related to that day. I believed Penn State should also pay attention—our students needed to recognize what was happening outside Happy Valley, Pennsylvania, and the United States. So I asked my dean and the provost for authority (and a small budget) to organize a university-wide series of events throughout the fall semester. They agreed.

"Hey, Jason and Bruce," I said over the backyard hedges to our neighbors on an unseasonably warm afternoon that spring, clinking three ice-cold bottles of Yuengling in my hand, "How about a beer?"

Our neighbors were Penn State faculty, Bruce in music and Jason in English; they collaborated on writing operettas and other musical pieces. "You bet," they answered, like lambs to the slaughter.

"I've got an idea I bet you'd like," I said, and laid out my plan that they would write and produce a Broadway-style musical about the Day of Six Billion. "And I want a show with real tunes, like *The Sound of Music*; none of this *Les Misérables* stuff. Have another beer."

To my amazement, they did like the idea—and immediately set to work on the six-month process that was required. We premiered the musical *The Diamond Child* that October, to an audience of more than 1,500, each of whom brought packaged food for the local food bank as their price of admission. The show was splendid, with the kind of tunes that I was expecting.

That evening, Sharon and I loaded the cans into our aging van, which sunk to the axle on groaning springs. On Saturday, we delivered the food—driving very gingerly—to the local food bank, with the assistance of the visiting Ohio State cheerleading squad.

The Diamond Child was the marquee event for a semester's worth of programming. We had seminars offered by departments across campus, a statewide poster contest for middle-school students, a five-part series on public television, a semester-long seminar course, and outreach to local churches to encourage services about "Caring for Creation." We reached the most people—about 96,000 of them—at the halftime of the Penn State–Ohio State football game. The public-address announcer, reading from my script, told the crowd that during the game, the world's population would increase by the size of the crowd; then the marching band formed the number 6,000,000,000 on the field and played "It's a Small World."

Leading the Day of Six Billion program at Penn State wasn't in my job description—or in anyone's job description. That's the whole point. I created something that benefitted the entire institution that wouldn't have happened without my inability to curb my enthusiasm. And it has served me well throughout my career. When asked during my interviews at NC State for both dean and provost what accomplishments I was most proud of, I listed this program. And I got both jobs.

The second strategy for being a university citizen is to wade into faculty governance. Given that working with faculty is the fundamental task of the provost, having some experience with faculty governance is almost required. As I wrote earlier, being elected as a faculty representative is pretty easy—just agree to run. Once elected, spend a bit of time watching how it works, not with the jaundiced view of many faculty members, but with the goal of understanding what shared governance means in a university. Then, take on some tough and important jobs, like chairing the committee that hears faculty appeals on tenure and other grievances.

Faculty governance doesn't just occur through the Faculty Senate or other institution-wide body. Governance is shared through university-level committees that conduct a range of business, from curriculum review to athletic oversight to animal care; usually the members come from throughout the faculty, not just from the elected group. Participating in such committees is not only good for the résumé, but also as a way to understand the broader university. For example, if you are a laboratory scientist in biology or genetics, you are likely to think that animal care is pretty straightforward: Follow the well-established protocols for tending to laboratory mice. However, being on the university's animal care and use committee will require addressing the ambiguous questions of managing livestock on the university farm or catching, marking, and releasing black bears—on the university forest or in China.

Opportunities for faculty governance come naturally to faculty members who work with their heads up. When I was an associate professor at Virginia Tech, I needed a series of slides to illustrate approaches to nature as revealed in art and architecture (Frank Lloyd Wright's Fallingwater as opposed to Jefferson's Monticello or Eiffel's Tower). I had learned, somehow, that the Art Department kept a slide library, and I met with the art historian in charge to see if they had the slides I needed (to my surprise, they did; the university is a wonderful place!). We discussed my interest, and I could sense his delight that someone from "over there" had crossed the Drillfield to his side of the campus. What I missed was his delight that he might have found the required scientist to serve on their interdisciplinary humanities curriculum committee; almost immediately, I was appointed to a university function that gave me visibility and perspective.

My experience in art history could as easily illustrate a third aspect of becoming a university citizen—participating in the larger academic life of the institution. Just as understanding faculty matters is essential to a future provost, so is understanding academics from the institution's perspective. Whereas most faculty members think of teaching and learning in terms of the solar system of their courses and the major in which they teach, the academic enterprise extends far out into the galaxy. Every stage involves faculty participation, experience that is invaluable to the aspiring provost.

For example, think about the process for choosing the summer reading for incoming students. This might seem an easy task, largely an academic exercise of a few literary types in the liberal arts. But it is fraught with danger. Remember, thousands of parents are going to buy this book for their college-bound sons and daughters; a lot of those parents are going to get exercised about the choice. Select a book to help students understand Islam, and brace for the backlash from the patriotic and religious sectors. Designate a coming-of-age book with explicit language, and wait for—well, you get the idea. Experience of this kind helps steel the aspiring provost for the controversy when he funds the GLBT center or has to defend an art exhibit that disturbs some community sensitivities.

Participating in the creation and reformation of academic policy is equally valuable. Much of that job is virtually invisible, but also essential to the operation of the university. The academic calendar needs to be scheduled, syllabus requirements need to stay current with state and federal mandates, financial aid needs to be allocated legally and ethically, student suspension policies need to be adjusted, and dozens more. Because the provost is responsible, directly or indirectly, for all these matters, a tour of duty in the academic policy trenches is time well spent.

My fourth bit of advice on becoming a university citizen is more general: Find some unexpected ways to contribute to the overall university life. Here are some examples, just to illustrate that the aspiring provost needs to love—and live—the entire university:

- Volunteer to lead some aspect of the annual charitable campaign.
- Join the board of the university day care center.
- Teach a study abroad course.

- Become an officer in one of the university's honor societies.
- Serve the arts program as a docent or board member.
- Volunteer for the safety committee (they will love you for that!).
- Participate in some form of strategic planning.
- Advise students in undergraduate research.
- Serve as a conversation partner for international students (and invite them to the Fourth of July fireworks).
- Join the campus sustainability effort.
- And say yes to any of the scores of requests that you typically delete without reading because they are sent to "faculty everyone."

If you take this advice, you will learn early whether you are cut out for university administration or not. If participating in these university activities wears you out and you are generally wishing you could go back to the lab or art studio, then you probably aren't going to be happy in the central administration. But, if these activities juice you up so that you go home and can't stop talking about everything that happened today, then you are a prime candidate for the administrative yoke.

You'll never be bored and will always keep learning.

Bruce and Jason had one more learning surprise for me as we discussed the dimensions of putting on a Broadway show for the Day of Six Billion. They obviously saw my excitement rising as the idea started to emerge. They said, almost in unison and without hesitation, "We'd like you to be the executive producer."

I was flattered and immediately said yes, imagining myself contributing to improvements of the script, music, casting, costumes, and direction. "What does an executive producer do?"

"Pay for it."

64

A STUDENT OF THE UNIVERSITY

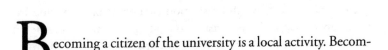

Becoming a citizen of the university is a local activity. Becoming a student of the university is global.

In the preface, I guessed that one reason provosts don't write about their experiences is they consider them too parochial. The responsibilities of a provost relate to running one particular university, not to running all universities or some other university. So, local experience will only go so far toward the making of a future provost.

The companion strategy to citizenship is scholarship. Not scholarship in your particular academic field, of course, but scholarship of the academy (when we're waxing scholarly we like to call the joint "the academy," which sounds all, like, scholarly, like). Just as study abroad provides valuable education to an undergraduate student, broad study of "the academy" provides valuable education for the aspiring provost. And it is available in several modes.

First, stay current with what others are saying about the university. To be specific, read *The Chronicle of Higher Education*, *Inside Higher Ed*, and similar news outlets about the academy. I know, those *Chronicles* keep showing up every week and piling up on the coffee table in the reception area, like a towering obelisk to your inefficiency. Add to that weekly issues of *The Economist*,

Sports Illustrated, and the Sunday *New York Times*, and it is more than an aspiring Renaissance Man or Woman can carry, let alone read.

So, be reasonable—pick and choose what you read, take the medicine in small doses. After a while, just like in all other news, the themes start repeating themselves, so the workload gets less intimidating. I started cutting my administrative teeth on *The Chronicle* before I was even a department head. Our school director would route his subscription around to whoever asked to see them; by keeping the issues in circulation, they didn't build up on his coffee table. I added my name to the list (partially so he'd know I was interested in this administrative stuff). At first, all I read were the clever and sometimes humorous commentaries by faculty members agonizing about tenure and unfair workloads, detailing the decline in student quality, and railing against the evils of athletics. Later I grew into the articles about low graduation rates, growing student loan balances, and intrusive boards of trustees. I mostly tsk-tsked because such things could never infect my university. It was only later that I learned that every university is a carrier of these diseases, and an epidemic can break out at any time.

The Chronicle and its peers serve a valuable role. They describe the higher education landscape, through faculty, administrative, and governmental eyes. How are attitudes toward nontenure-track faculty members changing? Is *high-impact learning* new, or just a new name for what we've always done? Why did that provost or president resign? What is the NCAA thinking about? What are the hot curricula that we should consider adding? How have recent high-profile faculty dismissal cases been handled? Is assessment gaining or losing ground? What are leading schools doing about their intellectual property?

Besides, the cartoons are great.

Second, while weeklies are good for current events, the formal literature about higher education is probably more valuable. I don't mean peer-reviewed journal articles, but rather trade books written by and for university administrators (like this one). If you want to become a provost (or dean), put down the journal of whatever-you've-been-reading-for-a-decade and pick up a book about higher education. You'll learn a bunch. After I read Jane Tompkins's *A Life in School,* I adapted her habit of sending post-cards to herself and her students, to capture random and interest-ing thoughts (I taped mine to my door). After reading *McKeachie's Teaching Tips,* I completely revised my approach to a lecture-laboratory course I taught. After reading Howard Gardner's *Frames of Mind,* I stopped thinking that only glib people were smart. And after reading Jane Smiley's *Moo,* I began a 17-year chuckle that continues to this day. For our twentieth anniversary, Sharon gave me Henry Rosovsky's *The University: An Owner's Manual,* with this note: "Because I know you'll need this someday." And, as usual, she was correct.

Books come and go, but there are typically books that grab the academic community's attention for long enough that we all should read them. Ernest Boyer's *Scholarship Reconsidered* has been the basis of policy discussions of faculty performance for decades; a would-be provost who can't speak to Boyer's ideas won't survive the airport interview. Similarly, Allan Bloom's *Closing of the Amer-ican Mind* was the catalyst for much thinking in recent decades, and Richard Light's work on student success is required reading. Maybe this one will be the next. . . . Beyond the direct literature on higher education leadership, though, a number of other sub-jects belong in the aspiring administrator's shopping cart.

Management books also can be instructive, and the aspiring provost needs to be conversant with a new book or two every year. One of the most valuable insights I get from management books is how different the university is from business. Almost none of the advice that management gurus give to their readers is applicable in public universities (which is, of course, why we don't run universities like businesses). John Kotter's classic *Lead-ing Change* was particularly revealing, because almost none of the conditions he says are needed for change exist in the university; so, is it any wonder that we change so reluctantly? But read those books anyhow, just so you can dissemble confidently when board members ask if we're going "from good to great" or whether we are "getting to yes" in our latest dustup with the faculty.

As an administrator, I always kept a short row of books on my desk, so visitors would think I was a scholar, just like the carved wooden monks gracing my bookends. Books like *The World Is Flat* and *How to Think Like Leonardo Da Vinci* convey just the right sort of image—classical yet contemporary, thoughtful yet daring. When I was dealing with a particularly nasty set of faculty matters at one school, I set *Coping With Difficult People* where everyone could see it. I recommend putting a few Post-it notes in each book—sticking out a bit, to give the impression you've read them. For a time I had the book *First, Break All the Rules* facing out on my desk. Eventually, I moved it, because faculty members kept coming in asking to break all my rules.

Another crucial subject area for students of the university is teaching and learning. Because provosts are in charge of teaching and learning, they need to know how to do it well, at least in principle. This is also an area of expertise for which faculty members are rewarded long before they openly confess to any administrative leanings.

Every university offers recurring workshops and seminars about how to improve teaching and learning, and the aspiring administrator should be a regular customer. What does service-learning really mean? How can I write better tests and assessment tools? What options do I have for making a 200-student class more than student nap time? Not only does this help keep you in the know regarding current thinking on pedagogy, but it helps make you a better teacher.

Eventually, you need to put this learning into practice. The aspiring provost's classes should be laboratories for trying new ways to improve learning. Experiment with being the "guide on the side." Teach an online or hybrid course. And publish the results of the experiments in educational journals, along with essays about your views of teaching, in your discipline and in general. It will not only pay off in better teaching, but you'll be noticed and rewarded for trying—eventually, you'll be asked to contribute to those workshops and seminars, adding further to your credentials as an academic and university leader. If you persist, you'll probably win an award or two for teaching—that'll get the search committee's attention.

(If you are keeping score, you'll notice that I haven't mentioned becoming a research leader. I have two reasons for this omission. First, I assume that every aspiring administrator has successfully passed the research hurdle, that is, tenure. Most tenured faculty members don't need to be told to do their research—that lesson is pinned to the bulletin board. If anything, a faculty member's training and innate tendencies usually draw him or her toward research and away from the coalition of the willing. This book is about getting the experiences that an active research program actually works against. Second, the idea that a dean or provost needs to be a top-tier researcher is a red herring. Faculty members on a search committee will typically make sure that "being a respected researcher" is on the list of qualifications for a provost, but that will never be the deciding selection factor. Provosts need to be interested in the institution, not in their research.)

The essential subject area in the aspiring provost's education is diversity. It is not enough to say you value diversity—you also need to know why you value it and how to convert that value into action. My bookshelf houses as many books about diversity as it does about teaching and the university in general, and I'm confident I've learned more from the diversity books. Don't believe that you can enhance diversity just because you say you aren't biased and are a good person; the first isn't true, and the second isn't sufficient. You are unlikely to know how to advance diversity unless you've spent some time exploring the topic with experts, through workshops, reading, and on-the-ground participation. Take every opportunity provided to learn how to be more proactive about detecting, confronting, and reversing discrimination—and your university will provide many. Study the educational rationale for diversity in the university, which is the ultimate defense for affirmative action and other programs that often come under scrutiny and attack.

The final big subject for study is the world—I saved the best for last. Keep your passport current and invest in some good compression socks. Every university today says it wants to be global (check your strategic plan, I dare you), but I doubt that many know what that means beyond sending more students on study abroad. So, it behooves the aspiring administrator to learn what a truly international university would look like—topics such as what's in it for a public university, how the educational process might change, how faculty performance might be evaluated differently, how research is conducted internationally, and scores of other questions.

In addition, given today's global educational marketplace, Americans need to understand how education is done in other countries. Problems with matching our academic systems to those of partner institutions in Europe have led to obstacles that have proven very resistant to removal. For example, some European universities are so decentralized that individual departments decide on their own academic calendars. A U.S. student might find it impossible to schedule one course in his major in economics, say, and another course to fulfill a general education requirement in art history. So, taking opportunities to visit universities in other countries to become familiar with their policies and processes is excellent preparation for being a global provost. And if you figure out a way to explain the Bologna Accords, give me a ring.

Finding opportunities for international experience brings me to the last point of preparing to be a provost. Many formal programs offer experience that benefits an aspiring administrator. ACE Presidential Fellowships are the most famous, of course, almost certainly a ticket to a higher administrative post, at the home institution or elsewhere. But any opportunity that provides international or interdisciplinary experience is an expression of your desire to learn more broadly about the academy and its work.

My own career changed dramatically, thanks to a Kellogg Foundation National Fellowship. I was in the second year of the program, in which about 50 faculty members, mostly associate professors, and nonprofit professionals spent 25% of our time for three years expanding our understanding of the world. The idea, they said, was to take competent specialists and make them generalists—the "*T*-shaped" qualities that we hear so much about today. At our closing seminar, I asked the president of the foundation what they would like to see as outcomes for their large investment in this program. "Oh," he said, "a couple of university presidents and provosts would be just fine."

65

ONE OF THE GUYS

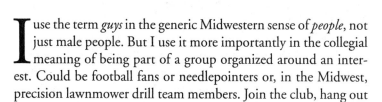

I use the term *guys* in the generic Midwestern sense of *people*, not just male people. But I use it more importantly in the collegial meaning of being part of a group organized around an interest. Could be football fans or needlepointers or, in the Midwest, precision lawnmower drill team members. Join the club, hang out together, be one of the guys.

The proof of your sincerity to become an academic administrator will ultimately be shown by the extent to which you are already walking the walk. That requires getting beyond the borders of the campus, where you have proven to be a good citizen, and beyond the library and teaching center, where you are a dedicated reader and student. It requires participating in the broader community of people with an interest in academics.

Let's start small. I'd wager that every academic disciplinary organization of any size has a subgroup about teaching; certainly all of the ones that I've belonged to have them. Join that organization and grow to be its leader. The faculty members in that group will be like you—interested in more than just their disciplinary subjects. Use those contacts to learn about their issues and concerns, how they do things better (or worse) than you. At the annual meeting, contribute to the group's educational mission in as many ways as possible. In addition to your usual research presentation (you know, the ones that got you tenure), make a presentation in the education session. Create a program for student travel to the meetings and for mentorship during the meetings. Work on committees trying to develop online courses to share among schools—or whatever the interesting academic topic is at that moment.

Early in my time at Virginia Tech, I joined the Education Section of the American Fisheries Society, the major professional and scientific group in my discipline. After being as active as possible for a couple of years, I was elected president (the group was small then, and getting elected to an office there was about as easy as getting elected to Faculty Senate). One thing led to another, and soon I was coediting a new fisheries textbook, a totally volunteer project of the group that would become the highest-selling fisheries textbook of our generation.

Now, figure out some way to link the institutions that share your interests through some sort of special project. Perhaps three schools can get together for a common experience; last summer, I led a nine-day doctoral seminar on climate change among NC State, the University of Surrey, and the University of São Paolo. Perhaps two schools can create a speaker exchange; Virginia Tech and NC State did this for a couple of decades after I started it with a colleague I met through our education group. One year, I put together a speaking tour for a water resources professional from England who visited several leading fisheries schools, and we all shared the expense. The point is to get experience reaching across institutions to create value—and to make a name for yourself as a can-do and will-do person.

Most disciplines today also have specialized meetings from time to time about some aspect of the academic trade—teaching, advising, enhancing diversity, leading study abroad, enhancing undergraduate research. Take every opportunity to participate, parlaying your academic activities on your home campus into regional, national, or international visibility and contacts.

Fast forward a few years to when you've become a department head, associate dean, or dean. Those same disciplinary organizations will probably have groups devoted to the leadership of academic units, a deans' council, or a department heads' section; just like earlier, you should join, participate, and lead. I was an early participant in the Council of Environmental Deans and Directors (a subunit of the National Council for Science and the Environment); I began to understand universities and their many ways of organizing around environmental topics from those meetings and colleagues. Although many faculty members and some university officials regard participating in these groups a waste of time, I disagree. This is where you find your peers and grow to understand academic administration in a larger context. These groups also tend to be active on national funding issues—advocating to Congress for federal appropriations like student loans, special projects, and land grant allocations; working with federal agencies with higher education programs like the U.S. Department of Agriculture, EPA, and NASA; and developing relationships with major federal research programs like NSF, NIH, and the Department of Defense.

These organizations and contacts are also the route to participating in academic reviews. Most universities around the country, and certainly all that receive core federal funding, conduct regular reviews of their academic programs. Being invited to participate is not only a great credential, but it is also an opportunity to learn how other schools conduct their business and to sneak off with their best ideas. As anyone who has ever been involved in these activities knows, the biggest beneficiary is the reviewer, not the reviewee.

The next step is to graduate to similar groups that serve the university as a whole. Participation at this level generally distinguishes a person who is eager to cannonball into the deep end of the administrative pool from one who hesitantly keeps one foot anchored in her discipline while the other tiptoes around in the administrative shallows. A little exploration will turn up many opportunities to learn the academic ropes from a university perspective.

At Penn State, I attended leadership seminars of the academic arm of the Big Ten, called the Committee on Institutional Cooperation; other athletic conferences have similar arrangements, although not as comprehensive as the CIC. For a time, I was involved in the Council for Undergraduate Research. The

Higher Education Resources Services (HERS) group offers continuing education for women interested in administrative roles. NACUBO, the National Association of College and University Business Officers is the peer organization for chief financial officers and their staff. Because the provost and CFO need to be best friends, some of NACUBO's programs target the essential partnership that these two positions must have to advance an institution. Many other organizations also offer learning opportunities, such as the seminars and workshops held by the Harvard Institute for Higher Education. All it takes to participate and become a leader in most of these activities is to walk up and say hi.

At the highest level are a set of nonprofit organizations that focus entirely on higher-education leadership. This community is dominated by a group called "The Six." Together, these six groups represent most brands of higher education, from community college to the top tier of research universities. In general, these organizations list the improvement of university administration as one of their primary goals. Except for one of the six, they offer programs that anyone in higher education can attend and provide opportunities for developing expertise and a peer group. The six, in alphabetical order, are:

- American Association of Community Colleges (AACC)—Because chief academic officers play a major role overall at community colleges, many AACC leadership programs relate directly to provosts (known more often as chief academic officers in community colleges). The AACC also supports an affiliated organization, the National Council of Instructional Administration, that is oriented directly to the responsibilities of provosts and their immediate academic staff.
- American Association of State Colleges and Universities (AASCU)—The AASCU focuses on smaller public universities than the APLU. This group has a dedicated annual conference on academic affairs, led by and intended for provosts.

It also operates a selective development program for aspiring administrators, the Millennium Leadership Institute, similar to the ACE Presidential Fellowships.

- Association of American Universities (AAU)—Whereas the other organizations listed here are simple membership groups, the AAU is different. It is a selective group, open only by invitation from the organization. Consequently, their programs are restricted to their 62 members. They have a formal Provosts' Group that conducts an annual CAO meeting as well as other programs. The AAU publishes an "Acronyms and Resource Guide" that lists major organizations related to higher education administration, as well as many other government and more specialized groups (it is available to all on the AAU website).
- American Council on Education (ACE)—The ACE is the standard-bearer of programming for aspiring and current university leaders. It has a series of programs relevant to provosts and is the origin of the national presidents' and provosts' surveys. ACE operates an Institute for New CAOs, and the ACE Presidential Fellowships are the most prestigious training opportunities for aspiring administrators. In February 2013, ACE announced the formation of a group dedicated to the work of provosts, the first comprehensive organization for all provosts from any type of higher education institution.
- Association of Public and Land-Grant Universities (APLU)— APLU is the recently adopted name of the former NASULGC; it tends to represent the larger public universities, especially the one or two land grant universities in each state. The APLU has a formal Council on Academic Affairs, which is the peer group for university provosts. The council has its own annual meetings, as well as sessions during the comprehensive meeting of APLU each year in the late fall. In addition, the subunit called the Commission on Food, Environment

and Renewable Resources (CFERR) includes an Academic Programs Section that is particularly relevant for provosts and academic deans.

- National Association of Independent Colleges and Universities (NAICU)—This organization represents private institutions. Although NAICU does not have a specific provosts' group, much of the programming is relevant to the academic mission. Their website includes an informative guide to other organizations in higher education under the heading "higher education resources."

As I headed to the computer to finish this chapter, I said to Sharon that I was having difficulty ending the book. It could go on for much longer—more issues, more nuanced insight, better stories to tell. Almost every day, in conversation with a faculty or staff colleague, I remember another situation that begs to be included in the text. A dinner with E. O. Wilson, perhaps, or the debate around how we should accommodate a multi-handicapped student who was unable to attend traditional classes, or being accused of censoring the student newspaper.

But if the end must come, why not end with a new beginning?

I opened my e-mail (a wonderful displacement activity), and found a message titled "Request for advice on career development." The writer was a former colleague who had been an associate dean and then moved to another university as a vice provost. We had often talked about higher education leadership when he was at NC State. Now he was seeking my perspective about how to get to his real goal—provost. He was currently applying for the provost opening at a small public university, but my sense was that he was much more interested in the kind of position I had left.

Of course I agreed to be his *mentor* (his word, not mine, the crafty devil; so how could I refuse?). He had included his résumé and letter of application. I could have just copied them here to replace the pages in the last three chapters. Here was a true citizen of the university, having progressed through disciplinary, interdisciplinary, and university-wide stages of service that reached into all the crevices of the institution. Here was a true scholar of the university, having participated in an impressive list of learning opportunities, including a yearlong sabbatical relating to higher education administration, with the grants, publications, presentations, and awards to prove it. And he was also one of the guys, belonging to and leading several groups of like-minded persons at all levels from discipline to world.

As I read his résumé and letter, though, I realized he didn't need my advice at all. He had assembled an impressive set of credentials, to be sure, and he certainly didn't need me to tell him to shore up this or that weakness. None of that mattered. What mattered was that those accomplishments and activities were consequences of one essential truth that jumped off every page: He loves the university. He doesn't just love his discipline, college, or administrative unit. He loves it all. You simply cannot do what he'd done, can't keep up the enthusiasm and energy, unless you love the place and all it means. Get that right, and everything else will follow.

But don't give up your tenure.

REFERENCES

Austensen, Roy A. (1997). Faculty relations and professional development: Best practices for the chief academic officer. In James Martin & James E. Samels (Eds.), *First among equals: The role of the chief academic officer* (pp. 21–40). Baltimore, MD: Johns Hopkins University Press.

Bergquist, William H., & Pawlak, Kenneth. (2008). *Engaging the six cultures of the academy.* San Francisco, CA: Jossey-Bass.

Berliner, Herman. (2009, February). Perspectives of a long serving CAO. In TIAA-CREF Institute, *Chief academic officers and the future leadership of American higher education* (p. 304). New York: TIAA-CREF Institute.

Bloom, Allan. (1987). *The closing of the American mind.* New York: Simon and Schuster.

Boyer, Ernest L. (1990). *Scholarship reconsidered: Priorities of the professoriate.* Princeton, NJ: The Carnegie Foundation for the Advancement of Learning.

Brooks, Glenn E. (1984). Aphorisms and maxims for chief academic officers. In David G. Brown (Ed.), *Leadership roles of chief academic officers* (p. 306). San Francisco, CA: Jossey-Bass.

Brown, David G. (Ed.). (1984). *Leadership roles of chief academic officers.* San Francisco, CA: Jossey-Bass.

Bryant, Paul. T. (2005). *Confessions of an habitual administrator: An academic survival manual.* Bolton, MA: Anker Publications.

Cornell University. (2011). *History of Cornell's provosts.* Office of the Provost, Cornell University, Ithaca, NY. Retrieved from www.cornell.edu/provost/

Eckel, Peter D., Cook, Bryan J., & King, Jacqueline E. (2009). *The CAO census.* Washington, DC: American Council on Education.

Edelstein, Mark G. (1997). Academic governance: The art of herding cats. In James Martin & James E. Samels (Eds.), *First among equals: The role of the chief academic officer* (pp. 58–78). Baltimore, MD: Johns Hopkins University Press.

Ferren, Ann S., & Stanton, Wilbur W. (2004). *Leadership through collaboration: The role of the chief academic officer.* Westport, CT: Praeger.

Gardner, Howard. (1983). *Frames of mind: The theory of multiple intelligences.* New York: BasicBooks.

Glickman, Maurice (1984). Goals, academic direction, and faculty development. In David G. Brown (Ed.), *Leadership roles of chief academic officers* (pp. 77–84). San Francisco, CA: Jossey-Bass.

Hartley, Harold V., III, & Godin, Eric E. (2010). *A study of CAOs of independent colleges and universities.* Washington, DC: Council of Independent Colleges.

Hickey, Robert. (2011). How to address a provost? Posted on Robert Hickey's blog, *The protocol school of Washington's honor & respect: The official guides to names, titles, & forms of address.*

Hynes, William J. (1984). Strategies for faculty development. In David G. Brown (Ed.), *Leadership roles of chief academic officers* (pp. 31–38). San Francisco, CA: Jossey-Bass.

Kotter, John P. (1996). *Leading change.* Boston, MA: Harvard Business School Press.

Lorden, Joan. (2009, February). Creating the pipeline for academic leadership. In TIAA-CREF Institute, *Chief academic officers and the future leadership of American higher education* (pp. 4–6). New York: TIAA-CREF Institute.

Martin, James, & Samels, James E. (Eds.). (1997). *First among equals: The role of the chief academic officer.* Baltimore, MD: Johns Hopkins University Press.

Mayhew, Paula Hooper. (1997). Creating common ground: Student development, academic affairs, and institutional diversity. In James Martin & James E. Samels (Eds.), *First among equals: The role of the chief academic officer* (pp. 104–116). Baltimore, MD: Johns Hopkins University Press.

McKeachie, Wilbert J. (1978). *McKeachie's Teaching tips: A guidebook for the beginning college teacher* (7th ed.). Lexington, MA: D. C. Heath and Company.

Mortimer, Kenneth P., & Caruso, Annette C. (1984). The process of academic governance and the painful choices of the 1980s. In David G. Brown (Ed.), *Leadership roles of chief academic officers* (pp. 43–48). San Francisco, CA: Jossey-Bass.

O'Meara, Timothy. (1984). The Notre Dame long-range plan. In David G. Brown (Ed.), *Leadership roles of chief academic officers* (pp. 8–99). San Francisco, CA: Jossey-Bass.

Oppelt, John. (1984). Sustaining faculty leadership. In David G. Brown (Ed.), *Leadership roles of chief academic officers* (pp. 1–38). San Francisco, CA: Jossey-Bass.

Palm, Risa. (2009, February). Understanding a lack of CAO interest in the presidency. In TIAA-CREF, *Chief academic officers and the future leadership of American higher education* (pp. 6–7). New York: TIAA-CREF Institute.

Rosovsky, Henry. (1990). *The university: An owner's manual.* New York: W. W. Norton and Company.

Smiley, Jane. (1995). *Moo: A novel.* New York: Fawcett Columbine.

Smith, Robert V. (2006). *Where you stand is where you sit: An academic administrator's handbook.* Fayetteville: University of Arkansas Press.

Smyer, Michael A. (2009). Age, generational and gender considerations. In TIAA-CREF, *Chief academic officers and the future leadership of American higher education* (pp. 8–10). New York: TIAA-CREF Institute.

Teague, Peggy Shaw. (2000). *Chief academic officers: Their characteristics, experiences, and pathways* (Unpublished doctoral dissertation). North Carolina State University, Raleigh, NC.

Tompkins, Jane. (1996). *A life in school: What the teacher learned.* Reading, MA: Addison-Wesley.

Walton, Karen Doyle, & McDade, Sharon A. (2001). At the top of the faculty: Women as chief academic officers. In Jana Nidiffer & Carolyn Terry Bashaw (Eds.), *Women administrators in higher education: Historical and contemporary perspectives* (pp. 85–100). Albany: State University of New York Press.

Wheatley, Margaret J. (1994). *Leadership and the new science: Learning about organizations from an orderly universe.* San Francisco, CA: Berrett-Koehler.

Winstead, Nash. (1999). *The provost's office: An informal history.* North Carolina State University Libraries, Raleigh, NC. Retrieved from www.lib.ncsu.edu/universityarchives/universityhistory/provosthistory

Wolverton, Robert. E. (1984). The chief academic officers: Argus on the campus. In David G. Brown (Ed.), *Leadership roles of chief academic officers* (pp. 7–18). San Francisco, CA: Jossey-Bass.